THE
HOUSING
DEBATE

Stuart Lowe

First published in Great Britain in 2011 by

The Policy Press
University of Bristol
Fourth Floor, Beacon House
Queen's Road
Bristol BS8 1QU

Tel +44 (0)117 331 4054
Fax +44 (0)117 331 4093
e-mail tpp-info@bristol.ac.uk
www.policypress.co.uk

North American office:
The Policy Press
c/o International Specialized Books Services (ISBS)
920 NE 58th Avenue, Suite 300
Portland, OR 97213-3786, USA
Tel +1 503 287 3093
Fax +1 503 280 8832
e-mail info@isbs.com

British Library Cataloguing in Publication Data
A catalogue record for this book is available from the British Library

Library of Congress Cataloging-in-Publication Data
A catalog record for this book has been requested

ISBN 978 1 84742 273 6 paperback

The right of Stuart Lowe to be identified as author of this work has been asserted by her in accordance with the 1988 Copyright, Designs and Patents Act.

The statements and opinions contained within this publication are solely those of the author and not of the University of Bristol or The Policy Press. The University of Bristol and The Policy Press disclaim responsibility for any injury to persons or property resulting from any material published in this publication.

The Policy Press works to counter discrimination on grounds of gender, race, disability, age and sexuality.

Cover design by The Policy Press.
Front cover: photograph kindly supplied by Corbis
Printed and bound in Great Britain by TJ International, Padstow.
The Policy Press uses environmentally responsible print partners.

MIX
Paper from
responsible sources
FSC® C013056
www.fsc.org

In Memoriam
Professor Kathleen Jones (1922–2010)
Founding Professor of the Department of Social Policy
and Social Work, University of York

Contents

List of tables and figures

Tables

Figures

Foreword

The critical examination of housing policy has tended to be marginalised. Insufficient attention has been given to the interactions between housing and other aspects of human welfare. There has been a tendency for housing to be regarded as simply a commodity supplied by the market, with a limited need for residual policies for those who have difficulty in participating as market actors. This marginalisation is a reflection of the perspectives of powerful political and economic actors. Within the government machine, housing policy responsibilities have moved confusingly between Whitehall departments over the years, and in any case much decision making of key importance for housing has come from the departments governing the economy and the taxation system.

This dominant perspective has been challenged by some social policy scholars, recognising how our access to – and opportunities within – the housing market need to be seen as fundamental for our well-being, and in many respects as a source of reinforcements for social inequalities. Stuart Lowe belongs within this group of scholars, and considers that mainstream social policy scholarship can still do more to integrate understanding of the overall dynamics of housing policy and housing systems with wider social policy analysis.

That is a very relevant view for our time. But to understand where the housing system is now requires an analysis of how we got to the present situation. Stuart shows how, in the context of the long lives of property and the importance of ownership (in the British system, among others), the contemporary housing situation must be seen as a product of its history, and in that respect one that is slow to – and hard to – change. Yet there is a need to change, and in addressing that need, the interactions between the housing market and the rest of the economy require more attention.

The 2007–08 crisis makes this sort of analysis particularly necessary. One justification offered for the excessive lending that generated that crisis was that mortgages were being extended to people hitherto excluded from owner occupation: possibilities for asset accumulation were, it was said, being extended. The crash shattered those dreams and inevitably the poorer borrowers suffered most. The reality is that asset accumulation (even in housing) has reinforced widening inequality, perhaps increased it, and certainly embedded it. The conventional political response has been a concern with the fall in house prices, damaging the asset accumulation dream of a lot of people in 'middle England'. Yet there are good reasons for arguing that in the UK houses are overpriced, and that the reliance on housing asset accumulation as personal saving is damaging to the economy as a whole.

Outside the world of owner occupation, support for renters in the UK increasingly comes through the benefit system. Stuart's historical analysis shows clearly how this has come about. The government today, among its measures to deal with the public expenditure element of the crisis, is curbing the cash available to poorer households through the housing benefit system, a clear example of 'blame the victim' politics. Stuart's comparative analysis suggests there are better ways of addressing the issues about the participation of lower-income households in the housing system.

I welcome this book therefore as an incisive contribution to our understanding of an area of public and social policy that is currently at a critical stage, where innovative thinking such as that offered by Stuart Lowe is particularly needed.

Michael Hill
Series Editor

Preface

A debate can have several different levels of argument. Sometimes there is a dispute about facts and 'what happened'. On other occasions the debate is about deeper theory and the question 'why'. Often it is difficult to separate out these empirical and conceptual layers. In recent years, this issue has been much discussed among the students in my department at York University who have been exploring the policymaking process and particularly the new institutionalist literature. How does social change occur and what causes it? How do we know? The core of this thinking takes place in the policy analysis module taught with my colleague John Hudson. Badgered by our students to explain in writing the complexities of this field we wrote our *Understanding the Policy Process: Analysing Welfare Policy and Practice* (2004, 2009). Here we suggested an approach built on incorporating macro-, meso- and micro-level material. Globalisation forces, for example, are filtered through a middle layer of political and social institutions before delivery down to the street level. We called this the 'Big Mac' approach because of the need to bite through the whole bun (macro, meso and micro) to get the full flavour of the meal! These ideas inform most of what we teach and naturally have spilled over into the Housing Policy module that I teach to our undergraduates. *The Housing Debate* is structured around a number of different 'layers'. Once again students have been keen to see the ideas they work with in print and hence this book.

It is very much to be hoped that these ideas do not confine themselves to the classroom, but spread into the 'real world'. Our Masters students, quite often returning to study after periods as practitioners, comment on how valuable their thinking about the policy process was in their jobs. They come back for more! It follows from this, and also in the spirit of Michael Hill's series, that the book is intended to reach out to the wider world of practitioners. Bringing together theory and practice adds up to more than the sum of its parts.

—

A note of thanks to colleagues other than John Hudson. Student friends and other friends and colleagues who have read and commented on parts of the manuscript or simply discussed the issues with me are quite numerous, but some names stand out. In no particular order, Paul Keenan, Dan Horsfall, Beth Watts, Jo Jones, Yong-Chang Heo, Stefan Kuehner and Caroline Hunter all loom large in this, even though they may not realise it. Susan Smith and Beverley Searle have latterly added stimulus to the debate. Jim Kemeny's influence is often lurking in my thinking and at the twilight of his career may I say that, in my view, his work should be much better appreciated, for it is more subtle than some commentators have realised. Many thanks to Michael Hill for reading the first draft so carefully and for his useful comments. Finally, thanks to my wife Sue for being tremendously patient!

At the Oxford Union and other debating societies a specific proposition is posed for claim and counterclaim. The motion in *The Housing Debate* is the following: 'This house believes that there is a close connection between housing systems and types of welfare states and, moreover, that the growth of home-ownership and associated mortgage markets in recent decades has created the foundations for asset-based welfare in which families use personal wealth – mostly derived from housing – to buy into a mixed economy of welfare.' I know there will be differences of opinion about some of the material contained herein, but that is what a debate is for. Bring it on!

Stuart Lowe
Department of Social Policy and Social Work, University of York
March 2011

1

The foundations

OVERVIEW

This opening chapter outlines the core themes of the book and puts in place some of the concepts and technical terms used in the analysis of housing policy and housing systems. Attention is particularly drawn to the connection between housing and the development and pattern of welfare states and it is argued that there is a symbiotic relationship between them. The rise of home-ownership is shown to be particularly significant for how we need to think about and understand welfare states in the 21st century. The growth of globalised mortgage markets is critical to this story. The idea of the housing stock, of 'flows' of dwellings, of the balance of households to dwellings and of housing tenure are all outlined providing a foundation for interpreting contemporary housing policy. Different types of housing systems are introduced, notably the distinction between nations that have 'social market' housing or are dominated by home-ownership. These distinctions turn out to be important for how we think about the housing–welfare state connection.

Key concepts

flows of housing need, 'home', home-ownership, households, housing and demography, housing stock, housing tenure, integrated rental markets

Introduction

The significance of housing to people's welfare and well-being – having a roof over our heads – is hard to beat in terms of significance. Article 25 of the Universal Declaration of Human Rights lists housing as being an essential right necessary for health and well-being and Article 12 notes that the home is a private sanctuary in which citizens must be free from undue interference of their privacy (UNGA, 1948). Home is the central focus of most people's lives, where we keep our clutter, build our closest relationships and in many ways define who we are as individuals (see Box 1.5). For this reason alone, housing policy is a major concern of governments and one purpose of this chapter is to outline the key issues that most modern states focus on in this field of public policy. These areas of policy typically include:

- the quantity of houses (including flats) that need to be built in relation to the current and forecast number of households;
- the type and size of properties required to meet the needs of modern family types; and
- ensuring an acceptable standard of housing.

But this is only half the story; for housing is, as the UN Articles hint at, a very private domain and so does not easily fit as one of the 'pillars' of the welfare state, such as education, social security or the health services, which are mainly provided by the state or are basically income transfers managed by a state-run bureaucracy.

One of the main differences is that with housing normally a much higher proportion than with health or education is supplied and distributed through the private sector (although this is not the case, for example, in the US where health care is predominantly a privately provided service). It is common to talk in terms of 'the housing market' rather than housing as a service. Even in societies with a high proportion of state-owned housing or where the state attempts to oversee the rental part of the housing market (such as in Germany and Sweden), home-ownership and private landlords (the two main components of the private market) together make up the majority of housing. In addition, the vast majority of housing whether state-owned or market-based is built by private construction companies:

- A high proportion of housing in most countries, typically between 60% and 80%, is supplied through the open market.

- A high proportion of the resources expended on housing is in the form of capital expenditure on 'bricks and mortar' and the purchase of building land. The other pillars of welfare – social services, schools, health care – are mainly services delivered to people and are very labour-intensive (ie most of the expenditure is on salary costs) and social security is principally a bureaucracy facilitating income transfers.

The housing and welfare state connection

Housing has been described as 'the wobbly pillar under the welfare state' because of these features, particularly since state housing programmes are vulnerable to cuts during periods of public spending retrenchment and austerity budgeting (Torgersen, 1987). Indeed, as can be seen in the UK case over recent decades, housing has been squeezed out of the government's welfare portfolio through a steady and systematic transfer from public to private ownership and massive cuts in building subsidies. In the most recent incarnation of this following the Comprehensive Spending Review in October 2010, the Coalition government have cut three quarters of the social housing programme, and in the Localism Act 2011 have abandoned the idea of tenancies for life, effectively ending the historic, statutory role of state housing as the provider of permanent and secure homes for low-income households.

'Housing' – meaning all housing in both the public and private sectors of the economy – has a subtle connection to society in general and to the wider welfare state. Unravelling this and making sense of how we should think about housing as an issue in the 21st century is the core of this book. The problem with the wobbly pillar analogy is that it is cumbersome because it does not really capture these wider and sometimes complex connections. For example, some people think of housing as only about the state sector – the idea of it as a social right that the state should enforce like compulsory education. Others think of housing more as a private commodity that is bought and sold in a market and that the function of the state, if there is one, is

3

to regulate transactions and the financial industry that supports home purchases. This confusion between housing as a social right or as a commodity has dogged the subject for some time. In fact it is both (Clapham et al, 1990).

For similar reasons, the comparative welfare state literature mistakenly downplays housing mainly because of its reliance on the open market. Housing does not fit very easily with the somewhat ageing tradition of research on core welfare state pillars. Wilensky, for example, rather unconvincingly argued that housing was too difficult to incorporate into his comparison of OECD countries because of the 'bewildering array of fiscal, monetary and other policies that affect housing directly' (Wilensky, 1975, p 7). Even in the new generation of studies about welfare state 'families of nations' and 'regimes' that emerged in the 1990s, housing was at best a marginal analytical variable. Esping-Andersen (1990), Heidenheimer et al (1990), Castles (1998) and Swank (2002), for example, all downplay the role of housing in their otherwise path-breaking accounts of welfare state change. Even in Esping-Andersen's *The Three Worlds of Welfare Capitalism* (1990), perhaps the most famous book in recent decades on the nature of public policy in modern democracies, and which explored the welfare state pillars of social security, health and education, the word 'housing' was barely mentioned and does not appear in the index.

The neglect of housing in these waves of research is no longer tenable. And from a UK perspective, the 'real-world' situation – with severe and seemingly sustained cuts in the social housing programme; the ending of tenancies for life, effectively creating a mirror image of the tenancy arrangements in the privately rented sector; tightening in the application criteria for housing benefit; and record low figures for house-building in the private sector – makes the neglect of housing in the public policy literature all the more incongruous. More than this, the recent banking crisis revealed the extent to which 'housing' in its wider sense was complicit in the events of 2007–09 because it was the massive scale of bad debt accumulated in parts of the US prime housing market (Mian and Sufi, 2009), but particularly in the US sub-prime market, with serious errors made by credit-rating agencies about the value of this debt, that triggered the crisis (Muellbauer and Murphy, 2008). The bursting of the global financial bubble following a period of unprecedented growth in house prices across most, but not all, of the OECD countries has had major economic and social repercussions (Hennigan, 2008). This was underpinned by the invention of new forms of financial trading, principally the process known as 'securitisation'. This is a way of bundling up mortgages into bonds that are then sold by the banks to investors, creating a supply of new capital, while offloading the long-term risks to other institutions. In this process, mortgage markets stopped being basically national and became truly global institutions (Renaud and Kim, 2007; Kim and Renaud, 2009). Home-ownership, which has grown in most countries, is not the product of some neoliberal agenda, but has expanded due to policy choices made, the evolution of welfare state regimes and recently the impact of the globalisation of mortgage markets, tempered by nationally specific institutional structures. New ways of funding mortgage markets and the many thousands of products that connected home-owners to globally sourced capital, powerfully influenced the way that home-owners began to think directly about their properties as commodities or investments, rather than as homes or accommodation (Smith et al, 2010; Lowe et al, 2011, forthcoming; see also Chapter Seven).

Until recently, almost the only scholar who investigated the place of housing in welfare state theory was Jim Kemeny. His pioneering work showed the kind of processes that might work through specifically 'housing' variables to impact on welfare state development. Even before the recent developments, his work showed the kind of processes that were shaping outcomes. Kemeny's key observation here was that owner-occupiers come to have a particular outlook towards taxation and spending on public services because the life-cycle patterns involved in the costs of buying a house are normally very front-loaded. Home-owners have to save up for a deposit and mortgage payments are expensive at a time when income tends to be low. This compression of costs at the beginning of a housing career eases after the mortgage is paid off, usually over 20–25 years. On the other hand tenants pay their housing costs out in a much more even way, perhaps increasing during the period of child-rearing, but basically rent is paid over the whole of their lifetime (Kemeny, 1995).

Kemeny's thesis inspired a key debate about housing and the welfare state, in which he and Castles deliberated whether housing leads or follows welfare state retrenchment. This argument explored the relationship between home-ownership and financial planning for old age and provided an important conceptual linkage between housing and welfare state theory. The 'really big trade-off' debate between Kemeny and Castles revolved around the front-loading of costs associated with purchasing a home, the implication being that relatively low housing costs for elderly owner-occupiers created disincentives for the state to provide good-quality pensions (see Kemeny, 2005). So there is a 'trade-off' between pensions and housing to the extent that, for some home-owners, cheap housing costs in older age, and the potential to release home equity by trading down or in some other way, can substitute for pensions and enhance post-retirement income.

Looked at in this way, 'housing' needs to be taken seriously as a key component of welfare state research. But much more than this, the stirrings of the idea of what is now referred to as 'asset-based welfare' can be found in Kemeny's earlier writings, in which he points to the connection between low tax/low spend welfare states and high tax/ high spend alternatives. In other words, political attitudes to welfare state spending can be significantly shaped by people's housing assets or lack of them. The key, however, to the approach in this book arises from the connection of these debates to the globalisation of the financial markets that over three decades up to 2007 washed huge amounts of capital across the world, a large part of it due to the trade in mortgage-backed securities as mentioned earlier. What has changed the agenda for the asset-based welfare state concept is the connection of these capital flows directly into individual household budgets, particularly through remortgaging. This made home-ownership not only a significant long-term asset for millions of families, but also an immediate source for spending – on consumer items and services – and at the very least, as Susan Smith and Beverley Searle talk about it, a 'bank' from which families from time to time and when needs arise dip into (Smith and Searle, 2008). As will be obvious, relying on this is a terribly perilous strategy and yet it underpins a great deal about the current UK government's social policy thinking.

The context in which all this was happening and its sheer scale and global reach gives fresh urgency to the need to renew our thinking about the relationship between housing and welfare states. This is the principal aim of this book.

Institutions and change

In order to explain why such dramatic change has occurred, we need to go back in time. This opens up a second dimension to the 'housing debate' and is built around the theme of the role of institutions in shaping policy. There is an inner dimension to the text that is founded on ideas developed in the new institutionalist literature. This research school, mainly working in the field of public policy, has made some of the most important discoveries in the social sciences in recent decades. New institutionalism emerged during the 1980s and since then has been particularly influential in the analysis of social change. As Thelen and Steinmo suggest, new institutionalism aims to 'illuminate how political struggles are mediated by the institutional setting in which they take place' (Thelen and Steinmo, 1992, p 2). In other words, they emphasise that institutions structure the impact of political actors.

Box 1.1: Defining institutions

Thelmo and Steinmo (1992) identify the key characteristics of institutions as:

- meso-level structures standing between the broad macro-level forces that shape policy (such as globalisation and demographic change) and the micro-level (of individual actors and where/when policy is finally delivered);
- having formal and informal dimensions: these can be either rules and laws or customs and norms;

- showing and creating stability and legitimacy over time: they are valued in themselves.

Examples:

- Election rules and voting systems.
- Political party systems and structures.
- Relations between branches of government.

Examples of housing institutions include: 'council housing', estate agents, private landlords and their organisations, house-builders, tenancy arrangements and building societies.

One of the key discoveries of this school was the critical importance of taking a long view of policy change. In a series of influential case studies, the so-called 'historical institutionalists' have demonstrated the impact of the past on current policy. The area of the welfare state and social policy has been particularly fruitful in this regard (Baldwin, 1990; Immergut, 1992; Skocpol, 1992; Pierson, 1994, 2001; Castles, 1998). Unfortunately, there are no 'housing' cases, probably for the same reasons that housing was neglected in comparative welfare state research, although there are many studies of 'the history of housing' that unwittingly provide quite a good substitute (Merrett,1979; Holmans, 1987; Ravetz, 2001).

At the heart of the historical institutionalist perspective is the idea that institutions foster stability and that social and political change is complex. In order to understand social policies (including of course housing), what they are like and why, it is essential to look over the *longue durée*, to see over quite long spans of time how policies have developed (see Box 1.2). Historical institutionalists argue that policy tends to evolve quite slowly and incrementally. This is because institutions are 'sticky'. Once they are set up, it is difficult to change them because of vested interests and what Pierson calls the fact of increasing returns. For example, once a particular type of pension policy has been instigated – either on a state-managed Pay-As-You-Go (PAYG) scheme or more geared towards the private sector – the more difficult it becomes over time to turn back (Myles and Pierson, 2001). The closely connected notion of 'path dependency' has been subject to some debate recently, particularly around the question of how and under what circumstances change takes place in otherwise quite stable situations (see Box 1.2). What causes major social/political paradigms to shift (see, for example, Howlett and Cashore, 2009)? The argument here is that change often occurs from within institutions as well as from external shocks such as wars or radical new governments, and that these processes are very subtle and difficult to evaluate.

The second institutionalist theme that runs throughout the text is the way in which macro-, meso- and micro-institutions work together in shaping policy. Institutionalists think of the meso-level as the bridge between wider macro-level factors and the micro-level, where the focus is on individual policymakers and the implementation of policy on the ground. A key point here is that meso-level institutions act as filters to macro-level forces and tend to foster stability. Swank, for example, concluded from his analysis of OECD countries that the impact of the powerful forces of globalisation on welfare states was mediated by domestic political institutions – the type of electoral system, the influence of strong trade unions and civil society, and a welfare state based on universalism with wide coverage and strong benefits (Swank, 2002). In other words, there was nothing preordained about the effects of globalisation leading, so it has been argued, to an inevitable convergence around neoliberal ideas and policies. Chapter Seven, which is a discussion of the globalisation of the mortgage market, comes to a broadly similar conclusion. Despite the release of huge flows of capital into what is now a world financial trading system and the creation of an international mortgage industry (following the deregulation of the banking system in the 1980s), the globalisation of mortgage markets was tempered by nationally specific institutional structures.

–

9

Housing's institutional structure

One of the complexities in the field of public and social policy that mirrors the earlier argument is that different policy areas are not governed by the same rules because their institutional structures are different one from another. What might be true for health policy is not necessarily the case with housing policy. As we have seen, Torgersen shows that much of the cost in housing is the capital investment in land and building, which has the knock-on effect of making it vulnerable to spending cuts (compared to health where most of the cost is in salaries and there are strong lobbies and interests among the medical professionals to defend jobs and salaries). Housing is also very prone to long patterns of change, but even radical departures, such as the Right to Buy council housing brought in by the Thatcher government in 1980, take decades to work through as sales do not occur all at once. Indeed, housing can fundamentally change only very gradually because the existing housing stock is massive compared to the rate at which new properties can be added. Governments publish house-building targets planned over decades of investment. This factor also makes housing vulnerable to the vagaries of what institutionalists refer to as the 'legislative attention span'; governments come and go quite quickly in terms of house-building targets and the speed with which houses can be built. In the British case, it took the dramatic events of two world wars to inject significant pace into the housing programme and even then man had walked on the moon before the post-war shortages had been dealt with!

Properly understood, 'housing tenure' is a key endogenous institutional structure of housing policy, housing's tectonic plates. These plates move only very slowly, but are subject to occasional shocks – earthquakes – when new landscapes emerge from the old. In the language of social science, long, historical and culturally embedded forces are quite 'path-dependent' and not easily changed. Sometimes society reaches a 'juncture' – a political shock such as a major war – which changes the direction of policy and begins to reshape society. While this is not the place for a full-on discussion of historical institutionalism, it is important to note that the early, more historical chapters at the beginning of the book are not just random historical accounts, but are designed to show the type of factors that impacted on the pattern and development of British housing policy without which it is not really possible to understand the contemporary debates and patterns of policy change. In the *longue durée* (see Box 1.2), the seeds of the home-owning society were sown in the crisis of 19th-century private landlordism, became layered into the social fabric of the nation in the interwar years, responded in a second wave of evolution to the deindustrialisation of the UK in the 1980s and 1990s, and then took off under the impact of the globalisation of mortgage markets until the banking crisis in 2007. This temporal sequence is not a random collision of factors, but builds up through the interplay of existing institutions, new power bases, the shock of two massive wars and the impact of globalisation. There is some complexity here, but institutionalists argue that it is possible to make sense of what happened and why.

Box 1.2: Ideas about change

A key theme in this book is that social scientists, including policy analysts, need to pay attention to what François Simiand called the *longue durée*, 'eventual history', his point being that many social processes take a long time to unfold. Pierson points out that much of recent political science has been based on short time horizons, set for example by the period of elections – four or five years. The trap is that we tend to see important things as unfolding quickly and misunderstand what is really happening. There are important things that we do not see, and as a result often do not account for in our analysis. Pierson suggests an analogy that helps explain this complex point using cases drawn from geological science. For example, what causes an earthquake?

> The explanation invokes a very slow-moving process: the build up of pressure on a fault line over an extended period of time. We would be very unlikely to focus our explanatory account on what happened in the days or weeks immediately preceding

the earthquake – the last, miniscule increment of pressure that triggers the event. In this case we have a 'quick' outcome but a very slow-moving, long-term causal process. (Pierson, 2004, pp 79–80)

The same could be said for global warming, with long-term man-made impacts creating a warming effect on the climate that triggers unexpected 'weather' events, sometimes with severe consequences for a local population. 'Weather' is not the same as 'climate'.

In the language of social science, long, historical and culturally embedded forces are quite 'path-dependent' and not easily changed. Sometimes society reaches a 'juncture' – a political shock such as a major war – which changes the direction of policy and begins to reshape society. Part of the analogy also incorporates the idea that the origins of policies are particularly important. The 'path' that is initially decided on is very difficult to retrace if things go wrong, like climbing a tree. Once the climber sets out up a particular branch the outcome of where she ends up is almost inevitable and going back is difficult. Moreover, a different climber starting from the same place but going up a different branch is likely to end up in a completely different part of the tree (Levi, 1997, p 28). First decisions are critical to what comes later.

In a sense, all this is history, but 'history' is not the point. The point is to try to illuminate what was happening and why housing policy became so significant as a field of social policy through the course of the 20th and 21st centuries. Albeit in very attenuated form for the purpose of this 'housing debate', what runs through these pages are some of the key institutionalist themes and claims, and in particular that telling the long story is key to understanding contemporary policy and the direction in which it is moving. These processes of change increasingly impacted on the shape of the wider welfare state, sculpting in the process a new social landscape.

Housing's conceptual and technical foundations

The rest of this chapter layers in some of the fundamental concepts and analytical tools that are used to describe, evaluate and design housing policy, in its most general sense. These are the basic elements that housing analysts work from, especially policymakers in central and local governments. The first of these is the idea of the housing 'stock' – all the historically accumulated structures, whether houses or flats – and then the closely related question that is at the heart of all assessments made by governments about housing, namely, the balance of households to dwellings – whether there are enough dwelling spaces for the population, usually clustered into 'households'. Governments usually also concern themselves with housing standards, at the very least to ensure that buildings are safe, but more likely in modern societies that they are healthy to live in. The next stage is to discuss briefly the idea of housing 'tenure', literally meaning how housing is 'held' (from the Latin verb *teneo, tenire* – to hold) or occupied, normally either as an owner-occupier or as tenant of a landlord. As we will come to see, this distinction is critical to how 'housing' connects to the wider public policy domain and especially the welfare state.

Box 1.3: Outline of the book's structure

The book has two main sections. The first part (Chapters One to Four) explains the development of British housing policy and how this evolved in relation to the welfare state, and the second part (Chapters Five to Nine) examines the current debate about this relationship in the light of the globalisation of the financial markets and the growth of home-ownership.

Chapter One: The foundations outlines the core themes of the book and describes the key analytical tools that are used to describe and evaluate housing policy. Some preliminary comments are made about housing, the idea of housing regimes and how these relate to welfare states.

Chapter Two: The origins of housing policy explains the emergence of the idea of 'housing policy' out of Victorian public health concerns, the demographic pressures that were building and the impact of the First World War in bringing the housing market crisis to a head with the plan for a large-scale state intervention.

Chapter Three: The birth of the home-owning society discusses the seminal interwar years when modern ideas of home-ownership were forged in a massive speculative house-building programme, and addresses the issue of why 'council housing' was the preferred solution to the provision of workers' housing.

Chapter Four: Home-ownership comes of age outlines what happened during the Second World War and its aftermath, focusing on the connection between housing, economic restructuring and the impact of these on the welfare state.

Chapter Five: The post-industrial economy and housing examines how globalisation compelled the British economy to restructure towards a services-based economy and the consequences of this for the welfare state in the 1980s and 1990s.

Chapter Six: Housing and welfare states discusses the reasons for the neglect of housing in the comparative welfare state literature and outlines why housing should be a central part of how welfare states are evaluated.

Chapter Seven: The globalisation of the mortgage market shows how the mortgage market was revolutionised after the deregulation of the banks in the 1980s, and how the characteristics of different mortgage markets created different outcomes despite the flood of global capital.

Chapter Eight: Towards asset-based welfare states examines the case for asset-based welfare and focuses on the UK case as an example. It shows how everyday life became 'financialised' and shows why there is a 'really, really big trade-off' between housing assets and attitudes towards domestic welfare decision-making. Some international cases of asset-based welfare states are discussed.

Chapter Nine: Conclusion provides an overview of UK housing policy following the 2010 general election and sums up the discussion about the significance of housing and welfare state change.

The housing stock

The housing stock consists of all the accumulated dwellings built in the past, representing many different styles of building, designs and building programmes. For example, in most European countries after the Second World War (1939–45), a high proportion of new housing was built in the form of high-rise blocks of flats producing a lasting impact on the urban landscape. In recent years some of the biggest of these have been demolished because of the social problems that became associated with them. But cities such as Stockholm, Budapest and Vienna are dominated by high-rise flats and have a tradition of such housing. Some historians have observed that this tradition is common to cities that had medieval walls.

In England, the country that first experienced the Industrial Revolution and as a result was the first to be rapidly urbanised, the building tradition was for low-rise property clustered around factories and, after the invention of the electric tram, in 'suburbs'. Because of this early start, it follows that a high proportion of the housing stock in the UK is old; over 25% of current stock was built in the 19th century despite subsequent slum clearance programmes and bomb damage in the Blitz during the Second World War.

Due to rising incomes and new technologies, the housing stock and housing standards evolve over time, so that what was once normal and acceptable can change quite quickly. For example, a high proportion of housing in the northern hemisphere (certainly north of the Alps in Europe) has double glazing and central heating, but only 30 or 40 years ago these were less common. Other key features for measuring housing standards are the size of the property, usually measured in square metres, how many rooms it has (especially bedrooms) and its location – where a house is and access to local amenities matter considerably to its value and the experience of living in it.

Box 1.4: Definitions

- The word 'housing' is both a noun and a verb. Housing, as a collective noun, refers to all the buildings in which people live and includes flats as well as houses. The verb 'to house' refers to the process or activity of housing.
- The word 'dwelling' is used to describe the physical buildings of any type in which people live/dwell.
- 'Household' is a technical word that describes a group of people who form a separate unit who regularly live at the same address. This, of course, includes not only families, but also people who live alone.
- 'Housing tenure' describes the way in which the household possesses the dwelling. It comes from the Latin word meaning 'to hold' (*teneo*). The main forms of tenure are ownership and tenancy (ie rented from a landlord).
- 'Home' describes the sense of belonging to a place and has very powerful emotional connotations. It is the place where we can be 'ourselves' (as the marriage vows state '... for better or worse').

It should be noted that languages other than English do not share some of these concepts or have other words to describe the complexities of 'housing'. For example, in Hungarian the words for 'housing policy' are 'lokacs politic', which refers to flats, not houses.

Repair and maintenance

One of the main functions of the state in relation to housing is to ensure that housing standards are maintained, both when properties are built (typically structural plans have to be approved), and as time goes

---

by that they remain in a condition fit for habitation. Governments in industrialised societies usually monitor housing conditions in regular surveys of the stock. This sometimes leads to renewal and renovation strategies and when necessary clearance of unfit property. Almost always 'slum clearance' is a state activity managed by local governments. Often these properties are owned by private landlords and the demolition programme involves replacing them with new state housing – housing that is owned and managed by local authorities, federal governments (such as the German 'Lander') or state-financed housing associations/ cooperatives.

The existence of this historical stock is another reason why housing is different from the other welfare state pillars. Housing is fixed and durable and the stock is added to very slowly; typically less than one per cent of new housing is added per annum. As a result, housing is much slower to change than the other public services and many housing problems arise from this historical legacy. Problems in the supply of housing are therefore initially expressed not through new building but in price – when demand cannot be met by new supply, house prices go up.

Stock and flow

Although it is a technical point, it is worth noting that it is not just the existing stock of housing that matters, but the flows of housing need – the shortfall between the households currently seeking a house, especially first-time buyers and young people trying to rent a flat for the first time, and the rate of new supply through house-building. The problem is that there may not be enough housing of the right type or price available in the areas where people want to live. In practice, many of the key housing policy issues concern how to deal with the flow of new needs. This concerns not only the quantity of houses that should be added to the existing stock to meet new needs (and any that have not been met in the past), but also a calculation of the amount of housing that should be supplied for people who cannot afford to be in the normal housing market. Most nations make provision, to a greater or lesser extent, for 'social housing'. In other words, social housing makes up the gap (deficiency) between what the market supplies and what is actually needed to house everyone. This flow of housing need can be thought of as water pouring into a bath and social housing is the plug! At the most extreme end of housing need homelessness can also be thought of as a 'flow'. Each day will find different people becoming homeless while others are taken into hostels and supported by government projects or find settled accommodation in the mainstream social housing sector or housing market. So there is always a flow of homeless people into and out of homelessness. This makes it difficult to count the quantity of rough sleepers on any one day. Because homelessness takes many different forms – from literally being without a roof through to overcrowding and being forced to share unsatisfactory accommodation of a poor and unhealthy standard – it is difficult to know where homelessness ends and more general housing need begins.

Box 1.5: The concept of 'home'

The idea of home is universally and instinctively understood. People who have lived abroad talk about 'coming home'. We intuitively think of home in relation to the wider world 'out there' beyond our front doors. The concept is closely bound up with creating our own self-identity – where we are most 'ourselves'. The sociologist Anthony Giddens suggests that the home is the main place where social life is sustained and above all reproduced (Giddens, 1989). The French sociologist Bachelard believed that the home was critical to our deepest psychic well-being and that rooms, pieces of furniture, nooks and crannies in the house – how they smell, their echoes and their secret memories – make the home a sanctuary; as he says, 'the house allows one to dream in peace' (Bachelard, 1997, p 87).

A good example of the idea of home in practice is the idea of domesticity that was invented in 19th-century England. Victorian domestic culture was imbued with a sense of the home as a retreat from a hostile world outside. This powerful culture with its strong moral purpose spread across the British Empire and took root in all the English-speaking nations. Throughout the 20th century, interest in the domestic interior persisted and found expression in the obsession with home decoration and the 'makeover' of rooms and gardens as seen in numerous TV programmes. The BBC's 'Changing Rooms' programme acquired cult status in the 1990s with a weekly following in excess of 11 million viewers. This sense of being acceptably fashionable is not a new idea and is a contemporary expression of conformity through homemaking.

In the 21st century, the digital revolution and the invention of the Internet transformed how people's homes were used with a huge increase in 'home-working', new types of leisure activity (home cinema) and 'home banking'. In the era of globalisation, when we all reside on a planet where time and space have new meanings, it is clear that the home is ever more important to people's social and psychological well-being. Home has always been the focal point of human life and this is as true in the 21st century as it was for our cave-dwelling ancestors.

The balance of households to dwellings

The next stage is to consider in more detail the issue of how many households there are and whether there are enough dwellings available so that every household has its own independent living space. The bottom line here is that in every society there are homeless people because there is simply an insufficient supply or not enough property at a price people can afford. Overcrowded houses, rough sleepers on the streets, housing in poor physical shape and excessively high house prices are all symptoms that there is something wrong with the balance of households to dwellings. It is the aim of most governments to try to promote a sufficient supply of an adequate standard of housing. What is deemed an adequate standard depends very much on the wider economic health of particular nations. What is then done about implementing the standard varies considerably according to the policy direction taken by governments of different political persuasions. As a general rule, governments try to advance housing standards in line with economic growth. More generally, as will be outlined later, different countries have long-run political and cultural traditions favouring more or less intervention in the process of supply and demand for housing.

How a particular nation responds also depends on circumstances that are often beyond their control. For example, all the nations of central Europe suffered dramatic setbacks in their housing programmes as a result of the two world wars during the 20th century; not only was there a combined total of over 10 years when almost no housing was built, but there was also considerable destruction of civilian property and demand from new households soared. In Britain, for example, the Second World War created a deficit of households to dwellings of nearly 2 million by 1945 (in a housing stock of only 12.5 million). It was this level of massive deficit that was the context for post-war housing policy in almost every European nation and took decades to solve.

The number of households grows faster than the population

An important feature of the issue of the balance of households to dwellings is the fact that in advanced societies, due to improvements in life expectancy and incomes, the number of households grows faster than the population (see Figure 1.1 for the UK case). In particular, the number of adults in the population increases, resulting in a larger pool of people potentially wanting to form a household. A household can be and often is a single person living on their own as well as different types of families and other groups of people who live together, such as students who share a house.

Governments trying to achieve a balance of households to dwellings need to take account of other basic demographic changes. For example, there has been a rapid growth in the number of single-person households. In Europe, this tendency began during the Second World War with an increase in the number of widows, but it is now primarily a product of increasing divorce rates and people who make a lifestyle choice to live alone.

Figure 1.1: Number of households in Britain grew faster than the population during the 20th century

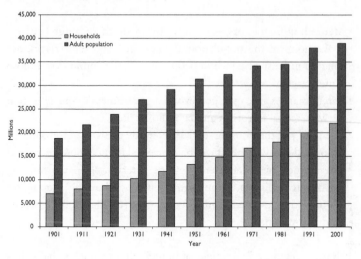

Source: Holmans (2000, p 13)

All these changes mean that there is both an increasing number of households relative to the size of the population and that their composition has changed – in general away from 'traditional' families and towards smaller households and less long-lasting types of relationship. It is a trend typical of those nations that have given up their manufacturing base in exchange for 'post-industrial' economies based on service industries (such as the USA, Britain and Sweden). Clearly, these changes increase the need for housing provision and the type of housing needed. The historic housing stock was not built for such family units and there has been a trend in many older industrial countries for the conversion of houses into flats. It should also be remembered that as people become more affluent, so they may out of choice over-consume the amount of space that they need and live in housing with rooms dedicated to music, their library of books, a lounge with built-in bar, a games room, an audio-visual room, as well as guest rooms.

To sum up the position, the equation of the balance of households to dwellings in any one country is a product of:

- demographic factors – such as the growth of single-person households in the population, divorce rates and remarriages, net migration (ie the balance of people leaving the country over those entering it);
- circumstances that may be beyond a government's control – such as wars, global terrorism and economic crises;
- the legacy of the housing stock that already exists – its size, where it is located and whether it can be converted to meet new needs; and
- the attitude of governments towards intervening in the housing market to build state housing, to influence housing production through the land use planning system or to subsidise housing repairs and renovation.

It is the growth in the number of households in a society that drives the expansion of the stock of dwellings. If the number of households exceeds the supply of new properties, then it quickly becomes apparent through evidence of overcrowding, sharing (especially young people forced to remain at home with their parents) and, in its most extreme, homelessness. In home-owning societies a critical indicator of the health of the housing market and the balance of households to dwellings are house prices. Although these are subject to economic cycles, in the same way as the wider economy, house prices that push the boundaries of affordability are a strong indication of a lack of supply.

Housing finance

Housing production is very expensive compared to average household income. As a result, governments often have to have regard not only to whether a sufficient quantity of housing is being built, but also to whether the 'consumers' (owners and tenants alike) can afford to pay the high costs. Because the cost of a house or flat can be anything between 5 and 10 times the size of annual household incomes, some mechanism is needed to spread out the costs over a long period of time. This is done in the form of long loans called mortgages. This credit is paid back over 20 or 30 years, but includes a large amount of interest on the outstanding debt. A legal contract is written such that if the household cannot afford the repayments the lender (normally a building society or bank) can repossess the property and sell it to reclaim the debt.

Since banks were deregulated in the 1980s this traditional model of housing finance has very largely been consigned to the dustbin of history. This is because mortgage markets have become completely global, with banks able to raise money through the wholesale international money markets. In particular, the invention of the process known as 'securitisation' has created a major supply of new capital (see Box 7.1 in Chapter Seven). Mortgages are bundled up into bonds – Mortgage-Backed Securities – and sold to investors who are looking for long-term and secure assets. Insurance companies and particularly pension funds buy securitised bonds because they need investments that will mature a long way in the future. As a result of these developments, mortgage markets stopped being basically national institutions and entered a new era of globalised bond markets producing massive amounts of new capital allowing originating banks to refresh their capital and pass the long-term risk (eg that interest rates will rise and create mortgage defaulting) on to investors. This key development is discussed in more detail in Chapter Six, but for now it is important to recognise the complete transformation and globalisation of mortgage markets because there were major social policy repercussions from this, particularly that home-owners were able to access housing equity by the process of 'remortgaging' (ie taking on new mortgage debt and releasing their capital to spend immediately *in situ* – without moving). Housing or home equity withdrawal (HEW) is a key aspect of the impact housing has come to have in shaping and reconstituting modern welfare states because home-owners have been able to buy welfare services through the private market and so break the circle of reliance on the state (Lowe, 2004; Smith and Searle, 2010). The consequences of this for the theme of welfare state change are discussed later in the book (see particularly Chapter Eight).

Housing finance in the British public rental sector of housing has been extensively described by Malpass, and there is no need to go over this ground here (see Malpass, 1990). As will be shown in these chapters, a key to this was the invention of the idea of subsidies towards the end of the 19th century, which created a 'historic cost' form of support for council housing; in other words, the bricks and mortar building/land costs of state housing were reduced, enabling rents to be lower than market levels. This system, which was embedded into local authority finance systems in the Housing Act 1923, was swept away by the Thatcher government in the Housing Act 1980. Instead of providing support to councils to provide housing at affordable rents – so-called 'bricks and mortar' subsidies – the idea was to push rents towards market levels and support low-income tenants through the benefit system. By this means, housing subsidies basically became part of the social security system.

Housing tenure

Apart from the stock of dwellings, its condition and the balance of households to dwellings, the next key issue concerns the balance of housing provision in the public and private sectors. As has already been explained, the deficit of housing between supply for people able to afford market prices and those who cannot is often made up by state housing rented at subsidised prices. Owning and renting are the two principal housing tenures. The idea of 'tenure' arises because housing is lived in (consumed) by private individual households behind their own front doors. This is a key difference between housing and the other welfare state pillars, because health and education are mainly services provided in a collective setting – a hospital ward, a school classroom and so on. In housing, there is a special conceptual language for describing the variety of forms that possession of the property takes. It is couched in terms of 'housing tenure'. In other words, who is it that has possession of the property? There are two principal types of possession:

- Owner-occupiers (or 'home-owners') who either own the property and the land on which it is built outright or who are in the process of buying it using a special form of loan called a mortgage. What generally happens here is that the lender (a bank or a 'building society') retains the title deeds until the loan is paid off, typically over 20 or 30 years.
- Tenants who rent their rooms, flat or house from a landlord who owns the property. Based on the payment of a weekly rent the tenant has legal occupation of the dwelling in a package of rights and responsibilities. The advantage of renting over ownership is that the tenants do not have to worry about the basic maintenance of the property and it is much easier and cheaper to move on.

Although there is a specific legal package of rights and responsibilities associated with each of the principal tenures, they are not in strict law as different from each other as might be imagined. In some countries, tenancy rights are so secure that they amount to control over the property normally associated with ownership. For example, the tenancy can be inherited by family members. In most legal systems around the world, a tenancy agreement means that the owner of the property (the landlord) gives up their right of possession for the period of the tenancy, although landlords often imagine that it is still 'theirs' and find it hard to accept that the house or flat is out of their control.

Types of housing systems

The balance between owning and renting is an important indicator of the type of housing system that exists in a country and, as will be shown later, can have wide-ranging consequences for the society. In most countries, there is a mixture of different forms of renting depending on whether the landlord is a private individual (or private company) or a public authority, for example, a local council, federal state, sometimes the national government itself or smaller agencies such as state-subsidised housing associations or cooperatives. There is a detailed discussion of this in Chapter Six because it is the foundation for how we need to think about how housing impacts on the nature of society in the circumstances of the 21st century.

The European model of housing

In Europe, with its long history of industrialisation and, as a result, urbanisation, housing problems, especially slum housing that was the source of disease, meant that intervention by the state was needed to sort out these problems. The capitalist free market left to itself was unable and unwilling to address the consequences of its rampant growth. It was also recognised that the reason for such poor-quality housing was the low level of wages against the high costs involved in the production of housing. This was the reason why housing standards in European towns and cities in the 19th century were so poor. Most countries in central Europe gradually adopted some form of 'housing policy' involving intervention in the market, either by giving subsidies to landlords to build better-quality houses or by directly building 'state' housing, owned by local authorities, government-funded housing associations and so on.

The two world wars in the 20th century also had a major impact on state intervention in the housing market. For 10 years (the combined length of the wars) almost no housing was built, and in central Europe there was massive destruction during the Second World War, especially on the Eastern Front where bitter battles were waged between Germany and the USSR. Life was chaotic – there were millions of civilian deaths, tens of millions of refugees, households broke up, marriages were accelerated. In the UK, which was relatively less damaged by bombing and civilian deaths, the number of households grew dramatically during the war. Everywhere, bombed-out housing needed to be rebuilt and the backlog due to the absence of building for nearly six years needed to be made up. This was the context for housing policy in Europe lasting several decades and involving large-scale state intervention in most countries to build 'social housing'.

There were, of course, many different approaches to how this should be done depending on previous traditions and particularly on which political parties controlled the government. Much of Central and Eastern Europe was taken over by the Communist Party and, in theory, housing markets were replaced by state construction companies and a state-managed housing system (the reality was very different – see Box 1.6). In Britain, the landslide victory of the Labour Party led to a massive expansion of state-owned and -managed 'council housing'. Elsewhere, as in terribly war-damaged Germany, state-funded housing construction and reconstruction operated through more plural housing systems involving local councils, federal/regional governments, state-sponsored housing cooperatives and associations and so on, as well as through financial subsidies to private landlords.

The product of this is that in many European countries the state was very active in housing policy. In countries such as Germany, Sweden, the Netherlands and Denmark, the division between public and private renting was not particularly significant because the government subsidised both of them. The landlords – whether public or private – competed with each other for tenants on the basis of the type of property rather than price because the local authorities oversaw local rent-setting. This model of housing is particularly associated with the corporatist nations of Northern Europe and was identified as a distinct 'housing regime' by Jim Kemeny (1981). He described this system as an 'integrated rental market' because of the close connection between public and private renting (see Chapter Six). But it is also characteristic of this model of housing that home-ownership does not dominate; people choose to own or rent more according to their housing needs and what they can or choose to afford, rather than thinking of their home as a financial asset, which is typical of the home-owning societies. Of course the 'European model' is only a general model of housing and many European nations do not conform to this set of ideas. This is particularly the case with the Southern European countries such as

Spain, Italy and Greece where access to housing is based on markets and families.

The conceptual basis of housing is explored in more depth later in the book. For now, it is enough to note that particularly the Central/Northern European nations have a historic model of housing that is very distinct. It will be seen that this model has come under attack in recent years, not least from the European Union. The point, however, is to show that these institutional structures are key to understanding how and why housing policy has changed and evolved in recent years, and that different housing systems operate according to different institutional rules. The UK is a particularly interesting case because uniquely in Europe it evolved during the 20th century from being predominantly a rental society, with most housing until the mid-century owned by private landlords, to the now-familiar home-owning society.

The USA and the home-owning societies

Home-owning societies are also varied in their institutional structures because they encompass societies as different from each other as the USA and China. In the mighty economy of the USA, a 'European' social market model of housing never developed because the government was not willing to become involved in housing to anything like the same extent. The tradition was to defend the free market and individualism. This means that it was expected that people found their own housing in the market either as owners or to a lesser extent in the private rented sector. A tradition of state-built housing did not develop there, very largely because there has never been a mainstream socialist political party. Neither did the US share in the destruction of housing during the two world wars. Indeed, the American economy grew by 3% during the Second World War. Without the need for reconstruction, in the face of an ideological legacy of individualism and where the divisions between Left and Right in politics were (and remain) narrow, American housing policy has taken a different route compared to most of Europe. Public housing was meant to be part of the New Deal in the 1930s (following the Depression), but it was never encouraged and was always stigmatised because of its role in housing poor families. Instead, there grew up a 'home-owning society' supported by tax relief on mortgages and a private rental system not hampered by rent controls or surrounded by political controversy. Very strong institutional support was put in place to promote home-ownership (see Chapter Seven).

There is a distinct cluster of 'home-owning societies' connected by a common cultural and linguistic inheritance as ex-colonies of Britain (the USA, Canada, Australia, New Zealand). Here the distinction between public and private renting is much sharper than in the European 'social market' model. Private renting is an unsubsidised open market in which rents reflect the current value of the property ('market rent'). Public rental housing, such as it is, is accessed through a bureaucratic procedure usually involving a means test (on income) and is targeted at the poorest households. Apart from the tax relief on mortgage payments, which are a form of subsidy, insofar as there are state subsidies for housing, they tend to operate through the social security system by helping low-income families to pay their housing costs. Britain is an unusual case because, while being the cultural source of the English-speaking cluster, it is much more connected to the European 'model' in terms of housing and has the shared legacy of the two world wars.

The UK was never a deeply corporatist nation with a historical legacy rooted in what Macpherson called 'possessive individualism', a tradition dating back to the 17th-century Civil Wars and arguably earlier (Macpherson, 1962). In the latter half of the 20th century, however, Britain went through a revolution in its housing tenure structure so that 70% of households are now owner-occupiers, state housing has been broken up and sold off and in recent years private renting has witnessed a significant revival. It has joined the home-owning cluster of nations and has become much less 'European' in this regard.

It should also be noted that a new breed of home-owning societies has emerged since the collapse of communism in Europe at the end of the 1980s, and a parallel story has emerged in China where free markets in housing have been encouraged within the framework of the communist state (see Box 1.6).

Two housing systems

In general terms, it is possible to divide most industrial nations into one of two broad housing systems:

- Mixed/plural systems in which public and private renting are clearly separated, but operate in the context of a more harmonised rent-setting system that is overseen by local authorities. There tends to be a diversity of types of landlords and no particular type dominates. Owner-occupation is important, but not a determining force. Overall, this system operates a balanced housing system and is commonly found in Northern and Western Europe.
- Home-owning-dominated societies in which there is a clear separation between public and private renting. Private renting is unsubsidised and fully commercial in pricing. Public renting is a residual state-run bureaucracy for low-income households. The housing system is dominated by owner-occupation and most households are compelled to buy. This is the system typical of the English-speaking cluster of nations.

Home-ownership has grown in some countries outside the English-speaking cluster in recent decades, although the changes have not been dramatic (see Table 1.1). It has grown from a low base in some countries and has fallen elsewhere, notably in Switzerland and Japan. In Europe, one reason for the growth of home-owning is that the state has pulled back from housing provision following the period of post-war reconstruction. From about the mid-1970s onwards, the state withdrew from direct provision because the crisis of post-war shortages was over and home-ownership began to grow as a result. British people tend to think that home-ownership is 'normal' and has grown everywhere. In fact, as Table 1.1 shows, the UK is an unusual case with unparalleled changes to its tenure structure. Only in the post-communist nations of Europe has there been anything as dramatic, arising in that case from rapid privatisation of the economies since 1990 when communism collapsed (see Box 1.6). The biggest impact on rates of home-ownership over the last three decades has been caused by the globalisation of the mortgage markets as discussed earlier. This provoked a major surge in house prices almost everywhere as new streams of credit became available in the context of a persistently low interest rate environment (see Chapter Seven). It was this change that has had a major impact on the nature of welfare states, or at the very least on the way people came to think about their homes, not only as places to live, but also as a major financial asset.

Table 1.1: Changing levels of home-ownership in selected OECD countries

	Early 1960s	1970s	Late 1990s	Change
Australia	63	67	70	+7
Canada	66	60	64	–2
UK	42	49	68	+26
Sweden	36	35	42	+6
(West) Germany	29	36	38	+9
France	41	45	54	+13
Switzerland	34	28	30	–4
Japan	71	59	60	–10

Source: Castles (1998, p 251)

Box 1.6: Post-communist housing

One of the most dramatic political changes in recent years was the collapse of the USSR and the other European communist states. Under the communist system, a large share of housing production was organised and managed by the state. There were, however, considerable variations to the balance of state and private housing. For example, in Hungary nearly 80% of new housing between 1946 and 1990 was self-built (private building firms were not allowed) – people used their own resources and labour. State housing was used as an incentive to ensure that key workers – doctors, teachers, engineers and so on – moved to where they were needed. Generally, the state provided cheap food and housing at very low costs, but in a very low-wage economy. In fact, housing was traded on a massive scale through a black market of cash and 'hard currency' deals. Most rural housing in all these countries was and remained owner-occupied.

When communism collapsed at the end of the 1980s, most of the economies were bankrupt and state flats were sold simply because local governments could not afford to manage and maintain them. Selling state flats at low prices was also a 'shock absorber' for the dramatic changes that were taking place in these economies as they adjusted to global market prices. Because private renting had been virtually abolished under communism, and because most state rental flats were sold, these countries have become 'super-owner-occupied'. Countries such as Hungary, Romania and Bulgaria have home-owning rates in excess of 90% of households. Other nations have retained some of their rental stock, but mostly the emphasis has been on rapid privatisation.

The economy of China has also been liberalised since 1988, although the country remains a communist state. A policy for the gradual privatisation of housing has also been followed, in parallel with the European post-communist nations. State flats have been progressively sold off and an open property market has developed alongside the marketisation of the wider Chinese economy.

Home-ownership has come to dominate post-communist European society and also China, producing a completely new variety of housing system, and it remains to be seen what the wider impact on society and the emerging welfare states will be.

Housing and the wider welfare state

Without being able to develop the point here in any detail, it is worth noting that many of the European societies that have retained a more 'social market' model of housing (the 'integrated rental' system outlined earlier) also tend to have welfare states that have developed along a high tax/high spend model with high rates of taxation, but high standards of welfare provision and lower demand or necessity for private provision in health, pensions, education and so on. One reason behind this is that housing costs tend to be lower (allowing taxes to be higher) and a tradition has developed of supporting expensive but high-quality welfare provision. The outcome of all this in any particular country depends on its history and culture and there are significant variations in this core model. Exploring the connection between 'housing' and types of welfare states is outlined in detail later in the book. Certainly, in the comparative and international welfare state literature, housing has generally been ignored, as was discussed earlier. A central aim of this book is to put that right. There is mounting evidence that housing is not only an important pillar of welfare states, but when looked at in the broadest sense has become a foundation. As noted earlier, the deregulation of the banks in the 1980s and the reinvention of financial structures into a truly global economy inter alia unleashed huge amounts of capital around the globe. It is through housing and reconfigured mortgage markets that these resources were connected to individual households.

In the home-owning societies, the emphasis has been on a different form of welfare state settlement that tends to favour a low tax/low spend model of welfare. Home-owners become resistant to taxes to provide state services that they can provide for themselves using their home as a financial asset. There is evidence, for example, that home-owners resist paying into pension funds because they calculate that in retirement their housing costs will be low (having paid off their mortgage), and that if needs be they can trade down to a cheaper house and so convert their housing equity into income. Housing, so it is suggested in this logic, is a better form of saving than a pension fund.

—

Storing up wealth in housing also enables families to fall back on this asset in hard times or when there is a need to bring forward an item of expenditure. The idea that there is a connection between housing equity and how modern welfare states have developed is the core theme of this book. This is not to say that this is a preferable or more effective means of providing welfare, but the fact of it is becoming increasingly clear even in the societies that have retained an integrated rental market and despite the bursting of the house price bubble in 2007.

Conclusion

This introductory chapter has outlined the case for rethinking the role of housing in public policy and particularly how it should be understood in relation to the wider welfare state. It has outlined the key themes of the book and established the conceptual framework in which the debate takes place. Key concepts and the language that shapes the knowledge base of housing policy have been described. What should be clear at this stage is that a central part of a 'housing debate' needs to focus on much, much more than housing as a social right (according to the Declaration of Human Rights). It needs to be understood not just as a roof over our heads, but, critically, as the means through which the wider global economy connects to individual households (see Chapter Eight). This process is very far from being understood in detail. As has already been suggested, something of a rescue mission needs to be put in place even before we explore housing's wider resonance because the comparative welfare state literature has marginalised it as too complex or difficult. And so the first step is to establish the rightful place of housing in the comparative welfare state literature. Indeed, in unravelling this neglect, what becomes clearer is how important housing actually has become in thinking about 21st-century societies and their welfare states.

The second inner theme of this book is to show how important it is to take a long look back at the sources of contemporary housing policy (or any policy field). In this approach, the *longue durée* is emphasised, that is to say, the deep cultural and historical patterns that underpin society and not just particular events. This is why Chapters Two to Four look back at the origins of housing policy in the UK case and how the home-owning society was constructed. These are our housing 'tectonic plates' and without thinking through how they got there it is very difficult to make sense of the current situation or to see the bigger picture – the social landscape on which welfare states were constructed. According to this institutionalist approach, the origins of social formations and policy are critical to the direction taken, and, as we will see, major differences have indeed grown up between the industrialised nations, with distinct housing systems. And so we need to take a close look at the early stage of state intervention into the housing market in order to chart the direction taken. The UK case is the focus here, but the logic is inherently comparative, each nation has its own narrative even though the starting point is often quite similar, especially at the end of the 19th century, at least in Europe: the question of how to provide housing for workers. In Chapter Two we start at the beginning: where did 'housing policy' come from?

SUMMARY

- Housing is a basic human right – the right to have a roof over one's head and a home that is reasonably comfortable – but it is also a key commodity that is the financial centrepiece of most people's lives. Housing markets are a focal point of the 'housing debate'.
- Housing has particular features that distinguish it from other pillars of welfare states, notably, that most of the cost of housing occurs as capital investment when it is built, compared, for example, with health services, where most of the cost is in paying salaries. As a result, housing is vulnerable to cuts in public spending.
- Key features of housing policy analysis are the stock of dwellings and the flows of new need, housing conditions, the balance of households to dwellings, and the type and structure of a nation's housing tenure.
- The structure of mortgage markets – the source of borrowing for house purchase and additional borrowing – is key to how housing markets operate, with important complementary effects on society.

- Housing theorists have identified two quite distinct models or regimes of housing. The home-owning society model is well-known and familiar to us, but rather less known are the integrated rental markets found in Europe in which home-ownership is much less prominent.

- Housing has important synergies with welfare state development, but has been almost totally excluded from the comparative and international welfare state literature. The aim of this book is to help show that housing, far from being neglected, should be a central focus of thinking about modern welfare states

Reading guide

Two of Jim Kemeny's books provide an excellent introduction to the broad themes of this text: (1981) *The Myth of Home Ownership: Public versus Private Choices in Housing Tenure* and (1992) *Housing and Social Theory*. His later books are more complex (and are recommended in later chapters). A useful collection of chapters focused on housing markets and the planning system is G. Bramley, M. Munro and H. Pawson (2004) *Key Issues in Housing: Policies and Markets in the 21st Century*. More detailed discussion of the content of this chapter can be found in S. Lowe (2004) *Housing Policy Analysis: British Housing in Cultural and Comparative Context*. For the UK, the best source of data and detailed discussion of households to dwellings and the development of the housing stock is A.E. Holmans (1987) *Housing Policy in Britain*. The themes in this chapter are written about in many journals such as *Housing Studies*, *The International Journal of Housing Policy*, *Urban Studies* and *Housing, Theory and Society*.

2

The idea of housing policy: the crisis of the late-Victorian housing market

OVERVIEW

There are points in time when existing patterns give way to new directions in policy and society. These 'birth' moments are critical to understanding the nature of the new forms and how they develop in the long run. The crisis of the late-Victorian housing market and, later on, the unexpected and traumatic events of the First World War triggered the demise of the normal institutional structure of housing at the time – renting from private landlords – and opened the way for two new forms – council housing and home-ownership. This chapter is an account of the social, demographic, political and economic forces that led to the idea of 'housing policy'. The questions of why local authorities became major providers of rental housing and why private landlords were unable to respond to the increasing demand for housing are outlined. The decades before 1914 contained in embryonic form important pointers to what was to follow the war. New ideas about housing were about to be born. It was the gestation time of the British home-owning society, new life forms came into being, quite unlike in most of the rest of Europe.

Key concepts:

'council housing', 'housing policy', housing subsidies, laissez-faire markets, urbanisation

Introduction

This chapter draws on the institutionalist approach to explain the sources of modern housing policy and shows the impact that housing policy had in helping to shape society. Its intention is as much conceptual as it is 'historical'. Understanding how and why societies change is the most complex task of the social sciences. As outlined in Chapter One, recent thinking suggests that in order to understand the here and now we need to discover the long cultural roots that underlie our social systems (Pierson, 2004). This same stream of work also shows that the impact of first decisions and even quite small variations at the beginning of the life of a policy can create major and long-lasting effects. In addition, it is now known that the timing of events is also a key driver of policy change. All these factors are in play here. For example, as we will see, coming more or less out of the blue, the outbreak of the First World War severely jolted Edwardian Britain, and in terms of 'housing', its timing made inevitable new directions in policy that had previously been only vague and highly contested ideas. Lest they be overlooked, it is also the case that the energy and commitment of a number of key personalities are important to the story of what happened.

How we think about and interpret the nature of the Victorian/ Edwardian housing crisis and the impact of the war are key to understanding the shape of housing policy in the 20th and 21st centuries. Decisions made then resonate down to the present day, when in many ways the early debates about 'state' and 'market' are being revisited following the housing market crisis in the USA beginning in 2007 and the ensuing 'credit crunch'. This is why in the next two chapters there is an emphasis on the seminal time for British housing, which was the period at the end of the 19th century and up to the outbreak of the Second World War in 1939. Between these dates, 'housing policy' emerged as distinct from public health – the concern with the demolition of 'plague spots' and insanitary property – and 'council housing' and a new version of 'owner-occupation' were invented. When the classic form of housing provision in the Victorian city, private renting, began to falter, it created what was known at the time as the 'housing question'. If private landlords would not supply new housing, who would? The answer to this engendered a quiet revolution in policy that, in time, turned Britain into the 'home-owning society' we know today and all that is entailed with this for the nature of society as a whole. So the fact that it started in the way that it did was a 'first cause' with major long-term significance, which, as will be shown, was quite different from other European nations facing the same question, particularly about the provision of workers' housing. The divergence of Britain from the rest of Europe at this time has enormous resonance for the contemporary 'housing debate' and it is very important to be clear about what was happening and why at this critical moment.

The focus is on the British case, and the aim in this chapter is not only to outline a narrative, but to show how this story was shaped by the housing fundamentals described in Chapter One, particularly changes that took place to household structure, the quiet revolution of housing tenure change and, above all, the issue of the balance of households to dwellings. All this was played out against the circumstances of the day.

Urbanisation and the private rental model of housing

Cutting a long story short, Britain was the first country to undergo a factory-based industrial revolution, and with it came urbanisation. Beginning at the end of the 18th century and continuing across the first half of the 19th, there were huge population shifts involving millions of households. As people relocated from country to town, housing was provided by factory-owners and investors who built to rent in a private market. By contrast to the situation today, 90% of households, of all social classes, lived in the private rented sector, and this was the case up to the early 1920s. For the great mass of the new 'working classes', this meant living in housing within walking distance of their work and often of a very poor standard, typically in tenements, 'two-up, two-down flats' or 'back-to-backs'. In this latter form of dwelling, built by speculative developers, terraces of houses shared a back wall with each house facing away from the other. Access and windows were at the front, with one living room coming in from the street where cooking was done on open fires or ranges. There was no mains water or piped sanitation; excrement and waste were collected by 'soil carts'. There were often no backyards, and these airless, stinking houses were often overcrowded, remembering that a normal family size would be on average six people, and frequently more, leading to an unimaginable situation if households were sharing, which, as we will see, was common. Styles and type of workers' housing varied considerably across the country, but conditions everywhere were grim. The reason for this abject standard was that wages were very low in relation to housing costs, bearing in mind that this was an unsubsidised free market made up of investors who required a yield from their capital, including the industrial entrepreneurs who paid the wages of their workforce, but were also their landlords. Low wages converted into low housing standards (Gauldie, 1974).

Private rental housing was a popular investment up to the end of the 19th century because it was literally 'as safe as houses', and until the decades before 1900 there was no obvious alternative for small-scale investors. Ownership was spread widely across the social spectrum with hundreds of thousands of small-scale, amateur landlords owning only a few properties. Income from this source was generally dependable and owners often used letting agencies as intermediaries. Different types of letting were accompanied by different levels of risk. For example, the normal arrangement at the bottom end of the market was the weekly let – rent paid out of wage packets – which often required intensive management and maintenance (which was the landlord's responsibility), whereas better properties let to the middle classes on long leases were a much more stable investment and maintenance was the tenant's duty. Then, as now, landlords often borrowed money to make their investments, but mainly from trusts and private individuals, with very little borrowing from banks or building societies (Kemp, 2004). The market was also subject to cyclical boom and slump fluctuations caused by wider economic conditions, but mostly by oversupply of new building during boom periods.

Problems began to hit the housing market in the late Victorian and Edwardian periods. Especially at the bottom end of the market, investors were becoming more cautious. The last house-building boom in the 19th century peaked at the turn of the century and was followed by a lengthy slump on an unprecedented scale that lasted until the outbreak of the First World War in 1914 when everything changed. Here are the seeds of the long and sustained collapse of private renting in Britain through to the late 1980s when it all but disappeared in its historic role. How we interpret this downturn in its fortunes is a key part of the analysis leading to a quiet social revolution in which state rental housing became prominent, and, above all, leading to Britain becoming a fully fledged 'home-owning society'. There is no doubt that, had the circumstances and the institutional structures of the Victorian housing market been different, there would have been a very different outcome, as there was in most of the rest of Europe where, even now, home-owning is a much less dominant force (see Chapter Five). How, then, do we account for the decline of investment in British private renting?

The late-Victorian housing crisis

It was abundantly clear that overcrowding and housing conditions generally deteriorated through the second half of the century for the great mass of low-paid workers concentrated in the inner urban areas. The plight of these people is vividly described in Charles Dickens' satirical novel *Hard Times* (1854) about a fictitious northern England town, 'Coketown'. Here, one can almost smell the stench of the hovels that were the norm for millions of households detached from the rest of society by their hand-to-mouth abject, pre-industrial poverty. This could not go on, but it was difficult to see what could or should be done in the circumstances of a laissez-faire economy in which state interference was treated with at best circumspection and often outright hostility. This is a situation that must be accounted for in the analysis of the period, given that average incomes doubled in the 50 years up to 1900.

Philanthropic factory-owners experimented with housing schemes for their workers and some enlightened developers such as the American businessman Peabody set up 'model dwelling companies' using new designs, aiming to run profitable but humanitarian housing companies, so called 'five percent philanthropists'. These projects helped by showing the way – with high-quality housing and improved management, albeit paternalistic – but they were a drop in the ocean compared to the scale of the problem. Recognition that there was a problem, at least in London, was apparent in the establishment in 1882 of the Royal Commission on the Housing of the Working Classes and in their report published in 1885. The Commission, whose members included the Prince of Wales no less, collected evidence of a measurable decline in housing conditions. Dockers and costermongers (sellers of fruit and vegetables from barrows – 'barrow boys'), among other occupational groups, were found to have incomes considerably below Booth's poverty line and, moreover, were paying a high proportion of their wages in rent. The conclusion was inescapable. These people were not feckless and undeserving, but were the victims of a housing problem not of their own making. It was a startling and salutary realisation, although attributed in the report to the temporary circumstances of a slump in the housing cycle. The problem is summed up by Morton:

> The inner urban poor were being driven outwards by a conversion of city centres to public and commercial uses but were being halted in their tracks by lack of access to newer, cheaper housing further out, of a kind which had eased similar congestion and high charges in the middle years of the century. (Morton, 1991, p 14)

As we have seen, average incomes rose significantly in the second half of the 19th century, although unequal distribution still left millions of poor working families at more or less hand-to-mouth standards. There appears to be little evidence of the trickle-down of better housing to poorer households as a result of rising real incomes, the impact of the new housing by-laws and the new suburban villas. It continued to be the case that the lowest-paid workers lived in dire poverty, unable to afford rent for better accommodation and forced to share in squalid, overcrowded hovels. There were vacancies in the market, but they were in the wrong places or the rents were unaffordable. The standard working day up to 1914 was 10 hours and the costs of transport relatively high. The reality for great swathes of low-paid workers' families was that they could afford neither the time nor the costs of transport to work away from their homes and so were trapped in the inner cities, unable to move because of their inability to travel (Holmans, 1987). Overcrowding and housing stress was an inevitable outcome. Until new modes of transport became more widely available and cheaper, rising real incomes were not sufficient in themselves to reduce high population density, overcrowding and sharing, and the attendant problems of morbidity, short life expectancy and a bitterly poor way of life. Thus, a key explanation for the persistence of inner-city Dickensian slums was not only low income, but also lack of accessible building land.

The birth of 'housing policy'

Following the report of the 1884 Royal Commission, it was not until the Conservative Prime Minister Salisbury returned to power in 1886 with the support of the Liberal Unionist Party that the political situation opened up the possibility of practical movement on the report's findings. As a price for their support, the Liberal Unionists demanded a bill to reform local government so that county councils would be elected and urban and rural district councils designated out of existing sanitary authorities, basically creating for the first time a relatively modern and, above all, a national system of local authorities with defined powers. The previous framework for the ad hoc provision of urban services was gradually incorporated into a system of local administration that lasted more or less intact until the mid-1970s.

With housing supply tightening and some local authorities already experimenting with building projects, the Housing of the Working

—

43

Classes Act was passed by Parliament in July 1890. The progressive London County Council was particularly influential in pressing for this legislation and almost immediately began to build new tenement blocks in London to rehouse families displaced by clearance or improvement schemes. In Poplar, for example, a considerable amount of land was purchased to accommodate the construction of the Blackwall Tunnel. Households affected by the tunnel were rehoused and the surplus land used for housing development. The 1890 Act was key legislation because it provided the context in which local authorities could intervene positively in this sort of project to address the housing crisis (Gauldie, 1974). In this sense, it can be understood as the first statement of 'housing policy' as distinct from local authority public health duties. It was very largely consolidating legislation. Parts I and II brought together the Torrens and Cross Acts (to do with slum clearances), but in Part I there was a new provision for local authorities to redevelop a site directly if no other agency came forward, and in Part III they were empowered to build and also to renovate and improve 'working-class lodging houses', defined (from an earlier 1885 Act) to mean individual dwellings. Through this somewhat arcane redefinition, a door opened that was to lead in the end to the mass provision of state subsidised 'council housing', at its peak in the 1970s accommodating very nearly one third of the whole population. As yet there was no financial support for these projects, and the default position was that any properties built under this legislation eventually would be returned to the private sector. These measures were thought of as temporary until 'normal' market conditions returned. It could not have been foreseen at the time that this was never again to be the case because the beginning of the end of the private rented sector was already well under way.

The beginning of the end of the private rented sector

The problems for private investors in property were both short-term and structural. New building standards via local authority by-laws, public health sanitary controls and clearance powers undermined the low-cost end of the market. There was no compensation for property demolished under public health legislation, insanitary housing being treated rather like contaminated food, as the liability of the purveyor. The extension of the franchise during the 1880s also served to damage the interests of private landlords because property taxes, particularly in the form of local rates, increased as new demands were placed on authorities to provide better and more local services to satisfy public demand. So it was that in the decades before the First World War landlords' profits were being squeezed from a variety of sources. There was thus a long-term, structural problem that was eating away at the core of the traditional market. This had been identified by the 1884 Royal Commission, although, as we have seen, not fully comprehended. On the other hand, new investment opportunities began to open up with the creation of joint stock companies and the maturing banking system, and many small-scale investors were turning to these even before the slump that hit the market about 1900 and lasted almost up to the war.

In the context of the normal boom and slump cycle of the Victorian housing market, this downturn was particularly sustained, deep and severe in its consequences. The slump was the final straw for many investors who withdrew their funds to much safer and easier financial investments. In the decade up to 1914, new house-building collapsed, possibly by as much as 70% (Kemp, 2004). This change of logic impacted particularly sharply at the bottom end of the market so that even before the catastrophic events of 1914 a new direction for British housing was implicit if not yet clearly defined.

Who was going to house the workers?

With collapsing investment in working-class housing came a political debate about whether or the extent to which local authority powers under Part III of the 1890 Act should remain permissive. The authorities were reluctant to do more than tinker with the problem in the absence of central Exchequer funding. Liberal philosophy argued that the source of such funding should be via taxation of property interests, and the Liberal government itself was already engaged in an expensive programme of social reform – old-age pensions, national insurance and so on – and, belatedly, in an arms race with the Germans. Nevertheless, it is clear that at the time of the bizarre and fateful assassination of Archduke Ferdinand in Sarajevo on the morning of 28 June 1914, the event that triggered the outbreak of war, the government was already planning a large-scale housing programme of some 120,000 houses, albeit thought of as a one-off intervention. It was a scale far in excess of anything previously attempted or achieved. The sum total of local authority provision by then was a meagre 28,000 new dwellings nationally, 90% of which had been built since the 1890 Act. This was a smaller contribution than that of the private model dwelling companies and the charitable trusts, which had a combined total of about 50,000 dwellings. The step increase in the municipal housing programme was a turning point. As Morton suggests, 'The notion predates the war, predates any decision on subsidy and had the support of both main political parties' (Morton, 1991, p 30). Moreover, it was unequivocally the decision that this programme of building was to be carried out by local authorities.

Why 'council housing'?

The municipal authorities picked up the mantle of the provision of rental accommodation because they had an established national structure since the Local Government Act 1888. Many of the larger urban authorities employed public health inspectors who had hands-on knowledge of housing standards and the technical aspects of house-building through their duties to implement by-law standards. Local authorities were empowered to compel developers to deposit plans for inspection and amendment if necessary and could inspect construction sites and insist on changes if the building contravened local by-laws – wider road layouts, airbricks, bigger and more windows and so on. Some of the more progressive authorities such as the London County Council, Sheffield and Leeds had already built high-quality houses under the terms of the 1890 Act, dwellings generally of better standard than those of the private model dwelling companies which, in any case, were mainly based in London and would not be capable of delivering a national house-building programme.

The reason why private landlords were never seriously considered as contenders for this national programme requires some explanation because it bears on the wider picture of how the housing question was addressed by comparable European nations. In the first place, having virtually abandoned the provision of housing before 1914, conditions for investors in the housing market worsened considerably during the First World War, making it difficult to see how investment would return even with subsidy. It must also be remembered who these investors were: a petit bourgeois class made up of thousands of small-scale, amateur landlords typically owning only three or four properties, held as an insurance against the future, and on the fringes of all the main political parties. They were politically disorganised and did not have a voice in the housing debates of the day. The Liberals, as we have seen, sought to tax property-ownership, the Conservatives represented an essentially rural rather than urban interest and the emerging labour movement was not inclined to support private landlords. Indeed, it was in local politics that the labour movement first flexed its muscles, experimenting, as we have seen, with their own housing provision – the first steps towards 'council housing'.

Box 2.1: The divergence of British and German housing

The moment when British and German housing policy diverged can be pinpointed to the period at the end of the 19th century when both countries faced the issue of the provision of workers' housing. There was a drastic shortage in both countries. In Berlin, for example, the population of the city fell in 1901 simply because there were no empty properties, overcrowding was at a peak and there was nowhere for people to live. In Britain, private renting was in abeyance, as outlined in the main text, and council housing was being considered as an alternative. In Germany, however, encouragement was given not to local authorities, but to housing cooperatives. Why did this happen? In the first place housing finance was made available in many European countries from social insurance funds. In the German case, non-profit cooperative building societies borrowed money at favourable interest rates from the fund established by the Invalidity and Old Age Insurance Fund Act 1890. In Berlin alone, by 1914, 11,000 houses had been built by this means. Albeit a relatively small number compared to the problem, it is far in excess of the number built by London County Council following the provisions of the Housing of the Working Classes Act 1890. The basis of the divergence in housing policy was already appearing. What was happening here? As we have seen in this chapter, British private landlords were politically weak. In Germany, private landlords were a more diverse group including powerful landowners and large-scale property companies. The three-class voting system of the Prussian state skewed election outcomes to favour the interests of large property-owners. Basically, the system divided the electorate into three, according to how much tax they paid. The top band contained only the very wealthy. The result was that a small number of high rate taxpayers had a disproportionate influence on national legislation and also on municipal government where the same system applied. As a result of this, private property interests were able to resist reform, especially the municipal housing option, and even made life difficult for the independent cooperatives.

In Britain, the influence of property-owners was much less, but as the trade unions grew and the Labour Party took root in the politics of the industrial cities, 'state housing' was the most acceptable alternative to the dwindling private rented sector. The labour movement in Britain did not have grounds for the same scepticism of the politically biased state as did their German comrades. The German Social Democrats refused to participate in 'bourgeois governments', but Bismarck's social reform agenda during the 1880s – based on social insurance schemes – was a carrot to the German workers designed to undermine socialism. The point here is that the municipal housing route was more or less blocked off in Germany. Instead, autonomous trade unions, friendly societies and housing cooperatives drew on the social insurance funds to build their own housing schemes over which they had management control including tenant selection. In Britain, although the model dwelling companies and housing cooperatives did have an early significance, the scale of the shortages required a nationally coordinated strategy that the local authorities were politically and administratively able to deliver, given sufficient resources.

Using cheap loans from the state, the German path was to develop a more plural system built around autonomous housing providers. The political systems and institutional structures of Britain and Germany weighted the balance of possible solutions to the housing question differently. As we will see later in the book, this divergence has persisted and is the basis for modern housing systems that remain dissimilar.

Council housing was not the route taken by the Continental labour movements, which regarded the state as politically biased and compromised – supporting the interests of large-scale and powerful landlords. Germany, France, Hungary, Austria and later the Nordic countries all have their own stories to tell, but in the main the municipal route was not an available option to supply workers' housing. Landlords and property-owners were able to block the municipal route, which they regarded as 'socialist' (Daunton, 1990). Using cheap loans borrowed at favourable interest rates from national social insurance funds, trade unions, non-profit housing cooperatives and housing associations were able to build and manage their own independent housing projects. British landlords were a politically disorganised class and did not have the powerful position at the centre of government enjoyed, for example, by German landlords as a result of the three-class voting system (see Box 2.1). The consequences of differences in voting systems is a key institutionalist insight and is very well illustrated here. The divergence of policies at this point in time was to have very long-lasting effects because already the logic of two different systems was in place. In the British case, the tired form of housing that had served Victorian capitalism for so long was replaced by council housing and, in a parallel development, home-ownership. The building industry was compelled to sell its products to those who could afford to buy, which as we will see was a new social class of 'white-collar workers' spawned out of a new services economy after the First World War. The key point for now is that the political and institutional structures of some Continental nations produced very different answers to the housing question compared to Britain. It is important to recognise that the roots of this divergence are very early indeed. As will be seen, this divergence provides an important perspective not only on the housing story, but also on how and why welfare states grew and were shaped by different political forces and social interests.

Conclusion

In this narrative account, some of the main building blocks of 21st-century housing were outlined. To start with, the idea of 'housing policy' causing the state to intervene in the laissez-faire Victorian housing market was the beginning of a major paradigm shift – of new ways of thinking about social problems – bringing with it new institutional structures quite unlike what had gone before. Local authorities were already building council housing and experimenting with new architectural forms, providing housing not for the poorest families, but for artisan workers who could afford the quite high rents charged. Private landlords were leaving the housing market in droves and, without subsidy and isolated outside the political arena, the structural and social demise of this sector of housing was already being layered into the fledgling 20th-century housing system. The decline of the private rented sector had been initiated and, apart from one brief moment at the end of the 1930s, there was no going back. New pathways were being laid down that were to shape the pattern of the future leading to our 'home-owning society'. This is why it is important to take seriously the *longue durée* because it is very difficult to understand contemporary social policy without seeing its roots, the moments when history turns and old institutional structures are sculpted into a new landscape. This was to be the foundation of an asset base of quite massive proportions and in time began to reshape the welfare state, so that the timing and sequence of these apparently distant events are very resonant in today's story, as we will see later in the book.

On the Continent, the issue of the provision of workers' housing was addressed rather differently and this early divergence had its roots in the different political/cultural institutional structures. Here also, then, we must take on board the need to understand how these origins, the gestation moments, impact on new policy directions. A path was taken that led in a significantly different direction so far as housing policy was concerned; more plurality of providers, incorporation of the powerful landlord classes (and the lesser private landlords), a less centralised subsidy system, all underpinned by different ideas about social housing provision, renting and ownership of property.

The impact of the First World War on the already stressed housing markets of Europe was like a massive crunching up of old tectonic plates. The consequences of this in Britain was the rise of council housing and, even more importantly, the birth of the home-owning society, both key features of the interwar years between 1918 and 1939, and this seminal time is the subject of the next chapter.

SUMMARY

- Housing in Victorian towns and cities was provided by private landlords for whom housing was an investment. Standards were very low because house-building was expensive relative to income. In a market economy, low wages meant low housing standards.
- The Housing of the Working Classes Act 1890 was the first real attempt at 'housing policy' as distinct from the demolition of slums, which was a public health question and did not involve rebuilding.
- Because wages were low and working days long, most working-class households could afford neither the time nor the cost of travel to work away from their homes, and so were compelled to live within walking distance of their employment.
- In the decade leading up to 1914, investment in the private rented sector collapsed. New investment opportunities began to open up with the creation of joint stock companies and the maturing banking system and many small-scale investors turned to these.
- Local authorities began tentatively to build houses and some progressive councils such as the London County Council, Sheffield

and Leeds had already built high-quality houses under the terms of the 1890 Act. Their dwellings were generally of better standard than those of the private model dwelling companies.

- Private landlords were a petit bourgeois class made up of thousands of small-scale, amateur landlords typically owning only three or four properties and on the fringes of all the main political parties. They were politically disorganised and did not have a voice at the heart of the housing debates of the day.
- On the Continent, the provision of workers' housing was accomplished by different methods not usually focused on local authorities. Instead, autonomous trade unions, friendly societies and housing cooperatives drew on central social insurance funds to build their own housing schemes.

Reading guide

There is a wealth of excellent, even classic, writing about the development of housing policy in Britain. Enid Gauldie's (1974) *Cruel Habitations* is a gem. A general and very readable history of housing that incorporates a wide knowledge of the cultural and architectural foundations can be read in J. Burnett (1986) *A Social History of Housing*, 2nd edn. S. Merrett's (1979) *State Housing in Britain* is a comprehensive account of the development of council housing; and P. Malpass (2000) *Housing Associations and Housing Policy* is a good account of the general context of early housing policy and the important but minor role played by housing associations, showing why they were not in the early period the preferred mass housing provider. Alan Holmans' (1987) *Housing Policy in Britain* is a tour de force containing masses of data compiled and analysed by a leading and influential housing economist.

3

The birth of the home-owning society: the interwar years (1918–39)

OVERVIEW

The First World War created major trauma to society and was a turning point in the history of housing in Britain. It was an event of such magnitude that it traumatised the whole social structure and left the nation reeling. The social fabric of Britain was ripped apart and a new economic order grew from the old and decaying structures. The housing market was in crisis because conditions for private investors were poor and there was a very large and growing deficit of dwellings to households. The state stepped in with a mass house-building programme. At the same time the private sector – in part supported by government subsidies – invented a new consumer-led form of 'home-ownership', meeting the housing demand created by new classes of white-collar workers. Meanwhile, the mass of ordinary manual workers continued to live in deteriorating housing rented from private landlords. The built environment of the country was transformed as public and private housing estates sprang up in and around every town and city. A new suburban way of life came into existence as transport links such as the London Tube expanded. Such was the scale of building that by the time the Second World War broke out, housing shortages were in sight of being solved. New institutional forms had been invented and the foundations of 'the home-owning society' had been laid down.

Key concepts:

affordability, 'owner-occupation', slum clearance, suburbanisation, 'white-collar workers'

Introduction

As in so many aspects of social and political life, the traumatic events of the First World War jolted Britain out of its Edwardian complacency. The threat of Bolshevism and revolutionary politics was looming on the Continent, and the British government was increasingly concerned about threats to the war effort from a radicalised workforce, a large part of which was engaged in arms manufacture. One alarming manifestation of this was a series of rent strikes organised by women working in armaments production in Glasgow. Landlord and tenant relations were already strained by changes to Scottish law on rent arrears and evictions. Moreover, landlords in the city tried to force up rents for the mainly female immigrant workers aiming to recoup earlier losses. In this very inflamed situation, the government had no real alternative other than to intervene, which they did with the Increase of Rent and Mortgage Interest (War Restrictions) Act 1915, limiting rents and mortgages to their pre-war levels. Not only was the immediate impact felt by landlords, but it made them far riskier customers for building societies compared with owner-occupiers (who were exempt from the mortgage interest restrictions on loans of over 10 years – after lobbying by the Building Societies Association) (Kemp, 2004). Rent control in the particular circumstances of Britain became an important long-term reason for the uneconomic position of private landlords. It was not terminal, as the revival in investment in private renting in the 1930s demonstrated, but we can clearly see now that this was the time when general family housing as an investment dried up. In the immediate aftermath of the traumatic events of the war, the housing shortages reached critical levels. If private landlords would not invest, at least for the time being, how was the housing crisis to be addressed?

Three key factors shaped the post-war housing strategy:

- a rapid increase in the number of new households;
- the conditions in the housing market after the war; and
- the restructuring of the economy.

The consequences of war

The scale of the shortages got much worse in the years up to 1918 – almost nothing was built during the war and there was a sharp increase in new household formations, meaning that the backlog of new need plus existing shortages stacked up to crisis proportions. These figures are sufficiently important to need some detail. Despite a brief recovery in the market just before the hostilities broke out, about one in eight households were sharing with another household, unable to afford even the lowest standard of housing of the day. Roughly 1,250,000 families simply could not afford even the most meagre standard of accommodation available at the bottom end of the market – two-bedroom terraces with outside/shared WC and a cold water tap. It is apparent, therefore, that an important reason for such a large number of households not having separate accommodation of their own was one of affordability rather than lack of supply. The war made an already serious problem much worse because there was very little building done for the duration of the conflict. The government itself calculated that the war had created a shortage of 500,000 dwellings, mostly arising from new household formation. This is a very big number when added to the existing pre-war shortage and this combined total is the backdrop against which the interwar period needs to be read.

A critical element for the interwar period and beyond was the rapid growth in the adult population – between 1921 and 1931 the fastest ever. As the population grew, the proportion of children fell while people aged over 20 became proportionately more numerous. The effect of this was to increase the number of people of working age. In addition, and very important to the demand for housing, there was a large increase in the number of married couples, almost the only way of forming a settled partnership in those days.

Earlier and more marriage, despite the loss of hundreds of thousands of young men in the war trenches – a factor that dampened the figures – plus a growth in the number of widows and the decline in the number of children, were all critical to the long-term trends in population and household formation and accordingly to the demand for housing. According to Holmans, for 50 years up to 1911, new households grew quite evenly by about 95,000 per annum, but this figure began to change remarkably quickly after the war and in the decade up to the outbreak of the Second World War in 1939 reached 175,000 (Holmans, 1987, p 64).

Table 3.1: Population totals for England and Wales

	Total population	Population aged over 20	Female married population
1911	36,071	21,683	6,630
1921	37,887	23,883	7,590
1931	39,953	26,997	8,604
1939	41,460	29,129	9,666

Source: Holmans (1987, p 61)

There were many more households in the population than previously and this had an inevitable impact on the demand for housing that no government could ignore, which made housing a key political issue.

The housing market after the war

The situation in the housing market was such that, even with subsidy, it was unlikely that investors would opt to build in the private rental market. Building costs were high in the aftermath of the war and interest rates remained stubbornly high as the government tried to protect the value of sterling against the gold standard. In these circumstances, it was unlikely that investors would be in a position to build, not knowing when rates and costs might come down. Although newly built houses and flats were exempt from rent restrictions after 1919, even for this unregulated section of the market wartime inflation pushed rental income down very significantly indeed. Rents in 1924 were in real terms between 25% and 30% lower than they had been in 1914. It simply did not make sense to commit capital in such an uncertain environment. The reduction in the real value of rents had the additional effect of increasing housing demand because income levels had significantly improved during the war. Many households could now afford a separate house of their own compared to before the war. Pre-war vacancies were quickly taken up, but this went nowhere near addressing the huge backlog of shortages. It thus became clear that what had been speculatively planned before the war became inevitable. Local authorities would have to be encouraged to mount a large-scale building programme and deliver on a bigger scale what had been foreseen in the very different world of the Belle Epoque.

The Addison Act and its relative failure

The decision to engage local authorities, as we have seen, pre-dates the events of the war so that what happened during the war made the outcome inevitable. The Ministry of Reconstruction spearheaded the post-war housing plan through its housing panel, which was established in 1917, and included on its committee Seebohm Rowntree and Beatrice Webb. They recommended a crash local authority building programme to overcome the immediate shortages, with a follow-up role to supply the nation's housing needs through a tightly controlled, state-subsidised building programme lasting for five years. This plan was enthusiastically advocated by Christopher Addison, the Minister of Reconstruction and a confidante of Lloyd George. Indeed, his advocacy of a new structure for the delivery of this plan, by breaking up the housing role of the Local Government Board, created a new governance of housing. A Ministry of Health was set up embracing the housing function (a situation that remained in place until the 1950s). Addison became the first Minister of Health, and the Housing and Town Planning Act 1919 took his name as parliamentary sponsor (the 'Addison Act') (Ravetz, 2001, p 75). The election of November 1919 resulted in a reduced coalition of Liberals and Conservatives led by Lloyd George. They won the campaign principally on the famous slogan of 'Homes Fit for Heroes' and quickly pushed through housing legislation. In order to appease the ratepayers and to persuade reluctant local authorities to build, the Exchequer's subsidy was very generous.

Box 3.1: Christopher Addison (1869–1951)

Addison, the son of a Lincolnshire farmer, had a long political career after first establishing himself as a distinguished medical doctor, specialising in anatomy. He married Isobel Mackinnon, a Christian Socialist, and she encouraged his increasingly radical political views. Essentially, Addison wanted to help alleviate the poverty and morbidity of ordinary working-class families. He entered Parliament in 1910 and his medical knowledge enabled him to help steer the National Health Insurance Act 1911 onto the statute books, the first of the Liberal reforms. This brought him to the attention of Lloyd George and on the outbreak of war he joined Lloyd George at the Ministry of Munitions. Addison was the powerhouse behind the idea of 'War Socialism' – of intervening in private industry to increase munitions production. Later, as Minister without Portfolio, he planned the post-war social reform strategy. Addison became President of the Local Government Board in January 1919, with the goal of transforming it into a Ministry of Health. He became the first Minister of Health in June that year. At the head of the Ministry of Reconstruction – which represented everything that was progressive at the time – he was responsible for a great deal of the post-war social legislation, including the Housing and Town Planning Act 1919. He was opposed by Conservative members of the coalition government and eventually withdrew and joined the Labour Party in 1923. He became increasingly radical during a period of being in and out of Parliament in the interwar years. He organised medical aid to the Republican fighters during the Spanish Civil War. According to the *Dictionary of National Biography*, Addison 'transformed the housing of the working classes from a capitalist enterprise into a social service'.

After the war he was raised to a peerage and became a Viscount in 1945 (aged 76). From 1940, he was leader of the Labour Party in the House of Lords, a position he held until his death in 1951. His statesmanship and political skill in the House of Lords smoothed the introduction of the National Health Service against an overwhelmingly Conservative-dominated House.

The scale of the Addison Act programme was, as planned, in a completely different league to pre-war council housing. It was designed as a temporary measure, albeit with a programme stretching to 1927, when it was assumed normal market conditions would have resumed. In the meantime, rental housing was to be provided by local authorities. Progress, however, was very slow. It proved to be difficult to get the programme moving in the face of skills shortages and with contractors and unions unwilling to commit themselves to this new and risky venture, especially with spiralling building costs, the same reasons that inhibited investment in the private rented sector. By the end of 1919, not a single house had been built and as late as March 1921 only 16,000 houses had been completed. When construction was aborted by the government in July 1921, only 170,000 council houses had been built or contracted. This was far short of Addison's target of 600,000 houses for the first three years, a target he regarded as the brute minimum to tackle the overall housing crisis. He resorted to lowering standards by introducing a new 'C'-type house (which had no parlour) and using prefabrication, but it was to no avail.

A second housing Act – the Housing (Additional Powers) Act 1919 – was designed to encourage the private sector to build for rent to working-class households, but this requirement was overturned in committee. It led to about 40,000 private-sector houses being built. But even with this boost to the numbers, only 340,000 houses were built in the five years after the war. This was insufficient to keep up with new household formation – which as we have seen was accelerating – let alone make an impact on the existing shortages. Addison himself was distraught at the inability of the housing industry to implement his programme, and later joined the Labour Party where he continued to crusade on the housing issue (Ravetz, 2001, p 80).

One of the reasons for the high costs was the emphasis on high-quality, garden suburb housing, modelled on Raymond Unwin's designs and philosophy (see Box 3.3). Rents were set by reference to the local market for working-class housing with additions for the superior build quality, which almost certainly put these houses out of reach of most wartime heroes. Addison housing was occupied by the families of the better-off 'respectable' working class and the lower end of the middle classes, families who could afford relatively high rents. This was the case for almost all council housing up to the early 1930s. There is remarkably little evidence about who lived in them, but it was certainly *not* the mass of ordinary manual workers. Bowley's research suggested that this new housing was let to 'the better off families, the small clerks, the artisans, the better off semi-skilled workers with small families and fairly safe jobs' (Bowley, 1945, p 129). Studies in London and Liverpool both confirmed this general pattern in the social composition of council housing.

The housing question was not being dealt with and the numbers crisis was rapidly deteriorating. That council housing was neither widely nor enthusiastically embraced is clear. It was accepted out of necessity due to the continuing and persistent shortages of housing. This position would certainly seem to explain the Housing Act of 1923 introduced by the Conservative Minister of Health, Neville Chamberlain. Chamberlain knew from his experience of local government what the best local authority housing could achieve and he allocated a significant, if considerably diminished, role to it in his legislation. The reluctance to accept council housing as an equal partner in meeting the housing shortages also helps account for why the rate of council house-building through the interwar period fluctuated very considerably and was never positively embraced, except by the short-lived Labour government of 1924. Merrett shows how council housing was persistently subject to cuts in subsidy rates and cost-cutting reductions in building standards (Merrett, 1979, p 248). Even before the Addison Act subsidy was axed, the average floor space of the model three-bedroomed dwellings had fallen.

Subsidies for the private sector – the Housing Act 1923

Under the Conservatives' legislation, council housing played an entirely subordinate role to that of private builders. The 'Chamberlain' Housing Act of 1923 provided building subsidies to *both* the public and the private sectors. The Treasury offered local authorities only £6 per dwelling over 20 years with no requirement for rate fund contributions. The aim was to limit the scope and scale of local authority housing programmes and encourage private builders to supply housing for sale to the working classes. Central controls were more stringent than under the Addison legislation and local authorities had to demonstrate to the Ministry that the private sector was not supplying the housing needs of the area before they were given permission to build. The 1923 Act was not repealed until 1929, but only 75,900 council houses had been built under its terms compared with 362,000 subsidised private-sector dwellings (see Table 3.2). Having been chairman of Addison's Slum Area Committee, Chamberlain knew only too well the plight of slum-dwellers, although he shared little of Addison's idealism. The 1923 Act provided local authorities with half the cost of clearance but this was inadequate to encourage any large-scale assault on the slums. This legislation hardened political opinion on both sides, especially in the Labour Party, that the state needed to be given stronger powers to deal with working-class housing needs.

The preferential treatment given to building for owner-occupation was a clear indication of how the Conservative government perceived the pattern of housing policy. Chamberlain himself argued unequivocally for owner-occupation as an ideologically preferred solution to housing provision. Writing in *The Times* in 1920 he argued that 'every spade-full of manure dug in, every fruit tree planted converted a potential revolutionary into a citizen' (cited in Feiling, 1970, p 86), but he knew also that there was a need for low-cost rental housing. He was nothing if not a pragmatic politician, as was apparent later in his career, when as Prime Minister he attempted to appease Hitler. There was, indeed, rather a greater sense of all-party recognition of the need for a housing programme supported by the state than is often recognised in the histories of this period. The issue was where the emphasis between public and private provision should lie. In the next major housing legislation, the pendulum swung decisively towards the public sector.

Table 3.2: Housing completions in England and Wales 1919–39 (000s)

Year	Local authorities	Private sector with state finance	Private sector without state finance	Total
1919/20	0.6			
1920/21	15.6	12.9	}	
1921/22	80.8	20.3	53.8 (a) }	251.8
1922/23	57.5	10.3	}	
1923/24	14.4	4.3	67.5	86.2
1924/25	20.3	47.0	69.2	136.9
1925/26	44.2	62.8	66.4	173.4
1926/27	74.1	79.7	63.9	217.6
1927/28	104.0	74.5	60.3	238.9
1928/29	55.7	49.1	64.7	169.5
1929/30	60.2	50.1	91.7	202.1
1930/31	55.9	2.6	125.4	183.8
1931/32	70.9	2.3	128.4	200.8
1932/33	56.0	2.5	142.0	200.5
1933/34	55.8	2.9	207.9	266.6
1934/35	41.6	1.1	286.4	329.1
1935/36	52.4	0.2	272.3	324.9
1936/37	71.7	0.8	273.5	346.1
1937/38	78.0	2.6	257.1	337.6
1938/39	101.7	4.2	226.4	332.4
Totals	1,111.4	430.2	2,456.9	3,998.2

Source: Holmans (1987, p 66)

Note: These figures reveal some remarkable data in the long story of British housing policy. In the early post-war years, the industry struggled to keep pace with the scale of the problem as new household formation accelerated, adding to the existing backlog. In a rather uneven pattern, council housing grew to well over one million dwellings by the outbreak of the Second World War in 1939, accounting for about 10% of households. The first private-sector boom was sustained by a large-scale state subsidy and the second boom of the 1930s produced huge numbers of private-sector houses – 'semi-detached suburbia' – without subsidy. The figures for private-sector completions between 1934 and 1939 without subsidy have never been exceeded, the largest single year being 213,000 in 1968. Why this was possible in the middle of a global recession with unemployment persistently high is accounted for by the growth of middle-income, salaried occupations and the availability of cheap agricultural land and few planning constraints. After the Second World War, Green Belt policy and planning constraints curtailed 'urban sprawl'.

The Housing Act 1924 (the 'Wheatley Act')

Within a matter of months, the fate of council housing entered a new and decisive phase. Equally as pragmatic as Chamberlain, and also with roots in local government, was John Wheatley, the Minister of Health in the first Labour government, which came to power for only nine months in 1924. Wheatley was a 'Red Clydesider'; a Glaswegian, Catholic socialist hardened by years of campaigning in Clydeside local politics. Quite how such a full-blooded socialist came to be a leading cabinet member in this government is not entirely clear. His ideal was to use municipal construction to replace the privately rented sector, and he had written about the nationalisation of private landlords in his pamphlets. In government, he stopped short of pushing his radical agenda, so that once again pragmatic solutions came to the fore. Instead, he opted to build on the existing system using a much-improved level of subsidy. Because the 1924 Act was in essence a financial measure, its parliamentary passage was easy and largely uncontested. Wheatley's intention, through the Housing Act, was to establish a long-term investment programme in high-quality council houses. His vision was that council housing would be a socially and geographically ubiquitous housing tenure. Authorities no longer had to demonstrate 'housing need' to get building permission. The subsidy was significantly increased to £9 per dwelling payable over 40 years, instead of the £6 over 20 years subsidy under the 1923 legislation, and the rate fund contribution to council house-building was restored. The private sector was also able to benefit from this subsidy so long as it could be shown that they were building for working-class households.

Wheatley used the terms of this legislation and his labour movement credentials to negotiate a deal with the trade unions in the building industry, removing many of the trade's restrictive practices that had so damaged Addison's hopes. This facilitated the housing drive in the public sector, but also spilled over into the private sector where deskilling in the construction industry accompanied by large-scale unemployment helped to create the conditions for the boom in house-building in the 1930s. Wheatley also forced up the rate of construction by setting production targets for authorities and withholding subsidy unless they met their quotas.

Wheatley's was a long-term, strategic view of council housing and is very different, therefore, to the housing legislation of the coalition and Conservative successors. Arguably it is this legislation rather than the 1919 or 1923 Acts that finally established council housing as a permanent feature of British housing. The 1924 Act restored the general needs position of council housing, which had been abandoned to a residual role in the 1923 legislation, and also re-established the debate about housing standards, arguing very strongly in favour of a higher quality.

The rise of the suburbs

In the period between the wars, the backlog of housing was addressed both by a large-scale state intervention – the building of council houses – but much more significantly in terms of numbers built, by the private sector in two house-building booms. The first in the 1920s was generated partly on the back of government subsidies to private builders and the second and most dramatic phase during the 1930s happened when house prices were relatively low in relation to income, there was plenty of available labour and, above all, the one factor that was uniquely a feature of the period, building land was relatively cheap and available. This was due to the very weak planning constraints at the time and particularly by the advancement of all sorts of public transport, electric trolley buses, the London Underground, diesel buses and a growing quantity of motor cars, all of which brought into play farmland on the outskirts of towns and cities. This is the key reason why house prices were affordable on modest middle–class incomes. This was an unprecedented period of suburban sprawl.

Box 3.2: Why did the Conservatives retain the Wheatley subsidy?

Although the Labour government was quickly replaced by a new Conservative administration, under Prime Minister Baldwin, the Wheatley Act subsidies continued in place until 1933, by which time over 500,000 houses had been built under its terms, nearly half the production of interwar council housing. For several years, both the Chamberlain and the Wheatley subsidies operated in tandem. An intriguing and not entirely clearly answered question concerns the reasons why a right-wing Conservative government did not immediately abolish Wheatley's generous subsidy. As with most questions of this type there are a series of contributory factors.

First, an important consideration was that investment in the privately rented sector remained at a low ebb until the 1930s and, in any case, was not meeting the needs of households at the bottom end of the market. There was no other source of large-scale building for rent, and the subsidy needed to be generous to persuade some of the more reluctant authorities, of whom there were many, to build.

Second, the attitude of Baldwin is also a key factor. According to Holmans' reading of this, the Prime Minister approved of the Wheatley subsidy for its role in tackling the shortages, and so, somewhat paradoxically, it is to Baldwin's 1924–29 Conservative administration that the establishment of council housing as a core element in the story of 20th-century British housing can be attributed (Holmans, 1987, pp 307–8).

Third, Ravetz argues that there was a continuing cross-party consensus over housing, arising from the fact that building costs had until recently been extremely high and that the Chamberlain legislation had given the building industry confidence in state-sponsored housing, whether public or private, and it was this combination of factors that led to the continuation of building under the Wheatley terms (Ravetz, 2001). It was not so much an issue of ideological choice, but of difficult decisions needing to be made about what to do in these circumstances. Because the Chamberlain and Wheatley subsidies were both on the statute books, it was obvious that local authorities would use the more generous Wheatley subsidy, while the simplicity of the Chamberlain system continued to support building for sale. Indeed, most of the 363,000 properties built for private owners under the 1923 legislation were constructed after the 1924 Act (which extended the terms of the Chamberlain subsidy beyond its original cut-off date of 1925). At any rate, in both cases it was much easier to negotiate with the more confident building industry, which was now much freer from trade restraints and embarking on the first flush of the boom in building for home-ownership. Shortages at the bottom end of the market needed to be tackled and the Wheatley system worked.

The growth of the working population also had a significant impact on the rise of the suburbs because the economy developed a new range of what were known as 'white-collar' occupations and the established professions expanded. Despite high and sustained unemployment through to the outbreak of the Second World War in 1939, this was almost entirely among manual workers where mining, textiles manufacture, engineering and so on – the core of the 'old industries' that had made Britain 'the workshop of the world' – came under pressure from foreign competition and the impact of the worst global recession ever recorded. Despite this, the housing booms in the private sector were sustained on the back of households enjoying the benefits of relatively secure, salaried jobs in what we now refer to as the services economy. Jobs in banking, insurance and financial services grew dramatically. The old professions were flourishing and newer posts in public administration expanded as the state, both central and local, became much more active with an expanded array of services. For example, careers in the new profession of housing management, formerly mainly a women's domain in the philanthropic tradition, rapidly expanded as a male career pathway.

A key element in the story is the financing of this boom in private-sector housing. One of the most secure investment forms that emerged after 1918 was the 'building society'. These societies had long historical antecedents in the activity of working-class self-build cooperation in the 18th and 19th centuries. The original societies were terminated once the building project had finished, but some 'permanent' societies continued to accept investment, which was then loaned for other building projects or as mortgages for house purchase. Some of the original principles were handed down to these societies, especially that of mutuality, that profits would be shared by society members. The intake of funds in the post-1918 years was astonishing with investors given a competitive rate of return compared to government stocks and the stock market, which reflected the world economic crisis. Building society investment was very secure and the societies sailed through the interwar economic crisis almost unscathed. The inflow of funds grew from £120 million in 1924 to £636 million in 1937, and was the seedcorn for the home-ownership boom. For example, in 1936 alone, 240,000 new loans were made and this was typical of the 1930s' scale of lending (Holmans, 1987, p 221). As will be seen in later chapters, financial products, of which these were an early variety, become a key part of the 'housing debate' after building societies were deregulated in the 1980s.

The suburban way of life

Opposed by backward-looking intellectuals such as the author E.M. Forster and the poet John Betjeman ('Come friendly bombs and fall on Slough, it isn't fit for humans now'), the coming of the suburbs made up of kitsch, mock-Tudor semi-detached houses with long gardens formed part of a new society. These new 'ideal homes' came with modern facilities – indoor WCs, bathrooms and the modern miracle of electricity. The left-wing social critic George Orwell railed against this new society of 'little people' who he thought were snared in an empty, meaningless existence between home and office. His novel

Coming Up for Air (1939) is a banal, satirical book about the suburban way of life with a strong nostalgic tone and an instinct (which proved correct) of another impending war. E.M. Forster wrote in his novel *Howards End* (1910) about the 'rust on the horizon', the new suburbs gradually and threateningly creeping outwards across the nation's green and pleasant land. England became a recognisably suburban society and 'the estate', both public and private, became integral features of the built landscape. Servants gradually disappeared – although being 'in service' was still the most common female occupation up to 1939 – to be replaced by consumer goods and electrical labour-saving devices (Ravetz, with Turkington, 1995). In this new world, housing standards between the working and middle classes began to converge. The architectural founding fathers of these styles – Raymond Unwin, Norman Shaw and Edwin Lutyens – all drew their inspiration from the Victorian Arts and Crafts movement led by William Morris. His utopian, anti-urban ideals were picked up, for example, in the work of Unwin who drew housing designs based around simple principles aimed at enhancing people's lives. His facades were broad and open and faced towards the sunniest aspect, through-rooms downstairs enhanced the sense of airiness, 'back regions' were sometimes placed at the front of the house, gardens were large enough to grow vegetables and fruit. These workers' houses were visionary, designed to create a way of life very different from the Victorian tenements and slums.

Box 3.3: Biography of Raymond Unwin (1863–1940)

Born in Rotherham, Unwin was educated at Oxford University, becoming an engineer and architect known mainly for his visionary ideas about workers' housing, inspired by Ruskin, William Morris and the Arts and Crafts movement. He became a close friend of the socialist philosopher Edward Carpenter whose utopian village at Millfield inspired Unwin's own beliefs in the healing and life-enhancing effects of housing designed on simple principles following a 'cottage garden' ideal. With his practice partner Parker, he designed the model garden suburb at New Earswick near York for the philanthropist Joseph Rowntree and then was involved in the design of Letchworth and Hampstead Garden Suburb (where he lived until the end of his life). Unwin joined the Local Government Board in December 1914. In 1915, he was seconded to the Ministry of Munitions to design the villages of Gretna and Eastriggs and supervise others. From 1917, he had an influential role at the Tudor Walters Committee on working-class housing. The committee report, which contained copies of his designs for New Earswick, was published in 1919, the year in which he was appointed Chief Architect to the newly formed Ministry of Health. That post had evolved into the Chief Technical Officer for Housing and Town Planning by the time of his retirement in November 1928.

Unwin's influence shaped the 'cottage' style of council housing, although he was angered by the loss of key design principles as the housing programme moved to mass production and financial constraints kicked in. His visionary ideas, rooted in an English tradition of vernacular architecture with simple and clear lines, were central to the social experiment that was 'council housing'. He held many positions at the centre of British architecture and town planning. He was a founder member of the Royal Town Planning Institute in 1913 and was President of the Royal Institute of British Architects between 1931 and 1933. He was knighted for his services to architecture in 1932.

Unwin's estates at New Earswick in York and Hampstead Garden Suburb and his new town at Letchworth were important social experiments. Unwin was appointed as the design consultant on the Tudor Walters Committee, which was convened during the war to develop the post-war housing strategy. His drawings for New Earswick were incorporated into the Design Manual that was sent to local authorities in 1919 when, under the Addison Act subsidies, they were encouraged for the first time to build. Unwin's intention was that the new 'council housing' should mirror his ideals. As we have seen, his vision very quickly ran up against the need for economy, but interwar council housing – the idea of the vernacular, brick-built cottage – was to remain as the archetypal building form for council housing and

—

narrowed the distinction, at least architecturally, between middle-class and workers' housing.

Socially, it was a different story, and part of the narrative of this period is one of a bitter class rivalry between public and private housing estates, especially after general needs subsidies were abolished and all that remained was the lower standard of building for slum-cleared families. Stories that these 'slum people' created bedlam and kept coal in the bath quickly circulated and did much to stigmatise council housing. The notorious 'Cutteslowe Wall' – a seven-foot brick wall topped by metal spikes – was built by residents of a private estate to keep Oxford City Council's tenants at bay. Where major roads, canals, railways and so on did not do the job, less dramatic fences and concrete bollards were common features around the country of the division between middle-class and working-class estates.

In the private sector, there was more choice of styles and house types according to income and the speculative building industry imposed its view of the 'ideal home', assuming rather than knowing that their 'semis' with mock-Tudor facades accorded with public taste. The sources of these styles were the renowned architects Norman Shaw (most well-known for Bedford Park in Chiswick) and Edwin Lutyens (architect/planner of New Delhi, the Cenotaph War memorial in Whitehall and mock medieval manor houses designed for wealthy clients). The designers of the new middle-class suburbs used a pastiche of Shaw's and Lutyens' domestic buildings. It was criticised by intellectuals as mere kitsch and revealing of the shallow intelligence of middle England. Despite this, the suburban semi-detached villa became popular places for home-building. Victorian domestic culture was reborn. 'The Bendix automatic home laundry makes a house an ideal home' trumpeted the adverts in the *Daily Mail Ideal Homes* magazine. These new objects of display – 'Hoovers', cookers, radios, even electric refrigerators, cars and electrical record-players – became important features in establishing a family's status in the neighbourhood and its sense of self-esteem. Home-ownership became synonymous with ownership of consumer goods, and the marketing companies frequently connected the two with the gendered nature of life. The housewife inhabits the ideal home. Although space was needed for the new labour-saving devices, quarters to accommodate domestic servants were not now needed and housing design changed accordingly.

It should not be forgotten that the availability of mortgages and the rising real incomes of those in work – personal disposable income grew by about one third between 1920 and 1939 – enabled sitting tenants of private landlords to buy their houses from their landlord if he was willing to sell. Nearly a third of mortgage advances were for this type of transaction as people felt there was perhaps a greater security in owning their home during a time of economic uncertainty. During the interwar years, over one million private tenants bought their home as a sitting tenant, a comparable figure to the number of new council houses built, and boosting as a result the rapidly growing numbers of people joining the home-owning society.

Housing the poor?

Let there be no mistake. This quiet revolution in standards and tenure structure did not affect the housing conditions of the great mass of poor working-class households who continued to inhabit, as they had done throughout the passage of the century, ageing and ill-equipped accommodation supplied at the bottom end of the privately rented market. Even with the high level of subsidy under the 1919 Act, council house rents were well out of the reach of the poor working classes. Even when the Wheatley Act allowed rate fund contributions, designed to moderate rents, and open the way for lower-income households, the tradition of paternalistic landlordism operated against the worst-off families. The Poor Law tradition of deserving and undeserving poor was very much alive and kicking in the allocation and management of the new council housing. In his work as a journalist, George Orwell visited the north of England in the mid-1930s and wrote about what he had seen and experienced in his *The Road to Wigan Pier* (Orwell, 1937). He was appalled at the squalor that he saw and was sharply critical of a political system that left millions of people in this predicament.

Box 3.4: Extract from George Orwell's *The Road to Wigan Pier* (1937)

As you walk through the industrial towns you lose yourself in labyrinths of little brick houses blackened by smoke, festering in planless chaos round miry alleys and little cindered yards where there are stinking dustbins and lines of grimy washing and half-ruinous w.c.s. The interiors of these houses are always very much the same, though the number of rooms varies between two or five. All have an almost exactly similar living-room, ten or fifteen feet square, with an open kitchen range; in the larger ones there is a scullery as well, in the smaller ones the sink and copper are in the living-room. At the back there is the yard, or part of a yard shared by a number of houses, just big enough for the dustbin and the w.c.s. Not a single one has hot water laid on. You might walk, I suppose, through literally hundreds of miles of streets inhabited by miners, every one of whom, when he is in work, gets black from head to foot every day, without ever passing a house in which one could have a bath. It would have been very simple to install a hot-water system working from the kitchen range, but the builder saved perhaps ten pounds on each house by not doing so, and at the time when these houses were built no one imagined that miners wanted baths.

For it is to be noted that the majority of these houses are old, fifty or sixty years old at least, and great numbers of them are by any ordinary standard not fit for human habitation. They go on being tenanted simply because there are no others to be had. And that is the central fact about housing in the industrial areas: not that the houses are poky and ugly, and insanitary and comfortless, or that they are distributed in incredibly filthy slums round belching foundries and stinking canals and slag-heaps that deluge them with sulphurous smoke – though all this is perfectly true – but simply that there are not enough houses to go round. (Orwell, 1937, ch 4)

Slum clearance

Against a background of economic crisis and mass unemployment (3 million by 1931), the second Labour government (1929–31) was increasingly limited in its ability and will to continue the provision of general needs council housing, despite the persistence of large-scale shortages, still in excess of 1 million potential households to dwellings. The new government defended the Wheatley subsidies from threatened termination, and through the Housing Act 1930 introduced a new subsidy to encourage local authorities to clear slums and rebuild (ie no net contribution to overcoming the shortages). The clear intention was to upgrade the conditions of the millions of slum-dwellers so far untouched by 'general needs' council housing. Local authorities were required to submit plans for their slum clearance programme to be achieved in five years. Subsidies were related to the number of people being displaced, and this was useful in helping larger families to be rehoused. Budgetary constraints and the low incomes of these households meant that such a programme was going to be of limited scope and was achieved only at the expense of further reducing the design and building standards, which included the more widespread use of flats, under the influence of the 'modern movement'.

The 1930 Act also required local authorities to set 'reasonable' rents with powers to set up rent rebate schemes. The aim here was to enable authorities to protect low-income tenants from higher rents. However, rent rebates were not popular with tenants, who saw them as divisive and degrading because they were means-tested, and very few authorities had rebate schemes running by the outbreak of war in 1939.

The economic crisis that swept the world in the late 1920s and 1930s led to the defeat of the second Labour government in 1933, which was replaced by a National government, led by the Labour leader Ramsay Macdonald, who was expelled from the Labour Party, many party members considering him a traitor. The Wheatley and Chamberlain subsidies were abolished in the first round of spending cuts, leaving in place only the slum clearance subsidy. Local authorities were urged to clear the slums in five years and then to eliminate overcrowding, although

73

there was no indication of how the latter aim was to be achieved in the absence of general needs building subsidies. The termination of the Wheatley subsidy was viewed by the political Left as a betrayal of the vision to provide decent accommodation for every family. Working-class housing had in effect been abandoned, except for those in the worst conditions (Bowley, 1945, p 140). The only saving grace was that the system of rent pooling under the 1935 Act, in theory, made re-lets more affordable and opened up access even for applicants from slum properties.

By 1939, the balance sheet of British housing was transformed. Speculative private builders had constructed very nearly 3 million properties (430,000 with state aid). Over 1 million sitting tenants had bought their home from their landlord using a mortgage (which, of course, did not add to the housing stock, but impacted on tenure structure by depleting the private rented sector while expanding home-ownership). Getting on for 1 million flats and houses at the middle and upper end of the market had been built for private investors during the 1930s. About 10% of households lived in council housing, 32% were home-owners and still the majority tenure was private renting, but with a downwards trajectory – most of the slum clearance involved dwellings in the private rented sector and landlords at the bottom end of the market were getting out in droves, albeit that the sector temporarily grew during the 1930s when conditions at long last made investment in rental housing profitable, mainly in London and along the south coast and almost all at the middle and upper end of the market. As Kemp points out, a novel feature of this development was the involvement of property development and finance companies looking for a return on capital by investing in property (which included office blocks and shops). Even at the lower end of the market there was a short-lived revival and Kemp estimates that 350,000 private rental dwellings were built between 1933 and 1939 at rateable values of £26 aimed at those unable to afford home-ownership (Kemp, 2004).

Housing standards between the middle and working classes were converging. 'the estate', distinctly public and private, had redefined the English landscape and a new suburban way of life had caught on and was being heavily marketed. Unlike most industrialised European nations, a very large part of the question about the provision of low-cost workers' housing had been addressed through the single means of local authority provision, a pattern very different to our Continental neighbours. The home-owning society was already the dominant force, forging not just a new housing revolution, but, with an umbilical connection, also the consumer society, a society that was put on hold with the outbreak of the Second World War. Still a majority of the population lived in houses without electricity or inside WCs, and cooked on ranges or the open fire. The balance of households to dwellings had been significantly improved during the interwar decades, but was still in deficit by about 500,000 in 1939, and this figure and the urban slums were carried forward to whatever was to follow the uncertainties and traumas of a new war.

Conclusion

These chapters can only be 'short histories', selective accounts that outline some key features of how housing impacted on the shape of society while itself reflecting social change. The significance of the interwar period for the housing debate is seminal. In a few short but action-packed years, the country changed from being one in which families of all social classes and ranks rented their housing from private landlords to one in which completely new institutional forms appeared with dramatic impact. Domestic servants rapidly disappeared, although being 'in service' was still the most common occupation for single females in 1939. For middle-class housewives, a peculiarly English culture of domestic respectability and repose began to shape their social lives. Electrification of new housing brought a revolution in housing standards and enabled labour-saving devices – 'Hoovers', cookers, washing machines, electric irons and so on – to transform the daily drudgery that was previously the lot of most women. Coupled with the development of the electric tram, the Tube in London, buses and the mass-produced car, Britain became the recognisably suburban society that is familiar to us in the early decades of the 21st century but was then quite new. At the same time, the division between public council housing and lower-middle-class home-ownership became the source of a spiteful and bitter class rivalry despite the fact that housing standards were converging.

—

75

What was happening between the two world wars was the creation of two historical 'tectonic plates'. Home-ownership bubbled up like molten lava, eventually solidifying into a new structural crust underpinning society. A new tectonic plate had come into being that would have unimaginable consequences for the shape of later social policy. At the same time, state housing in the form of council housing created another tectonic structure. For a while, these housing forms grew quite autonomously, albeit with some frictions and tensions as described earlier in the chapter, but in time there was to be a massive collision of these two very different forces. It was this collision that shaped the new social landscape of the 21st-century home-owning society.

For the story that is to be told later in the book about the emergence of a form of 'residential' capitalism and the connection between the continued growth of home-ownership and welfare state change, the 1930s seem a very long way away. But this is one of the inner themes of the approach outlined in these chapters. The *longue durée* matters a great deal to how we think about the nature of social change and how contemporary debates are resonant with what took place many decades ago. Here we simply note that in the UK case the home-owning society was by 1939 already the ideologically and socially dominant form of housing. Timing is crucial. The interwar years were a period of rapid social and economic change in which a new kind of society, the 'home-owning society', developed through the implant of millions of new houses, changing the landscape of the country, shaking the old social fabric and bringing with it a complementary consumer-led culture and economy of 'white goods', 'ideal homes' and domestic respectability. A substantial underpinning of this was the large scale of sales by private landlords to sitting tenants (40% of the growth of owner-occupation was due to this), taking advantage of the availability of mortgage funds in a new and expanding financial services sector of the economy. The home-owning society with the attendant mortgage markets were deeply layered into the UK's society and economy by the time of the fateful wireless broadcast by Neville Chamberlain, a little after 11.00am on 3 September 1939, announcing that war had been declared against Germany.

—

SUMMARY

- The scale of the housing shortages got much worse in the years up to 1918 – almost nothing was built during the war and there was a sharp increase in new household formations, meaning that the backlog of new need plus existing shortages stacked up to crisis proportions.

- The First World War had a traumatic impact on society and for the first time 'the state' became a major factor in people's lives.

- Including during the war, there was a rapid growth in the adult population and as the population grew the proportion of children fell while people aged over 20 became proportionately more numerous. The effect of this was to increase the number of people of working age with a surge in demand for housing.

- Investors in housing faced very adverse circumstance after the war. Building costs were high and bank borrowing was expensive because interest rates were high. By the mid-1920s, rents in real terms were 25% to 30% lower than they had been in 1914. It simply did not make sense to commit capital in such an uncertain and unfavourable environment.

- Addison hoped to build 600,000 council houses, but in the end only 140,000 were built, although this was far greater than anything before and marks the beginning of mass municipally provided housing, so-called 'Homes Fit for Heroes'.

- By the mid-1920s, the private sector was building at a very fast pace, supplying demand from white-collar workers with mortgages based on steady incomes. These houses were mostly built on greenfield sites. A new suburban way of life was born.

- Under the terms of the Housing Act 1924, put through during the short-lived first Labour government, 500,000 'council houses' were built, but mostly under the Conservatives. There was a bitter rivalry between residents on public and private estates.

- Slum clearance began in 1930, but most working-class families continued to live in ageing and poor-quality houses rented from private landlords, as witnessed by George Orwell in *The Road to Wigan Pier* (1937).

New consumerism – mortgages.

- By the outbreak of the Second World War in 1939, nearly a third of households were owner-occupiers and the 'home-owning society' had been born and intimately connected to new consumerism.

Reading guide

Easily the best reading about housing in the interwar period are Alison Ravetz's scholarly and readable books: A. Ravetz, with R. Turkington (1995) *The Place of Home: English Domestic Environments, 1914–2000*; and A. Ravetz (2001) *Council Housing and Culture: The History of a Social Experiment*. Both these books capture the sense of a changing society and culture. For the more hard-headed data on households and dwellings, nothing beats A.E. Holmans (1987) *Housing Policy in Britain*. Similarly, Stephen Merrett's (1982) book (with Fred Gray), *Owner Occupation in Britain*, contains much useful data and discussion of the economic, demographic and political context for the rise and progress of home-ownership up to the 1980s. Chapter Four of George Orwell's (1937) *The Road to Wigan Pier* is a classic eyewitness account and inter alia contains detailed descriptions of housing conditions in Barnsley in the 1930s. The rise of suburban society is described in Orwell's (1939) novel *Coming Up for Air* and E.M. Forster's (1910) novel *Howards End*. Both novels in different ways oppose the kitsch and socially disturbing changes wrought on the English social and physical landscape by the suburban way of life.

4

Home-ownership comes of age: the post-war decades (1945–79)

OVERVIEW

A new, radical paradigm emerged from the experience of war asserting the ideas of citizenship and new beginnings for society. Labour was elected with a landslide majority to deliver the Beveridgean reforms and establish a 'welfare state'. Post-war reconstruction was initially to be state-led. Housing policy was in advance of this new approach because the foundations of the home-owning society had been laid in the interwar era, but initially Nye Bevan insisted that council housing should lead the housing programme. In 1945, the deficit of households to dwellings was considerably worse than at any stage in the 20th century and it took nearly three decades to put this right. Conservative governments failed to revive the private rented sector via the Rent Act 1957 and so continued to build council housing. Slum clearance and sales by private landlords to sitting tenants depleted the private rented sector. By the mid-1960s, as owner-occupiers became a majority of the electorate, the Labour Party backtracked on its image as the party of council housing and the economic and political power of the forces of globalisation beckoned.

Key concepts:

Beveridgean welfare state, paradigms, rent decontrol, residualism, state versus market, welfare consensus

Introduction

The connection between housing and welfare state development and change entered a revolutionary phase after the Second World War. New ideas about the future of the UK emerged from the traumas of war. This is a point that has been emphasised throughout the book; that housing policy and how it connects to wider welfare concerns are shaped by ideas, in this case by the broadly accepted parameters within which the state can act. The policy process and decision-making always occur within a framework of ideas, sometimes referred to as a paradigm (see Heffernan, 2002). Although not uncontested, the major political parties and the wider political community generally operate around a set of core assumptions. In normal times, this creates stability, but from time to time paradigms are compelled to shift and change. The war and its aftermath was just such a 'moment' when a window of change opened. This was graphically illustrated by the outcome of the post-war general election in July 1945 when the electorate made a very hard-nosed decision to reject the heroic war leader Winston Churchill and elected the Labour Party with a landslide majority of MPs on a tide of popular belief that the sacrifices of the war years should lead to a renewal of Britain's social and economic life. The 1942 Beveridge Report had indeed promised as much by its attack on what he called the 'five giants' of 'want' (poverty), 'squalor' (inadequate housing), 'disease' (ill-health), 'ignorance' (lack of educational opportunity) and 'idleness' (unemployment) (Beveridge, 1942). It was explicitly argued that these issues should be thought of as a whole package rather than, as was previously the case, that social insurance was one of a number of technical items of government expenditure. In other words, what was proposed by Beveridge was a 'welfare state', rather than disconnected welfare policies. Arguably, the key theme of this approach was its emphasis on social rights as a consequence of citizenship (Marshall, 1950).

And so it was that the Labour government led by Clement Attlee enacted major social reform – the Education Act 1944 guaranteed free education up to the school leaving age; the National Insurance Act

—

1946 and the National Assistance Act 1948 improved and rationalised state–run income support schemes for people in various types of need; and the National Health Act 1946 made health care free at the point of use (for an overview, see Fraser, 2003; for detailed discussion of the record of this government, see Hill, 1993; Gladstone, 1995; Glennester, 1995; Jones, 2000). It is quite a challenge at this distance in time to appreciate just how strong the mood was for the use of state intervention and for fundamental change to pre–war society. People had been asked to 'pull together' during the war and there was a strong expectation that because the state had run the war, so it should spearhead peacetime reform. This extended beyond welfare policy and made dramatic inroads into major sectors of private industry. Coal–mining was nationalised under the National Coal Board in 1946, shareholders in the Bank of England were bought out by the state and the four great private railway companies were taken over by the state on 1 January 1948 creating British Railways under the British Railways Board. All of these and much of private industry had been incorporated into the war effort by the state. As with social policy, much of what happened was a continuation of wartime practice that had marked the break with the much more market–oriented approaches of the pre–war governments (Hill, 2003).

Crucial to all this was the assumption that the free market was inefficient and that there were limits to what it could do in crisis circumstances. This was a radical departure from the interwar period during which the state floundered in the face of the economic recession that soon plunged into a full–blown depression, which the markets seemed to have created and were unable to solve. The response to mass unemployment was a weak attempt to ameliorate the worst problems and, just at the time when society needed support, emergent welfare services were cut back. The long tradition in Britain with its laissez–faire liberal market economy was one of private solutions to individual welfare with history traceable back to Victorian philanthropy. Through the Poor Laws there were deeply entrenched ideas about the 'deserving' and 'undeserving' poor, remembering that low–income workers were a majority of the population at the time. The Poor Laws and private charity were the main arms of 19th-century welfare. The state was more active in some areas of welfare than others. In education, for example, by the end of the century the state was filling the gaps left by the voluntary/Church schools so that it was compulsory for all children to attend some form of education between the ages of five and 12.

Although it is rather simplistic as a comparison, the Liberal welfare reforms between 1906 and 1914 had established what Briggs referred to as a 'social service state' and not a 'welfare state', in short, the former gave very limited financial support to selected groups of the population and failed to meet the needs of the very poorest sections of the community (Harris, 2004). The Liberal reforms had made some progress – free school meals for some children, contributory health and unemployment benefits, and limited old-age pensions. The extent to which these measures were genuinely trying to develop a 'welfare state' has been disputed by historians, but it does seem clear that the old paradigm of self-help hung over them. Old-age pensions were introduced to remind younger workers of the need for thrift rather than to sustain the elderly. The interwar years did build on the idea that the state should manage a wider spectrum of welfare provision, but social reform at this time was patchy and reluctant and still essentially 'Victorian' in approach with quite a strong weight of moral judgement attached.

The position of housing in the period at the latter half of the 19th century was rather different. As was shown in Chapter Two, 'housing' emerged out of the slum clearance/public health theme as a clearly distinct issue of 'policy' at a very early stage. This early start places housing in a rather different place to the other aspects of social policy, which were still below the horizon until the Liberal government of 1906. Housing, despite the state's involvement in slum clearance, was a fully commercial activity. Even the philanthropic housing reformers such as the American businessman Peabody expected to make a 5% return on investment. Nevertheless, housing policy was 'early' and this complicates the post-1945 story for how we should think about the role of housing in the era of post-war reconstruction and the rise of the full-blown welfare state.

Why was housing policy 'early'? History of housing

The reason why intervention in the housing market occurred sooner and more substantially than in other areas of welfare comes back to the earlier discussion about 'timing' and why we need to examine timelines and consider the *longue durée*. 'Housing policy' grew out of the paradigm shift that occurred towards the end of the 19th century as the social consequences of urbanisation hit home. As will be recalled from Chapter Two, the 1884 Royal Commission on the Housing of the Working Classes had worked their way to the conclusion that housing in London was unaffordable for low-income workers. This was quite a revolutionary idea at the time and represented an emerging new paradigm, opening the door to the unthinkable idea that some form of financial subsidy might, at least temporarily, be needed. For the first time, there was a reluctant recognition that in some circumstances the laissez-faire Victorian housing economy needed supporting by the state. As we saw, issues of public health and slum clearance were precursors to the Housing of the Working Classes Act 1890 (and consolidated in Parts I and II of the Act). The state was contemplating major, albeit temporary, intervention into the housing market in the face of the investment crisis in the *decade before 1914*.

Such was the scale of housing shortages that, well before the First World War made intervention inevitable, a plan to engage local authorities in building 'council housing' under the terms of the 1890 Act was in place. As we saw in Chapter Three, the consequences of the 1914–18 war and the demographic changes taking place in society induced Addison to envisage a programme of 600,000 state-built houses, and he was bitterly disappointed at the record of achievement and the diversion of subsidy to the private sector in the Conservative government's Housing Act of 1923. However, as the 1920s and 1930s progressed, state housing became a major factor in providing housing for working-class families and later on beginning to tackle the problem of the slums. The short-lived first Labour government's Housing Act 1924 was seminal, although most of the building under this legislation took place under Baldwin's Conservative government (see Box 3.2 in

Chapter Three). Albeit that this housing did not provide for poorer households, by 1939 over 1 million council houses had been built, accommodating 10% of the population. This was a much greater scale of intervention than a 'social service state' and engaged both political parties in funding a major state-built programme with increasing standards of accommodation (see Chapter Three). *State intervention into the housing market on the scale of a 'welfare state' was in motion several decades ahead of Beveridge's plan to tackle the 'five giants'.*

By the same token, we saw how nearly 3.5 million houses were built in the private sector during the interwar period, creating a new suburban landscape of the ubiquitous mock-Tudor 'semis', lampooned by George Orwell and the poet John Betjeman, but nevertheless the source of a new type of lifestyle for millions of families. In other words, in 'housing', massive changes had taken place in the two interwar decades and the pattern of change in the quiet 20th-century revolution from a private rental to a home-owning society was already established. Here was the answer to the crisis of late-Victorian housing when the 'housing question' was posed. If private landlords would not supply new housing, who would? It was to be 'council housing' and home-ownership, two completely new institutional forms already changing the trajectory of housing policy with a wider impact on interwar society, as has been discussed.

Later in the chapter we will see that 'early' state intervention into the housing market and the creation of 'council housing' as a monopoly supplier of subsidised rental housing was a crucial part of the explanation for its conversion in the 1980s and 1990s into a much smaller sector of 'social housing' with a different and more residual function. The significant detail of this is buried in the complexities of the subsidy system – and we will discuss this later in the chapter – but, in a nutshell, once capital costs were paid off and the historic subsidy was factored in, by the late 1970s large swathes of this early state housing had few costs attached to it. As a result, in theory rents should have gone down, but this maturing stock of low-cost state dwellings, so it was thought, would undermine the private sector and this competitive advantage was not to be allowed (Kemeny, 1995).

—

But there was a prior question to answer in the immediate wake of the Second World War. It will be recalled that the private sector was building at breakneck speed in the 1930s and was rapidly depleting the deficit of households to dwellings by 1939, down to 'only' about 500,000 houses. Why not pick up these threads and once again let the private sector drive the post-1945 housing programme?

A state- or market-led housing programme?

Unlike during the First World War, between 1939 and 1945 there was very considerable physical damage to the housing stock. During the Blitz and later the unmanned 'doodlebug' attacks, about 450,000 properties were destroyed or rendered uninhabitable. But the main problem for the stock position was that very little housing had been built during the war, remembering that private-sector builders had been putting up on average 250,000 new properties per annum in the six years before 1939 and slum clearance by local authorities was picking up pace following the Housing Act 1930 (see Box 3.2 in Chapter Three). Six years of lost production was a big figure to add to the properties destroyed by bombardment from the air. Furthermore, there was a deficit of dwellings to households of about 500,000 carried forward from 1939. These are big numbers for a dwelling stock numbering a little over 12 million at the time. Very little routine repair or maintenance was done and it should be remembered that much of the housing stock consisted of ageing Victorian terraces. As many as 2 million houses did not have gas or electricity and would therefore have no lighting except candles or oil lamps. Nearly 60% of dwellings did not have hot running water (Holmans, 1987, p 138). Britain entered the war with a considerable legacy of poor housing conditions and this was also carried forward to the new era.

Moreover, the depletion of the nation's housing stock and its poor condition needs to be read against the other side of the stock equation, numbers of households. During the war new household formation accelerated rapidly arising from early marriages (2 million during the six war years) and also from an increase in family dissolutions. Millions of households were forced to share, and it was common for newly married couples to live with their in-laws and for families to take in lodgers. One expression of this after the armistice was the mass invasion of hundreds of disused military camps, involving some 40,000 people. This form of self-help was not discouraged by the authorities, although the squatting campaign in disused flats and hotels in London and some other major cities had to be broken up eventually.

As can be seen from Table 4.1, so bad was the balance of households to dwellings that it took several decades to restore the position back to where it was in 1939 and some time later still before there was an equilibrium, although this was short-lived, as we will see later. The point here is that the huge housing deficit was the context in which housing policy was framed until almost the end of the 1960s. Here we come back to the question of how the immediate post-war crisis was to be dealt with. Was the private-sector building surge from before the war to be resumed or would the state manage the peacetime housing campaign? In their 1945 election manifesto, the Conservatives promised to provide housing subsidies to both the public and private sectors. Labour politicians had mixed views about what to do and it was by no means clear whether the local authorities or home-ownership would spearhead the housing programme or a hybrid as before. However, the appointment of the Welsh socialist politician Aneurin Bevan as Minister of Health quickly resolved the position.

Bevan had responsibility for the housing programme and was vociferously opposed to the private sector being involved, arguing that developers should not 'suck at the teats of the state'. His vision was similar to that of John Wheatley, the equally radical Scottish Minister of Health in the 1924 Labour government. They believed that housing policy should not be socially divisive and that local authority housing should provide for all social classes. Accordingly, the speculative building industry continued the wartime practice of supplying under a system of licences. Between 1945 and 1951, 80% of new house-building was allocated to local authorities and 20% to private house-builders. In the event, the Labour government oversaw the building of 1,017,000 dwellings before it was defeated in the election of 1951. Of these, 146,000 were 'pre-fabs', small factory-made bungalows built in 1946–47 as an emergency measure, but nevertheless this scale of programme was impressive and was the first large-scale positive investment in public housing since the Wheatley legislation. It should be noted that the high quality of both 'Wheatley' and 'Bevan' housing reflects the vision of two socialist politicians who held ministerial office at a time of national political crisis. Although capturing the mood of the time, we should not forget that the influence of the ideas and personalities of leading political figures can be decisive in shaping policy. In terms of housing standards, much of the groundwork had been put in by government committees during the war, on this occasion by the Dudley Committee which, while not as dramatic perhaps as the Tudor Walters Committee during the First World War, certainly set the tone for post–war housing standards (see Box 4.1).

Table 4.1: Dwellings and households, 1900–2000

England and Wales	Dwelling stock (000s)	Potential households (000s)	Vacants (%)	Sharing households (000s)	Households– dwellings balance (000s)
1901	6,710	7,007	n/a	n/a	−300
1911	7,691	8,143	(4.4)	(1,200)	−450
1921	7,979	9,289	(1.5)	1,732	−1,310
1931	9,400	10,583	1.7	1,948	−1,180
1939	11,500	12,000	n/a	n/a	−500
1951	12,530	14,194	1.1	1,872	−1,660
1961	14,646	15,426	2.1	886	−780
1971	17,024	17,144	3.8	780	−120

Source: Holmans (2000, p 14)

Notes: Figures in brackets are estimates.

The key data in Holman's table is in the right-hand column showing the impact of 10 years of war. As Holmans sums up, 'For half the century the housing scene and the pressure on policy was governed by the legacy of war' (2000, p 15). In this context it can be seen that the situation in 1951, already six years after the Second World War, was by some way the worst position during the 20th century.

—

Box 4.1: The Dudley Committee

The Dudley Committee was appointed by the Ministry of Health in 1942 in order to prepare to raise housing standards after the war. Expectations were bound to be high that the sacrifices of the war years should lead to a better society, although, as Ravetz observes, and as was the case after the 1914–18 war, 'a fleeting optimism was followed by compromise and consensus' (Ravetz, 2001, p 95). The Dudley Report, published in 1944, reiterated the basic design philosophy of the Tudor Walters Report, that high-quality housing design and high building standards were not only essential, but also led to an enhancement of society. However, it was critical of the uniformity of the Tudor Walters estates and promoted the idea of a mixture of different dwelling types, not just the tedious '12 houses to the acre' concept, but embracing flats and maisonettes. The new planning ideal was built around the 'Radburn' estate layout – an American experimental settlement drawing on the British garden suburb movement. The estates have a central 'green' and were built in a radial pattern. In the age of increasing car ownership they had separate circulation systems for cars and pedestrians. Having been reimported into Britain, the advantages of the design concepts were lost because garages for cars were clustered away from the dwellings and the houses were built in short terraces, rather than detached or semi-detached units as in the original Radburn estate. Radburn became the ubiquitous model for council house-building in the 1960s and 1970s, but was not a success because of difficulties distinguishing the rear and front of the dwellings, the linking footpaths (which people did not stick to), car-parking problems, centralised children's play areas and so on, all contributing to an unsatisfactory estate set-up.

The standard of houses advocated by the Dudley Committee was high. Floor areas increased from the 750–800 sq ft which was the standard for interwar council housing to 900 sq ft for three-bedroomed houses, with an additional downstairs WC for larger households. Bathrooms were to be provided on the same floor as the bedrooms. Parlours were dropped in place of larger single living rooms, with the addition of a large dining room/fitted kitchen in place of a scullery. Electric or gas cookers replaced ranges and open fires for cooking and houses were to be given outbuildings for storage, the pursuit of hobbies and DIY activity. The Committee on the Costs of House Building estimated that these improved standards increased costs for a standard three-bedroomed house by 35%. This increased standard was one of the reasons why immediate post-war building targets were not met and, under funding pressures, the Dudley Committee standards were very much reduced in the 1950s.

Given the poor state of the economy and the disruption to the building industry caused by the war, the Labour government's achievement was considerable. But problems developed as time went by and in the end the housing programme fell significantly short of what had been intended and what, indeed, was needed. A significant part of the problem was that local authorities had to rely on private contractors, over whom they had no direct control, to build council houses. Labour and materials shortages compounded this problem and the very severe winter of 1946–47 also held up the building programme. These difficulties led to restrictions being imposed on tender approvals in 1947 and a further round of constraints were implemented following the economic crisis of 1948. In the cabinet, Morrison argued that the private sector should be given a greater role (Campbell, 1987) and it is apparent from the histories of this government that the social programme was to an extent compromised by their (expensive) ambitions to continue Britain's role as an international power. Local authorities did achieve the building of 100,000 dwellings in 1948, and on balance the scale of achievement by a state-directed housing programme was much more impressive than the public–private mix in the aftermath of the First World War. Nevertheless, the government fell very far short of its target and this was one of the main causes of Labour's defeat in the 1951 election, in which housing was a key issue.

The post-war welfare consensus and the Conservative Party view of housing policy

The post-war housing crisis was not in dispute and the institutional mechanisms for dealing with it were already well established during the interwar era. Welfare state historians talk about a post-war welfare consensus, which marks a break with previous practice, although with housing this was not really the case, as we have seen. The new paradigm brought with it a number of key features that, although disputed, were generally agreed. First, there was an acceptance of the Beveridge-inspired reforms and equally an endorsement of the Keynesian approach to economic management so that the new welfare state was underpinned by the belief that state intervention in the economy should guarantee full employment. There was, in short, a political economy of welfare that had moved the nation very far beyond the prevarications and inadequacies of the pre-war 'social services' society. Political commentators coined the phrase 'Butskellism' to signify the close accord of the Conservative and Labour Parties on this basic direction of national life (Butler and Gaitskell were Chancellor and Shadow Chancellor in the mid-1950s). This was a somewhat shallow interpretation of what was happening in reality. With the 'Tory' tradition in command, the Conservative Party basically took a pragmatic view of social policy with their basic instincts – of support for individualist solutions and the free market and scepticism (at the very least) of the large state – never far from the surface. Their attitude to housing policy is a good illustration of this.

The Conservative Party's manifesto for the 1951 election pledged to build 300,000 houses per annum by a combination of public and private provision and this commitment was a major plank of their election victory. Harold Macmillan, the first Minister for Housing and Local Government, outlined a strategy that favoured the expansion of owner-occupation, but accepted the need for authorities to make up any deficits in production targets. Initially, this meant that the council house programme was in the ascendant and new building starts increased sharply from 164,000 in 1951 to 227,000 in 1953. During 1953, the private sector built 81,000 so that the Conservatives' pledge to build 300,000 houses was redeemed. It was not until 1957 that the number of dwellings started reached parity between the two sectors.

The general thrust of Conservative housing policy was very clear. Under normal conditions, the private housing market was regarded as the default provider. Council housing was used to make up the deficit in housing production, given the massive scale of the imbalance between households and dwellings – a fact that became much clearer after the 1951 Census – and otherwise continued its special role in slum clearance and replacement housing. Policy was driven by a pragmatic and reluctant acceptance of the continuing place of municipal housing provision in the nation's housing strategy. As Kemp pointed out, this was particularly apparent in the restructuring of policy that took place between 1954 and 1957: '[The] Conservative Government reaffirmed its faith in owner occupation as the most desirable tenure and attempted to engineer a revival of private renting while seeking to circumscribe the role of local authorities in new construction' (Kemp, 1991, p 52).

The decline of the private rented sector

One of the distinguishing features of the Conservatives' view of housing was that investors in housing – private landlords – were waiting 'out there' for the economic conditions to become suitable and they would then come flooding back into the market. This turned out to be very far from the truth in the circumstances of post-war Britain and we must briefly account for this because the reasons why the private rented sector (PRS) not only did not revive, but continued to decline, have an important bearing on the progress of the home-owning society.

We need to recall the position inherited from before the war as it stood in 1939 because it sets the context for what happened. After the First World War, 40% increases in controlled rents enacted in 1919 and 1920 nevertheless left rents lower relative to incomes than before the war (Holmans, 2000, p 17). Also, newly built private rental housing was not subject to control at any time. This patchwork of controls over rents in the private sector was put on ice in 1939 when all rents were frozen at their September levels for the duration of the conflict and it was this long-standing situation that remained untouched until the Rent Act 1957. The problem was the same as it had been after the First World War. At the bottom end of the market, yields from rental income were simply too low to produce a corresponding investment surge. The paradox was that rent control had made rental housing in most of the market much more affordable to millions of households, but there was virtually no supply more than already existed at such low rents. It was this gap that subsidised provision (by local authorities) was designed to fill. This logic was essentially the same after the Second World War. The difference was that the conditions in which the market operated were far worse than in the 1920s and up to the mid-1930s (remembering that as many as 900,000 houses and flats were built by private investors mostly in London in the 1930s when interest rates were lower and building costs had fallen; and mostly, but not only, housing at the upper end of the market – see Chapter Three). The cost of property bought on the open market to provide accommodation suitable to the standards of the day, let alone built from scratch, required rents to be set that were simply too expensive for millions of households.

The government announced their intentions to deregulate the PRS (to allow market levels of rent) in 1956, the same year that local authority subsidy was abolished. The approach was outlined unequivocally by Macmillan (cited in Kincaid et al, 1962): 'Local authorities and local authorities alone can clear and re-house the slums, while the general housing need can be met, as it was to a great extent before the war, by private enterprise.' The Housing Repairs and Rents Act 1954 restarted the slum clearance programme and encouraged private-sector improvement. It was made increasingly clear that, as the private sector recovered from the war, local authorities' general needs function was to be run down. It was no surprise that the Housing Subsidies Act 1956 abolished the general needs subsidy. This legislation also gave considerable encouragement through the subsidy system to local councils to adopt high-rise building techniques when replacing slum-cleared properties.

Whether the relaxation of rent control and the abandonment of general needs subsidy really was a coherent strategy is open to question because it

—

entailed considerable risks after a decade of reliance on council housing to bring down the shortages. Faith in the power of market forces, and especially the entrepreneurial spirit of private investors in the rental sector, was deeply rooted in Conservative mythology.

The aim of the 1957 Act was to allow landlords greater freedom in rent-setting by the decontrol of tenancies of certain rateable values and new tenancies. The Act decontrolled all of the more expensive properties (see Box 4.2) and decontrolled the lower end of the market when there was a change of tenancy. The intention was to establish a creeping decontrol of the sector and so bring about its revival. It should be noted that under the law as it had been since 1915, controlled tenants had a full legal security including succession rights for widows and close family members. Decontrolled premises lost virtually all these rights including statutory protection against eviction other than the right to one week's notice (lengthened to four weeks in the 1957 Act). It was this context that allowed unscrupulous landlords, notably Rachman, a particularly nasty landlord with an extensive property portfolio in London, to hound tenants out of their homes.

Box 4.2: The Rent Act 1957

Apart from a very limited attempt to increase rents in the Housing Repairs and Rents Act 1954 – increases were permitted when landlords spent specified amounts on repairs – rents in the private sector both for furnished and unfurnished tenancies remained as they were in 1939 at the beginning of the Second World War when rents were frozen. Prices, however, had risen sharply during the war and afterwards. Holmans estimates that prices for consumer goods and services had risen by 105% between 1939 and 1951 and the price of building maintenance nearly trebled (Holmans, 1987, p 409). The Rent Act 1957 was a radical measure aimed at deregulating a large part of the PRS. Its main parts were:

- decontrol of lettings at the upper end of the market, above £30 rateable value (£40 in London), including *de jure* ending security of tenure;

- decontrol on vacant possession of lettings below that level;
- on lettings remaining under rent control, the rent was to be set at a level twice the gross value for rating purposes; and
- decontrol of lower rateable values by Statutory Instrument rather than primary legislation.

An across-the-board increase in private rents thus became possible by the simple means of a rating revaluation. A revaluation was conducted using 1939 prices in order to get consistency across the different types of property and it was this level that was the benchmark for the new rent levels (twice the gross rateable value). The system thus permitted increases in the order of 150% compared to 1939 levels. The system was fairly slow to kick in, and in the light of worries about security of tenure the Conservative government opted not to use its discretionary powers to extend decontrol. Rent increases were for some households quite sharp and in the absence of a housing benefit system anyone not in receipt of National Assistance paid the full increase out of their own pocket. But it was the implication of loss of security of tenure and the threat that unscrupulous landlords would exploit this loss that blighted the legislation and gave rise to 'Rachmanism'.

In fact, in so far as tenants had to pay higher rents they were induced into owner-occupation, and as house prices began to accelerate, landlords were encouraged to sell into the market. The main impact of the Rent Act 1957 was on properties that could *not* be sold because these could now be let unfurnished without security of tenure or limits on rents charged. Thus, there was an incentive for landlords to get rid of controlled tenants, at which Rachman and his henchmen were particularly skilled. The Rachman scandal haunted the Act. Private landlordism did not 'revive' as had been forecast by the government and, as Kemp suggests, 'Decontrol thus proved to be a necessary, but not a sufficient, condition for the return of the private investor in rented housing' (Kemp, 2004, p 41) (see Box 4.2 for more detail). Affordability was also a considerable part of the explanation for the poor condition of much of the PRS, for reasons which must now be clear.

—

The strategy, if such it was, of axing local authority subsidy and switching to reliance on the private sector alone for general needs provision lasted only three years. As we have seen, after decades of neglect the economic logic of private investment in rental housing did not make sense. Accordingly, further decontrol was abandoned and subsidies for general needs housing provision by local authorities were reintroduced. Once again a Conservative government turned to council housing as the mainstay of its strategy to provide rental housing for people unable or unwilling to buy into home-ownership. Evidence that homelessness was increasing compelled the government to act and their rethink was announced in a 1961 White Paper, *Housing in England and Wales* (MHLG, 1961), and given legislative force in the Housing Act 1961.

In working out the housing stock accounts, we should remember the squalid condition of much of the housing in the PRS by referring to Orwell's eyewitness accounts during his travels in the northern industrial counties before the war, especially his detailed observations of miners' houses in Barnsley (see Box 3.4 in Chapter Three). These were mostly privately rented houses and were the focal point of the slum clearance drive that began in the 1930s and resumed after the wartime emergency abated in the mid-1950s. Of the 1.3 million properties that were cleared by local authorities between 1938 and up to the mid-1970s (when large-scale slum replacement ended), over 80% were in the PRS and resulted in a net gain for council housing of about the same order (because slum-cleared families were normally rehoused in new council houses and flats). In addition, in the early 1960s as the economic logic for investing in private renting collapsed and house prices began to move in real terms ahead of the retail prices index and incomes, landlords began to sell their properties as they had done before the war, where they could with vacant possession. This also caused a huge net change in the pattern of housing tenure because most of these sales were to owner-occupiers. Between 1938 and 1975, 2.9 million privately rented properties were sold by their landlords, 2.6 million of which transferred into owner-occupation. This compared with 3.9 million newly built owner-occupied properties in this period, and thus it is apparent that *about 40% of the growth of home-ownership was due to the transfer of formerly privately rented stock.*

The account, therefore, reads that in 1938 there was a stock of approximately 6.6 million privately rented units equating to 58% of the stock as a whole. By the mid-1970s, this had been reduced by a combination of bomb damage, clearances and transfers into owner-occupation to 2.9 million, just over 15% of the total stock at the time. Such a dramatic reversal of fortunes was, nevertheless, the working out of patterns, policies and social changes put in place before the war and, as was shown in Chapter Two, had antecedents in the crisis of the Victorian housing market. The severity of the circumstances created by the 1939–45 conflict intensified what were structural and long-term pressures and it is doubtful whether anything could have been done to reverse its fortunes. By the time the 1957 legislation was enacted, the British PRS was already many decades beyond redemption. Slum clearance and sales to owner-occupation were simply nails in its coffin.

Council housing continues to be built

The Conservative government was forced to reconsider its laissez-faire strategy in the face of the evidence on homelessness and the further decline in private renting. The Housing Acts of 1961 and 1964 gave authorities considerably enhanced powers to compel landlords of multiply-occupied houses to undertake repair and improvement of the property, but renewal policy was no more successful than attempted deregulation and from about this time it was recognised that housing renewal in the private sector was not going to be achieved through reliance on landlords. Grants to owner-occupiers were by contrast up to 70,000 per annum in the early 1960s and in order to avoid the further degeneration of the housing stock, it became apparent that the promotion of home-ownership and renewal were interdependent. More important here is the point that the continuing failure of private landlords to supply general needs rented housing and evidence of an increase in homelessness forced the government to reconsider the role of council housing. In the Housing Act 1961, general needs subsidies were reintroduced, although at two rates and in a complex system of local calculations. In order to demonstrate that private renting could be made to work and in the absence of any significant return on investment, the 1961 Act made loans available for establishing cost-rent housing societies, now called 'associations'. With the election approaching, the Conservatives pushed further in this direction and in the Housing Act 1964 set up the Housing Corporation aimed at encouraging housing associations to build for letting at cost rents and with powers to borrow up to £100 million a year from the Treasury. The encouragement of a so-called 'third arm' of provision through the revival of housing associations was held in check, however, as a result of the 1964 election, which returned a Labour government.

Housing was a key issue in the election and Labour under Harold Wilson won on a manifesto that included a commitment to build 500,000 houses. This period of Labour government, however, was not to be a return to the visionary years of Wheatley or Bevan. In the 13 years since 1951, the Conservatives had sustained the role of the local authorities, albeit reluctantly. Indeed, far more council houses had been built under Conservative or Conservative-dominated coalition governments than under Labour. Labour, nevertheless, was known as the 'party of council housing', but during the 1960s they began to distance themselves from this image and at some considerable pace. When they returned to power in 1964 their policy stance, compared to the 1945 government, was radically different. Merrett probably overstates the position when he says that 'The main shift was to accept the residualist principle of Toryism' (Merrett, 1982, p 42). The evidence needs to be evaluated with care. In the 1965 Housing White Paper council housing is pigeonholed into a number of defined roles:

> The Expansion of the public programme now proposed is to meet exceptional circumstances; it is born partly out of short-term necessity, partly out of the conditions inherent in modern urban life. The expansion of building for owner occupation *on the other hand is normal.* (Ministry of Housing and Local Government, 1965, emphasis added)

It seems most probable that this statement reflects several somewhat contradictory processes, which were inherent in the circumstances of the mid-1960s. Principal among these was that the nation was reaching the period that marked the end of the post-war shortages. There was, for example, significant weakening in demand for council housing illustrated in the emergence of so-called 'difficult-to-let' estates.

Initially, however, the expansion referred to earlier took place under Labour's 'National Housing Plan' and the rate of council house-building accelerated for several years reaching a post-war peak of 180,000 in 1967. This programme was reined back following the devaluation of the pound in November 1967 and never really recovered its former pre-eminence at any subsequent stage. The plan for 500,000 dwellings was dropped quietly from the policy statements as the economic crisis bit very deeply into Labour's social programme.

Box 4.3: The 1977 Housing Green Paper

For historians of housing policy the 1977 Green Paper is of more than passing significance, for it encapsulated Labour's thinking on housing policy at this time. It is generally regarded as a conservative paper, particularly in its advocacy of home-ownership (DoE, 1977). Forrest and Murie's characterisation of the 1977 Green Paper as 'Labour's capitulation to owner occupation and acceptance of a limited, residual role for council housing' (Forrest and Murie, 1990, p 32) is not a fair assessment because, in the first place, Labour always accepted that owner-occupation was 'normal' and, second, the Housing Policy Review argued quite strongly for the continuation of the public sector as a major supplier of housing, albeit at lower levels of output than in the past, and more targeted at locally identified needs rather than large-scale national plans.

The Green Paper described the historic role local authorities played in ameliorating the squalor of the Victorian slums and demonstrated the impact council housing had had in raising housing standards. There can be no doubt that Labour sought to narrow the scope and role of public housing, and sustain the existing trends in the tenure structure focused

---

on the expansion of owner-occupation, but Labour still regarded local authorities as bastions of this long campaign and considered that they still had an important future role to play, albeit in new circumstances and in a more pluralistic housing system.

Labour and owner-occupation

The housing policy pursued by the second Wilson and then the Callaghan governments (1974–79) had no real direction to it, even though the 1977 Green Paper outlined a general perspective (see Box 4.3). Global pressures and the closedown of the era of mass housing production led to a large withdrawal of state expenditure on housing. By 1977, public-sector completions had fallen to a post-war low of only 88,000. The withdrawal of investment in the development programme, often associated with the Thatcher governments after 1979, was in fact well established under the Labour Prime Ministers Wilson and Callaghan. These cuts were closely connected to the worsening economic situation in the country and were a direct consequence of restrictions on state expenditure imposed by the International Monetary Fund in December 1976. The long years of reconstruction were over and Keynesian demand management of the economy came under pressure from globalisation (Bosanquet, 1980). The pound fell in value against other major currencies, inflation was high and industrial disputes wracked the British economy. This changed environment for housing was managed by a stricter system of cash-limited controls on local authority capital expenditure, administered through an annual Housing Investment Programme (HIP). The HIP system, outlined in the 1977 Green Paper, aimed to give local authorities greater flexibility to plan their investment programmes while giving central government considerable leverage over the size of local authority budgets.

There remains the as yet unanswered question of Labour's attitude to home-ownership. Labour's advocacy of owner-occupation was, by the late 1970s, well established. In that sense, the 1977 Green Paper was a statement of a long-standing position and not a 'capitulation'. It was never supposed that council housing would be the only form of provision.

Indeed, it was Labour's default position that under normal circumstances owner-occupation would be the principal form of supply. In the 1965 White Paper, Labour described home-ownership as 'a long-term social advance' and contrasted the public housing programme (which it was argued should focus on short-term necessity and on exceptional needs) with the more normal 'expansion of building for owner-occupation' (Ministry of Housing and Local Government, 1965). Richard Crossman, the Labour Housing Minister at this time, was keenly aware of the need to limit his party's identification as the party of council housing, partly out of sheer electoral necessity. Owner-occupiers were nearly a majority of voters by the mid-1960s. It was also very clear that the ideas of the Labour Left were under pressure. This housing minister was politically very different from the Wheatley and Bevan tradition. In his famous *Diaries*, Crossman wrote that 'we only build council houses where it is clear they are needed', and he went on to say that the main aim of Labour's housing policy should be to encourage owner-occupation (cited in Boddy, 1980, p 19). Labour, always committed to reforms in all the main housing tenures, by the mid-1960s had a clear vision of home-ownership as a symbol of social advance, although 'Old' and 'New' Labour (left and right wing) differed considerably about the emphasis that should be put on this.

During the period of the first Harold Wilson government (1964–68), the fiscal advantages of owner-occupation were further enhanced, following the abolition of Schedule 'A' taxation on the imputed rental income of the home-owner in 1963 by the Conservatives. Home-owners were exempted from paying capital gains tax on the sale of their principal dwelling, tax relief was retained for home improvements and mortgage interest tax relief was retained when most other forms of tax relief were abolished. The abolition of Schedule 'A' taxation meant that owner-occupiers with mortgages were in effect being subsidised for the purchase of the dwelling as consumers and because they paid no capital gains tax reaped a considerable financial gain as investors when they sold. In order to widen the social base of home-ownership, a system of 'Option Mortgages' was introduced in the Housing Subsidies Act 1967 and allowed both local authorities and building societies to offer mortgages at 2% lower than the standard rate for households on low incomes. This series of measures considerably enhanced the position of owner-occupiers, but caused imbalances in housing subsidies, which now favoured home-owners against public tenants and was generally regressive.

Conclusion

It took well over two decades to deal with the post-1945 deficit of households to dwellings, by which time man had walked on the moon. The end of the shortage era was signalled in the Labour government's White Paper *Old Houses into New Homes* (Ministry of Housing and Local Government, 1968), which outlined the switch away from slum clearance and general rehousing towards the private rehabilitation of the housing stock through the voluntary take-up of improvement grants. Resistance had built up to the most excessive mass slum clearance 'rolling programmes' now threatening to engulf areas that by no stretch of the imagination could be considered to be slums. These were mainly old, urban terraced properties at the bottom end of the market and these owner-occupiers were much more difficult to compensate than private landlords, who were often thought of as supplying a substandard service. Home-owners were resistant to clearance and, indeed, very largely at their own expense, stabilised and then improved this older part of the dwelling stock. What happened in the 1970s and 1980s has been written about elsewhere (see, for example, Ravetz, 2001; Malpass, 2005). Here it is enough to reiterate that by this period home-ownership had become easily the dominant force in British housing and the home-owning society was maturing very rapidly indeed. The post-war Beveridgean paradigm, which had overseen the reconstruction of society and the devastated war economy after 1945, was coming under pressure from the new forces of globalisation, forces that were to destroy much of the superstructure of the old economy and challenge the logic and purpose of the old welfare state. It is within this *new* paradigm that 'housing' and particularly home-ownership was to have a much higher profile. Housing as a commodity collided full-on with housing as a social right. Moreover, the globalisation of the financial markets created new mechanisms for connecting households to global capital markets in ways previously unknown, with major consequences for welfare states. These are the themes of the next chapters.

SUMMARY

- A paradigm shift took place in the aftermath of the Second World War as the plans to deliver the Beveridge Report were implemented, creating a 'welfare state' with an emphasis on social citizenship.

- State intervention into the housing market on the scale of a 'welfare state' was in motion several decades ahead of Beveridge's plan to tackle the 'five giants'. The reason for this was the 'early start' of state intervention into the housing market arising from the Victorian housing market crisis.

- Due to German aerial bombardment (the 'Blitz') between 1939 and 1945, there was very considerable physical damage to the housing stock. Only small quantities of houses were built during the war and household formation was high creating a huge deficit of housing; about 2 million out of 12 million households did not have separate accommodation of their own.

- The post-war housing programme was led by the state in the form of council housing, building on the interwar model. Bevan ensured that the private market was strictly controlled so that 80% of new housing was built by local authorities up to 1951. There was no immediate return to the private-sector building boom of the 1930s.

- Under the Conservatives, the private housing market was regarded as the default provider. Council housing was used to make up the deficit in housing production and otherwise continued its special role in slum clearance and replacement housing. Policy was driven by a pragmatic and reluctant acceptance of the continuing place of municipal housing provision in the nation's housing strategy.

- Attempts to revive the PRS through the Rent Act 1957 failed. By the mid-1970s, the PRS had been reduced by a combination of bomb damage, clearances and transfers into owner-occupation to 2.9 million dwellings, just over 15% of the total stock at the time (it had been 58% in 1939).

- Because of the failure to revive the PRS, Conservative governments continued, albeit reluctantly, to build council housing such that by the mid-1970s nearly a third of the whole population rented council-owned properties, including high-rise flats, built mainly as replacements for slums.
- By the mid-1960s, as owner-occupiers became a majority of the electorate, the Labour Party backtracked on its image as the party of council housing. They began to present home-ownership as a symbol of social advance, although 'Old' and 'New' Labour (left and right wing) differed considerably about the emphasis that should be put on this.

Reading guide

There are numerous excellent books about the origins and evolution of the British welfare state. Among the best are M. Hill (1993) *The Welfare State in Britain: A Political History since 1945*; and D. Fraser (2003) *The Evolution of the British Welfare State since the Industrial Revolution*. Both these books take a broad view of the subject, putting it into its wider political context. In terms of housing history the sources mentioned in the last chapter are still relevant: A. Ravetz, with R. Turkington, (1995) *The Place of Home: English Domestic Environments, 1914–2000*; and A. Ravetz (2001) *Council Housing and Culture: The History of a Social Experiment*. Both these books are superbly written with great breadth of knowledge. The first half of Peter Malpass's (2005) *Housing and the Welfare State* is a useful and detailed account of the development of housing policy across the 20th century and both the previously mentioned books by Merrett – *State Housing in Britain* (1979) and *Owner Occupation in Britain* (1982) – are well-researched accounts. Very useful on the PRS is Peter Kemp's (2004) *Private Renting in Transition*.

5

The post-industrial economy and housing

OVERVIEW

Globalisation compelled the UK economy into a phase of rapid restructuring, turning away from the old industries in manufacturing and mining and towards a knowledge economy based around services. This new work replaced mainly male full-time jobs with part-time female work. This reconfiguration brought with it a new welfare state paradigm that began to replace the Beveridgean model with a 'competition state', a workfare system geared towards supporting directly efficient economic performance. A new social geography emerged with the services economy, which was located in surburbs and small towns, leaving behind declining inner cities in the heartlands of the 'old' economy. Two-earner households underpinned a new wave of suburban home-ownership. There were thus significant complementarities between economic restructuring, welfare state reconfiguration and the further embedding of the home-owning society. Meanwhile, council housing began a rapid descent as manufacturing industries closed down. Home-ownership began to play a prominent part in shaping people's welfare choices, especially after the mortgage market was reinvented, providing access to housing equity on a massive scale.

Key concepts:

counter-urbanisation, globalisation, residualisation, the competition state, the maturation crisis

Introduction

This chapter considers the macro-level forces that combined to shape a remarkable period of change between the 1970s and 1990s. We need to stand back from the detail of housing policy to see the bigger picture. This involves both relatively short-term changes, but also some of the factors at work over the *longue durée*. Sometimes the narrative needs to account for the layering in of key factors, in this case how the housing stock matured over the course of the 20th century, putting down foundations on which current developments are based – the tectonic plates of society, to rejoin Pierson's analogy. There is a considerable degree of complexity involved, but the aim here is to bring to the fore the analysis of major events that shaped social change. It was the confluence of some of these big-picture issues that shaped a period of very rapid change and the creation of a new welfare state paradigm that involved 'housing', particularly of home-ownership in the case of the UK, in a much more direct way than before. Housing until this period had been part of the society's background, a key issue, but managed more or less by government policy and the wider housing market. In the social sciences, it was a fairly specialist field of social inquiry and research often focused on state housing. One aim of the chapter is to show how macro-level forces shape policy contexts but do *not determine* the outcome of policy. The setting of policy agendas and how policy is eventually delivered is the function of meso-level institutions that filter wider social forces (Hudson and Lowe, 2009).

At this period, as Britain matured as a 'home-owning society', housing both shaped and was shaped by major economic change and played a key role in a reconfiguration of the welfare state, a new paradigm that broke with the outmoded Beveridgean model. The idea is to show how very significant housing was becoming because in almost all the welfare state literature and accounts of this period it has a very low profile. Why this was is explored in more detail in the next chapter because there is a deep theory problem.

Here, there is need to discuss what political scientists call 'complementarities' – the interconnection between quite disparate forces which spark off each other and shape social change. In this case, the emergence of 'the home-owning society' was an integral part of a bigger picture of economic restructuring, bringing with it a new social and political paradigm. This shift was not the result of aggressive and traumatic wars, as had previously happened, but the more gradual although equally disruptive impact of globalisation. New economic forces were reshaping the world's political and economic institutional frameworks. Transnational corporations began to wield enormous economic power and the invention of the internet unleashed a tool of awesome power with new information technologies creating global networks of communication through which, as Giddens shows, time and space have been reordered (Giddens, 1999). The great Spanish sociologist Castells argued that we live in an 'informational age' and that this is what defines modern capitalism – a networked form of powerful information flows (Castells, 1996).

Globalisation is a highly contested concept, but few social scientists deny its impact, particularly that the planet is indeed wrapped in a new and powerful economic shroud. However, *this does not mean that the nation state is dead* or that national political and economic institutions are irrelevant, far from it. Rather, nation states have been compelled to respond from within their existing traditional and institutional structures. There has been a 'loosening' of economic, political and social structures through which nations have reconfigured their core institutions or at least have responded to the redistribution of power that globalisation has brought in its wake.

Box 5.1: What is 'globalisation'?

Giddens argues that globalisation has involved the *stretching* of time–space pathways; that people around the world are connected to each other in ways that break from all previous historical eras, opening up ranges of choice, but also intensifying the related risks. The Spanish sociologist Castells argues that we live in a 'network society' and it is this informational age that defines modern capitalism.

A good way to think about it is as a series of processes and it is these that make globalisation different from familiar ideas of international trade, as Marx observed as early as the middle of the 19th century, capitalism spanned the whole planet, at least in ambition if not in practice. This is why he argued that the 'workers of the world unite' in an international struggle against capitalism. But this geographical spread, and as we will see later in the book, this 'sort' of capitalism is not the same as that arising from new processes of globalisation in the late 20th century. These processes have been neatly summed up by Held and McGrew (2000) in four themes:

- *stretching* of economic, political and social activities across geopolitical frontiers;
- *intensification* or growing scale of the interconnections between trade, finance, migration and cultures;
- *velocity* of all these processes has increased dramatically so that ideas, capital, information and people relate to each other much more quickly; and
- *deepening*, meaning that the effect of quite small local events can potentially have big repercussions elsewhere in the world: 'In this sense, the boundaries between domestic matters and global affairs can become increasingly blurred' (Held et al, 1999, p 15).

To revert to Pierson's geological analogy, it might be thought that globalisation has been like a massive earthquake that has shaken all the (social and political) tectonic plates causing fissures and ruptures all over the place. Globalisation does *not* mean a simple convergence of everything towards a common endgame. Globalisation has not overwhelmed existing structures despite its worldwide reach and power in unifying the international economy (see Chapter Seven for a discussion about the globalisation of mortgage markets).

Globalisation and the welfare state

In response to these new forces, the core institutions of the British nation state have been compelled to reconfigure. The old unitary state centred in London has been eroded, with the devolution of Scottish and Welsh politics, new styles of local government that are much more entrepreneurial in approach, the adoption of new public management methods within the civil service, and the privatisation of major areas of policy delivery and implementation (of which the sale of council houses is a prime example). In the words of Rhodes, the British state has been 'hollowed out' and has become a much more networked system in which the ties between the central executive and the rest of the country have been loosened (Rhodes, 1994). The post-war Beveridgean welfare state began to appear very expensive and cumbersome in an era when the pace of the new global economy quickened. It was argued that global capital had become so mobile that it could withdraw or threaten to withdraw its investment if conditions suitable for profit-maximising were not provided – with public spending, interest rates and inflation all low. Governments, as part of this strategy of responding to the needs of global capital, so it was argued, were compelled to reduce welfare state spending in what Woods called 'a race to the bottom' (Woods, 2000, p 1). The evidence, however, does not entirely support this rather unnuanced argument because welfare states have been surprisingly resilient due to institutional 'lock-in' in which long-run traditions and institutional practices have become embedded. Even anti-welfare state governments such as the Thatcher governments in the 1980s and 1990s did little more than contain welfare spending. Swank's analysis of the OECD countries showed that far from a retrenchment of welfare state spending through this period, in most countries expenditure had increased (Swank, 2002).

Nevertheless, there was a decisive shift away from the Beveridgean model and towards a much more entrepreneurial welfare state. The idea of the 'competition state', for example, argued that in the UK the old-fashioned, post-Second World War welfare state model (the Keynesian plan of full employment, economic demand management and welfare rights) has given way to a more market-sensitive system under the impact of globalisation. In short, in social policy this means an emphasis on individual responsibilities (through workfare programmes and active labour-market retraining), the marketisation and privatisation of public services, and the general replacement of insurance-style unemployment benefits. Cerny and Evans, the political scientists who propose this thesis, argued that there has been a 'paradigm shift' that has resulted in 'a new, loosely knit neo-liberal consensus on the state's role in a global capitalist economy' (Evans and Cerny, 2003, p 21). They went so far as to suggest that the central purpose of the welfare state in the UK is to serve the national interest as the country competes in the fiercely competitive worldwide economy.

The idea that the welfare state has become subordinate to economic policy surfaced also in the work of the sociologist Jessop, who argued that the old-style 'Keynesian welfare national state' had been replaced by the 'Schumpeterian workfare post-national regime' (Jessop, 1994). In this approach, there was an imperative for an open (international/globalised) economy with an emphasis on supply-side policies that promoted flexibility, innovation and economic competitiveness. Jessop argued that this change forced a downward pressure on social rights and that the shift to an open economy made it difficult to sustain high tax/high spend welfare states. The delivery of social policies, he argued, was no longer the prerogative of the state because they increasingly operated either from above or from below the level of the nation state through a diverse range of providers. As we will see later in the book, although not figuring in these debates, 'housing' was in fact a key player in this process of reconfiguration in the British case and elsewhere. The maturing of the home-owning society was part and parcel of this paradigm shift. As will be discussed in Chapter Eight, households began to think of their properties not only as a home and place of refuge, but also as a financial resource that acted as a cushion against difficult circumstances. This shift of attitude to thinking about homes as part of the self-provisioning of welfare needs is one of the pillars of a new welfare state paradigm that was emerging in the 1980s.

The rest of this chapter outlines the key themes in the economic restructuring of the UK away from a manufacturing economy and towards a services economy. This modernised economy brought into the labour force millions of women, often in part-time work, and gave rise to households with two incomes. On this basis, home-ownership became affordable and in the new geography of the services economy, a new wave of owner-occupied suburbs became prominent on the urban landscape. To an extent, women were incentivised to work in order to buy housing and build up their homes. The 'home-owning society' thus has complementary connections to the new economy and social and physical landscape of Britain. In the new welfare state model that began to replace the outdated Beveridgean regime, housing wealth began to play an important role. Meanwhile, urban decay and degeneration afflicted all the towns and cities that had been the heartlands of the old manufacturing and mining industries.

The post-industrial economy and the new welfare state

As we saw at the end of the last chapter, by the 1970s the balance of households to dwellings had equalised in crude terms. After the devastation and economic ruin of the war and the establishment of the Beveridge settlement, once again the tectonic plates of the economy were beginning to shift. A new paradigm was emerging within which housing was to play a more fundamental role. The home-owning society continued apace, but the great visionary experiment of state housing that had been such a key feature of the 20th century was about to enter a dark and long-drawn-out nemesis. In short, the coming of the post-industrial economy brought with it fundamentally different connections between housing and the welfare state. This newly emerging situation created key complementarities at the macro-level of analysis and these need to be accounted for especially because they accelerated the rise of the home-owning society.

Pressure was building up around the Beveridge-inspired welfare state as the Fordist economy with its male-breadwinner model of society began to break down. Although women had been very active during the 1939–45 war, further continued participation was discouraged by labour-market restrictions that set wages for similar work at significantly different levels for men and women. Women's withdrawal from the labour market after 1945 allowed male wages to rise in real terms and trade unions strengthened this trend. Women's generally lower educational qualifications also acted to exclude them in the 1950s and 1960s, and this operated at all levels of work pushing down right to lower/unskilled jobs. This labour force model was the basis around which welfare state entitlements were constructed, in particular that they were offered to households not individuals. In the housing context, it seems almost certain that women at home increased fertility so that the 'baby boom' era put further pressure on housing demand.

What was happening here was the first stirrings of globalisation, of the emergence of a new economic paradigm. The UK economy entered a phase of rapid economic restructuring and reconfiguration. The bare outline of this can be quickly sketched in. Between 1956 and 2006, the share of employment accounted for by the manufacturing industry declined from 48% of the civilian employed population to only 22%. Meanwhile, the share of jobs in the services sector grew rapidly to the point where more than three quarters of the UK workforce was employed in this sector, ranging from banking and financial services, retailing, education and higher education with spin-offs in science parks, design and research, leisure/tourism, computing, and a whole swathe of new work in the public sector. Government data showed that nearly one in five employed people worked in some capacity for the state.

This was not of course unique to the UK, as Table 5.1 shows, but for a country formerly 'the workshop of the world', such rapid and deep change was dramatic (not forgetting that there was also a collapse in coal-mining, which at its peak in the 1930s employed over 750,000 men – out of a total population of 38 million at the 1931 Census). By the same token, during the 1980s and 1990s manufacturing grew rapidly in the Asian/Pacific Rim nations, sub-Saharan Africa and Brazil. In Vietnam, for example, 900,000 jobs were created between 1990 and 2000 mostly in textiles and garment production under an internationally agreed Multi-Fibre Arrangement (Nadvi and Thoburn, 2004). Bangladesh

Table 5.1: Levels of change in the structure of employment (% of civilian employment by sector)

	Agriculture				Manufacturing				Services			
	1956	1973	1989	2006	1956	1973	1989	2006	1956	1973	1989	2006
Australia	12	7	5	4	39	36	26	21	49	57	68	75
France	26	11	6	3	36	39	30	23	38	49	64	74
Germany	17	7	4	2	46	48	40	30	37	45	57	68
Japan	36	13	8	4	26	37	34	28	39	49	58	68
Spain	44	24	13	5	30	37	33	30	26	39	54	66
Sweden	17	7	4	2	41	37	30	22	42	56	67	76
UK	5	3	2	1	48	42	33	22	47	55	65	77
USA	10	4	3	2	37	33	27	20	53	63	71	79

Source: OECD website.

grew in the same way with 75% of its exports dependent on finished garments. Meanwhile, 40,000 jobs were lost in the English Pennine towns (around Halifax and Huddersfield), which were the hub of the UK textile industry – indeed, these were the towns most associated with the early stages of the Industrial Revolution with their water-driven mills. China became a powerhouse economy and by the early years of the 2000s was easily the world's largest manufacturing nation. State-managed capitalism was able to put millions of workers into low-cost production, creating export-led growth, moving out from the industrial heartlands around the Pearl River delta in Guangdong province north of Hong Kong and the mushrooming conurbations around the Yangtze River delta. Detail on this can be read in many places such as Hudson and Lowe (2009), Dolan and Barrientos (2003) and Linden et al (2007), but the point here is to show the dramatic impact that globalisation had on the world economy in the last three decades of the 20th century.

Furthermore, it should be noted that decline in UK manufacturing and mining was very heavily concentrated among full-time male jobs. One of the most extraordinary features of the new global labour force was the extent to which full-time male work was taken over by part-time female employment everywhere in the world affected by these dramatic labour-market shifts. It was also the case that the vast majority of new services jobs in the UK were taken on by women, very many of them working part time. In this sense, they were not 'taking' male full-time jobs, but were being engaged in the new services employment market, not 'old manufacturing' and mining. In historical terms, it always was the case that women worked both inside *and* away from their homes, so what happened was a reassertion of old patterns in a very different form (Harvey, 1973; Giddens, 1990).

The male breadwinner economy also came under pressure from changes that occurred in the post-war services sectors resulting from their commercialisation and deregulation (Schwartz, 2003). This trend in public utilities, transport and telecommunications began in the US, which had always had regulated rather than outright owned utility sectors, but spread to Europe in the 1980s with increased competition and privatisation and a general pressure towards commercialisation. As Schwarz sums up the situation, 'the security of breadwinner male employment in the service sector evaporated in ever-hotter competition in service sector markets' (Schwartz, 2003, p 83). In short, what happened was the unwinding of the male breadwinner model of employment in both the less skilled bottom part of manufacturing and mining and in the utilities markets where large numbers of full-time male jobs were lost. Generally, what was happening was that much of the new services work in retailing, banking and financial services, tourism and catering, and the expansion of public-sector services and research suited female job-seekers because they could often be worked part time or on flexitime, fitted with family responsibilities and required skills and aptitudes that were not of a gendered nature.

The reintegration of women into the labour market was not only a UK phenomenon. Between 1970 and 1996, female labour force participation in the OECD nations rose to 65%, although with considerable variations between nations. At the same time, male participation fell from about 90% to 83% during this period. A key social trend here was the gradual expansion of female participation in higher education, running parallel with the 'knowledge economy' and the growth of university places. This quickly brought into play a new generation of educated women competing in open access labour markets (such as teaching) with numbers of women in university about on a par with men by the 1980s and in recent years women substantially surpassing the numbers of men in many countries (Jonsson, 1999). Especially in the Nordic countries, the early growth of public services to support a reconfigured welfare state model brought female education early and in significant numbers. There was a complementarity at work here because public services grew in order to sustain female labour force participation through the provision of crèches, maternity/paternity leave and so on. These are important foundations for the more specific 'housing' dimension to the end of the male breadwinner society, which brought with it new and key connections between housing and welfare state change. The first stage in this is to look briefly at the 'geography' of what happened in tandem with these shifting social and economic tectonic plates.

A new geography

The impact of economic restructuring on the housing domain was at the time little understood, but in retrospect it is quite clear to see that key geographical shifts were beginning to kick in alongside the new services economy because the new economy tended to be located in *different places* to the old manufacturing and mining centres in and around the great northern cities. Just at the time when council housing, built largely to service the housing needs of manufacturing workers and their families, reached its maximum spread, economic restructuring was accompanied by major population shifts pulling in the opposite direction. This took the form of a process of counter-urbanisation, of a movement of people away from the old industrial centres to smaller towns and suburban locations. The services economy not only brought with it new types of jobs done mainly by women, but also created work in different places. A new social geography accompanied the new services economy.

Data published by Turok and Edge (1999) showed clearly the factors that were reshaping the social and physical landscape of the country. Male full-time work declined dramatically, even before the 1980s, and the impact of this was felt most acutely in the largest cities. At the same time, female part-time work grew equally dramatically, but in different places, principally in smaller towns and in the suburbs. Part-time jobs grew by 2.2 million in the period covered by Figure 5.1, which was nearly 60% of all new employment opportunities and this growth was made up almost entirely of female workers.

By the same token, major disruption occurred in the 'traditional' labour market. Male full-time employment declined everywhere, but the old industrial heartlands were particularly badly hit with the disappearance of 1.4 million jobs in manufacturing, which is about one third of the 1981 total. On the other hand, part-time work in services grew by 2.2 million, which was nearly *60% of the total of new jobs in the economy by 1996, a growth made up almost entirely of female workers*, and as Figure 5.1 indicates, this work was located in smaller towns, suburbs and rural areas. The overall picture revealed in this data is that economic restructuring was very geographically uneven. As Turok and Edge show, the major job losses were in the northern industrial conurbations and big cities while the economy rebranded itself in services in smaller towns and suburbs especially, but by no means exclusively, in the South of England.

Figure 5.1: Change in the composition of employment, 1981–96 (000s)

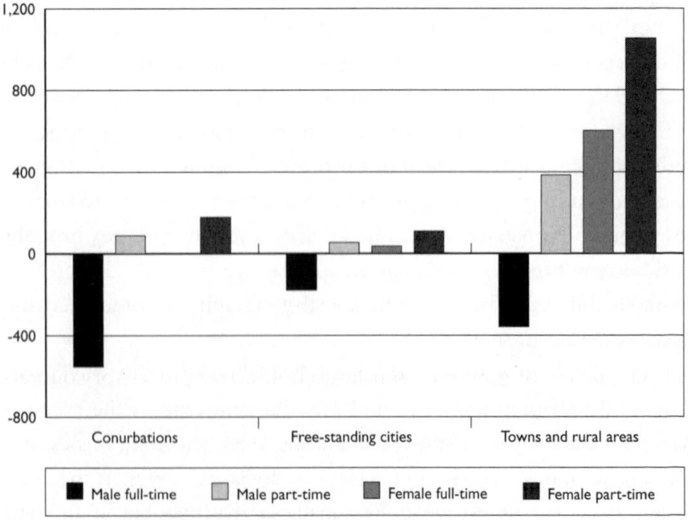

Source: Turok and Edge (1999, p 19)

Counter-urbanisation and home-ownership

The process of counter-urbanisation was closely allied to the continued expansion of home-ownership. A new wave of building took place. The housing market was in the main buoyant because two-earner households became the normal form of family life. *The connection between female labour force participation, economic restructuring and the continued growth of home-ownership were very closely complementary processes.* As the economy switched towards services, so the scale of female employment expanded. Indeed, by the end of the 1990s there were more women than men in the workforce. In history, women always did work outside the home although 'the home' has strong associations with female- and child-centred domestic functions and this was very strongly redolent of the Victorian era. Urban life was hostile, and beyond the front door the world was alien and potentially threatening. The home became a bastion of security and in this period very closely associated with social status. The disruption, confusion and plurality of city life drove families into their inner home life and to try to live in communities with like-minded people. As Ravetz with Turkington (1995, p 4) observe:

> Social gradations became crucially important to identity and security, most particularly at borderlines between classes. The most important of these in the eyes of Victorians, was that of separating 'respectability' from 'non respectability'.

So, women at home are a historical aberration; once again, in the 2000s, women are at the forefront of the labour market outside the domestic environment. The difference now is that they work for income in their own right, implying greater independence and considerable changes in the balance of power within households. The process of counter-urbanisation that took place in the 1980s and 1990s was essentially built on home-ownership by two-earner households. As a result, it created a direct incentive for women to enter the labour market. The home-owning society and its complementary appetite to consume was part of a key feedback loop in which women decided to take up paid work.

The new suburban era

As we saw in earlier chapters, patterns of urbanisation have always impacted in defining society in this way. As was shown in Chapter Two, 19th-century urbanisation led to the growth of particular forms of state intervention around issues such as street lighting, slum clearance and eventually the emergence of council housing. Similarly, the male breadwinner model of welfare associated with the post-war Beveridge settlement constructed a policy regime that supported and was complementary to this form of urban-based industrial society in which council housing played a large part.

In the services economy, however, it was the process of suburbanisation that came to define the era and this was inherently associated with owner-occupied housing. Everywhere, out-of-town shopping complexes were built, linked by ring roads and designed to be accessible by car. Science parks connected to universities and new private companies built on the commercial value of research, and office complexes for the insurance, banking and financial services industries, sprang up all over the country. This new landscape also incorporated the construction of tens of thousands of new owner-occupied properties on adjacent greenfield sites. Suburban home-ownership fed on this new economy with households routinely able to access two incomes (often from a combination of part-time and full-time work, but at least based on two incomes). This brought home-ownership into the financial compass of millions of households and, as we will see later in the book, the ability to buy expensive property in the housing market was underpinned by a revolution in mortgage markets following the deregulation of the banks during the 1980s. A complementary process at work here was the globalisation of the capital markets with the invention of the process of securitisation and related financial products that essentially created a global bond market in which mortgages were traded as bundles of long-term investment (see Chapter Seven). The point to note here is that it was the reinvented mortgage industry with thousands of products and in a low inflation environment that connected individual households to this new flow of global capital.

The significance of the growth of home-ownership for the definition and nature of the 21st-century welfare state in the UK will be discussed in the next chapters, but here it should be noted that the economic restructuring and the rise of the 'competition state' are part and parcel of the same processes of social change that were occurring at this time. The tectonic plates were shifting. New physical and social landscapes were emerging and these would inevitably lead to a reconfiguration of the welfare state, as we have seen; the Beveridge welfare state did not fit the needs of a country under fierce competition from a newly globalising economic environment, so that a 'welfare state' began to give way to a 'workfare state'. A critical feature of this paradigm shift was the emphasis in the new model on self-provision. Both the Thatcher and Blair governments in different ways shared a broad worldview about the political economy of welfare in which responsibilities for welfare shifted markedly towards individual responsibility and away from the Beveridgean notion of social rights.

As will be shown in Chapters Seven and Eight, a welfare state built on assumptions about private assets was central to this notion. This is why the growth of home-ownership is so significant to the narrative of this change. Owning property became a fundamental requirement of this new welfare settlement in which governments encouraged home-ownership as a socially responsible option. The reason for this was at first simply that outright ownership, once mortgages were paid off, reduced housing costs in older age and took pressure off retirement pensions. Elderly owners would also have the option of selling their property to sponsor access to residential care or nursing homes. The liberalisation of the banking system in the 1980s and the development of a massive global mortgage market created a completely new set of possibilities for home-owners through the process of equity withdrawal: in other words, people could extract some of the value of their home by remortgaging *in situ*, without moving. In this way, people's homes became banks against which they could from time to time draw in order to bring forward expensive purchases, but crucially to secure their welfare needs as and when costly treatments arose, school fees were needed, children required deposits to buy their own homes, and generally as a buffer against difficult times. The mortgage market became a conduit through which ordinary home-owners could be connected to flows of global capital with an enormous resonance for the nature of the 21st-century welfare state. In other words, what we saw in three decades before the banking crisis was the emergence of a new welfare state regime based on a residential form of capitalism (see Chapter Six). In this way, the competition state became a supercharged form of political economy. Neither Cerny and Evans nor any of the comparative and international welfare state scholars incorporated housing into their theoretical work. This is why the whole of Chapter Six is devoted to making this key conceptual connection.

Social housing residualisation

The restructuring of the economy over several decades also caused significant disruption to housing demand and supply around the country. Where manufacturing and mining were most severely affected, hundreds of thousands of jobs were lost over quite a short time frame. Compelling evidence of the geographical consequences of this can be found in the analysis of regional housing demand conducted over many years by Holmans and by Bramley. Evidence of the depopulation of the northern cities and the impact that industrial restructuring was having on local communities surfaced at first in problems of so-called 'difficult-to-let' council housing estates. Underneath this issue, however, were the shifting economic tectonic plates. As time went by, evidence of the impact on populations in the industrial heartlands became clearer. Webster, for example, showed that 'most big cities have lost two-thirds of their manufacturing employment since 1979, compared to a national loss of around a third' (Webster, 1998, p 48). In these areas, housing demand collapsed quite precipitously, as an example, Webster revealing that between 1981 and 1999, 20,000 local authority flats and houses had been demolished in Glasgow, representing over 10% of the city's council housing stock. Bramley presented evidence of extreme low demand for council housing in a study published in 1998 that showed a significant concentration of surplus housing in northern cities. He found that 22 local authorities (only 6% of the total) had a running total of 35,000 surplus properties per annum, 60% of the national total (Bramley, 1998).

It is clear from these research studies and others at the time (Lowe et al, 1998; Bramley et al, 2000) that the underlying cause of low demand for housing and the existence of large quantities of surplus housing was principally the result of economic restructuring. Old industries were replaced by new ones, but in different places, creating low demand in some areas, but also shortages especially in the overcrowded southern counties of England. In short, the opposite side of the coin from the growth of the new suburbs and the rise of services-based employment in smaller towns and cites was the sharp and socially damaging loss of population as core manufacturing industries closed down. The impact of this on local communities was devastating; housing markets collapsed (low demand was not only an issue for council housing), streets were abandoned, corner shops closed and the vibrancy of local neighbourhoods was shattered. Economic and social life ebbed away with alarming speed, making policy responses very difficult to coordinate. Keenan discovered that in the West End of Newcastle after the closure of the Vickers armaments and ship-building site on the banks of the River Tyne – resulting in over 20,000 job losses – local communities were destabilised as people moved away. He tracked 700 movers who stayed within the area, but eventually were forced to move out. These 'serial movers' often were in debt, became fearful as crime rates increased and struggled against vandalism because increasing numbers of houses were boarded up, so that life became unsustainable (Keenan, 1998). Pawson also concluded that the increasing frequency of re-lets of council houses as demand declined and families moved away created more unstable communities and a weakening of social cohesion (Pawson, 1998). Low demand associated with industrial decline and economic restructuring has diminished in recent years, and Bramley reports that the tendency to low demand in council housing declined between 2000 and 2005. It is also the case, however, that the scale of demolition of council housing in areas covered by the government's regeneration – 'Pathfinder' – areas is likely to have reduced vacancies.

Here is not the place to discuss in detail this issue and there are many studies of regeneration and the future of council housing (see, for example, Fitzpatrick and Stephens, 2009). What was happening during the 1970s–90s is relevant to the discussion of the welfare state because there is clear evidence here that social housing – once upon a time a proud achievement of British social policy – was severely impacted by structural changes in the economy simply because it had been built precisely to house the families of workers in the manufacturing and mining centres of the 'old' economy. In short, once labour markets declined in these areas then the social purpose of council housing also became redundant.

Thatcherism and the 'Right to Buy' council housing

This position pre-dated the onslaught on council housing arising from the election of the Thatcher government in 1979. Clearly council housing was already vulnerable, so the insertion of a highly ideologically determined view of state housing was a key indicator of the neoliberal paradigm shift. Policy analysts have shown how periodically established frameworks break down as new ideas and ways of thinking emerge. This is clearly what was happening here. As Heffernan suggests, 'Only when a status quo is considered "broke", and economic needs and political demands require change, can ideas be advanced to dramatically "fix it"' (Heffernan, 2002, p 750). These ideas are not necessarily 'new' as such, but it is the heightened attention they receive in policymaking and political circles that leads to a shift to new ways of thinking about old problems. This is similar to Hall's idea of 'social learning' as he describes the breakdown of the Keynesian paradigm:

> The 1970s were dominated by collective puzzlement and uncertainty about the economy, and the effort to regain control over it was an intensely intellectual quest marked by highly sophisticated debate in the media, the political parties, and the City, as well as among policymakers. The play of ideas was as important to the outcome as was the contest of power.

> For these reasons, it seems highly appropriate to describe this
> process as one of social learning. (Hall, 1993, p 289)

Hall argues that there are stages of change in which ideas gradually become accepted before a fundamental change occurs and a paradigm shift moves the whole political debate in a new direction. These moments are relatively rare because, in the main, political economies (of welfare) are generally quite stable. It is important to emphasise here that what happened to council housing had 'inner', specifically 'housing', dimensions (the maturation crisis), but also that the shift in perception about it needs to be read in the wider context of economic restructuring (globalisation) in which its social purpose was undermined, and that this was mediated through the institutional filters of the policy process itself with the design of the Right to Buy policy. It was a policy that had been around for some time and a number of local authorities had sold houses to tenants, but had always replaced them with new stock. This of course was not to be the case following the Housing Act 1980.

In its own terms, what happened to council housing must be read as a highly successful outcome. Once again, 'housing' was in a sense exceptional because it proved a much easier target for the Thatcher government's more general critique of the welfare state as profligate and supporting the undeserving poor. This was premised upon the belief that council housing was an inherently inferior form of housing provision compared to owner-occupation and represented a stumbling block to the creation of a nation of home-owners. It was, according to Thatcher, council housing above all else that was the anathema of modern British society. At the end of her three governments, council housing had been radically changed both in the quantity of housing stock, the geography of its distribution and, above all, in its social purpose. The long tradition of council housing established in 1919, which by the 1970s catered for the housing needs of very nearly a third of the population, came to an abrupt end. Instead, the tremendous social benefit of the long story of council housing that, as Feinstein et al (2008) demonstrated, in the post-war period was breaking the cycle of poverty, was tortured by Thatcher's

123

loathing for state housing and ended up reinforcing poverty by an entrapment of the least socially competent and poorest sections of the community. Its role in meeting the deficit of households to dwellings had been recognised by governments of all political persuasions throughout the 20th century.

Thatcher, however, picked up the banner of the property-owning democracy with a vengeance. This policy turn was innovative even by the standards of post-war Conservative Party politics, which had never been positively supportive of council housing, but had accepted its important role in the provision of rental accommodation, given the inexorable decline of the private rented sector. As we have seen, far more council houses were built under Conservative administrations than under Labour and generally they had accepted that council housing had a distinctive purpose and role in meeting certain types of housing need and making provision for slum-cleared families. In the 1980s and 1990s, however, the number of council houses fell year by year mainly as a result of the 'Right to Buy' policy enacted in the Housing Act 1980.

Box 5.3: The 'Right to Buy'

The Housing Act 1980 was one of the great pivotal 'moments' in the long history of British housing. The context of it was that, following the 1977 Green Paper, Labour introduced a Housing Bill that among other things would have introduced an element of tenant participation in council house management, a national mobility scheme to help tenants move more easily around the country, and a new type of tenancy for council house tenants – 'secure tenants' – giving them rights comparable to those enjoyed for many years by tenants in the private sector. The 1980 Act dropped much of Labour's programme, but used the framework of the 1979 Bill to establish secure tenancies, an extension of rights in line with Conservative thinking – emphasising individual rights (security of tenure, succession, to exchange, to take lodgers, to repair and bill the landlord, to improve) as against collective rights – and with the addition of the ultimate individual right, as they saw it, the right to buy the property, the right, as David Hughes puts it, 'to *cease* to be a tenant' (Hughes, 1991, p 94). This gave secure tenants a statutory right to purchase their dwelling after three years' occupancy with an immediate 33% discount and a 1% per annum sliding scale discount of up to 50% on the market value of the property. The Housing and Building Control Act 1984 reduced the qualifying period for Right to Buy purchases to two years and enhanced the size of the discounts; tenants of flats, for example, were allowed up to a 70% discount. In the decade from 1980, nearly one and a quarter million houses had been sold and the share of council housing in the overall stock of dwellings had fallen from 31.5% to 22.8%.

Between 1980 and 2000, the housing stock in the United Kingdom increased by over 3 million dwellings and there was a radical redistribution in the balance of housing tenures. Owner-occupation expanded by over 10% while council housing declined, mainly due to the Right to Buy, by almost 2 million properties. In 1980, local councils provided rental accommodation for nearly 31% of the nation's households. By 2008, the figure was only 16%. This dramatic quantitative decline has led simultaneously to a radical reshaping of the social composition of the sector and to its social purpose and future ownership. Right to Buy sales have been of the most valuable, high-quality suburban-style properties, leaving the core stock disproportionately represented by high-rise flats and low amenity inner-city and peripheral estates. A much higher proportion of sales has been in the South of England than elsewhere in the country. It is also clear that in the three decades since the 1980 Act, these properties have had a high resale value and have become integrated fully into the mainstream housing market. Research shows that former council houses have become attractive purchases for first-time buyers and also to families moving *from* an owner-occupied house. As Malpass and Murie suggest, 'Former council houses as a whole cannot be said to be at the bottom end of the owner-occupied market' (Malpass and Murie, 1999, p 256). Between 1991 and 1999, about 200,000 existing Right to Buy owners moved into the mainstream market. This means that the number of Right to Buy owners has grown at a much slower rate than in the 1980s, so that in 1998/99 there were only 1,452,000 owners remaining in the house they originally bought (there having been approaching 2 million sales since the 1980 Act). Other sales of vacant housing, demolitions and particularly sales to housing associations have reduced the local authority housing stock by some 3 million properties since 1980, over 60% since then (Jones and Murie, 2006).

The degeneration of council housing

A wider process of 'residualisation' of council housing was also at work in this narrative, which affected very large swathes of the historic stock of council housing everywhere. Here the long-term trends inside the financial structure of council properties collided with the loss of its social purpose. Long-term and shorter-term timing created a juncture that largely accounts for the speed of its decline and the residualisation of the stock. Although some of this stock was already ageing – remembering the interwar building programme – quite large parts of it became debt-free as subsidies ended and rental income was used over time to pay off any outstanding capital liabilities of this stock. This process was described by Kemeny as the 'maturation' of council housing and it allowed local authorities to cross-subsidise new building programmes, keeping rents in more expensive, recently built properties lower than would otherwise have been the case (Kemeny, 1995). Kemeny suggested that as the council housing stock inevitably matured and historic debts were paid off, the implication was that rents would not need to rise above what was needed for repairs, maintenance and to pay housing managers. In this way, public housing was different from the private rental stock because landlords normally have to charge a market rent based roughly on the value of the property. Without a real return there is no sense in investing in property compared to other investments.

Kemeny argued that in this way council housing could in theory have become more popular than private renting because of its inherently market-based advantage in having lower rents. Indeed, in other countries the historic maturation value implicit in this model of finance has been incorporated so that state housing 'leads' the market (Kemeny,

1995). Governments supply subsidy to private landlords while in return retaining control over rent-setting. As will be shown in Chapter Six, this logic is the basis of what Kemeny refers to as an 'integrated rental market' (examples being Germany, Austria and Sweden) where, as a result, home-ownership is much less a dominant force inside these housing systems. Housing costs here are much lower and the incentive to become a home-owner much less powerful. These integrated rental housing markets are also associated with high tax/high spend welfare states partly because of cultural differences with the 'home-owning societies', but also because lower housing costs enable families to afford high-quality welfare. Or, in the home-owning societies, the tendency is towards low tax/low spend welfare because housing costs are so high. As was shown earlier, the implication of the evolution of the competition state created an incentive for owner-occupiers to pay special attention to the equity stored in their properties and to think of their home as a 'bank', as a financial backstop if needs be. In this way, housing 'regimes' exert quite a strong influence on patterns of welfare state development, such that it is possible to argue that housing regimes and welfare state types are closely allied (see Chapter Six for a detailed discussion).

The slow death of council housing

Most council house purchasers were middle-aged, white-collar or skilled manual workers with grown-up children. There is also clear evidence in the research studies that Right to Buy purchasers were much better off than council tenants as a whole. This was especially the case in the South of England where house prices had been and remain considerably higher than elsewhere. Conversely, those households entering the public sector during this period were much more likely to be lone parents or young couples, who generally regarded council housing as a temporary form of accommodation. Analysis of income and employment indices has shown a marked trend for the poorest households to be concentrated very disproportionately in council housing. For example, 65% of households in the lowest three income deciles live in council housing compared to 16% of owner-occupiers (although this means that there is a very large absolute number of poor home-owners). It follows that the proportion of households in council housing with no earners or whose head of household is unemployed is also high.

These legacies of the Thatcher period of government are the product of a single-minded political will to transform the nature of the British welfare state. Although not successful in many aspects of this agenda, notably the failure to curb welfare spending, the case of housing was a success in reinventing the housing discourse – tenants became consumers, housing authorities became companies, large areas of housing became subject to competitive tendering and the whole pattern and shape of housing governance changed irreversibly. Council housing ceased to be thought of as a source of permanent housing for new households, homeless people or applicants on waiting lists and became a less stable and in many cases a much worse living environment, characterised by rapid turnover and demographic unevenness (a high proportion of young and old tenants). Indeed, the final symbolic nail in the coffin has been delivered by the Cameron–Clegg government in the Localism Act 2011 by ending security of tenure for council tenants, as was flagged up by the Prime Minister in a widely reported speech (PM Direct, Number10.gov.uk, 3 August 2010) and had been floated by previous Labour Housing Ministers (see Box 5.4).

Box 5.4: The slow death of social housing

The final nails in the coffin of the historic purpose of social housing and its place in the long story of housing over the last century are being administered by the Coalition government. The recent context is that the Labour government under Gordon Brown's premiership, following the path outlined by the Barker reviews (commissioned while Brown was Chancellor of the Exchequer), pushed for increases in supply both of private and social housing. In the Housing and Regeneration Act 2008 this programme and plans for regeneration were given institutional support through the establishment of the Homes and Communities Agency (HCA). The HCA took over the role of the Housing Corporation

(HC), English Partnerships and a number of functions of the Department for Communities and Local Government. At the same time, the regulatory functions over housing associations formerly lodged with the HC were taken over by another new body, the Tenants Services Authority (TSA). However, arising from the Coalition government's *Review of Social Housing Regulation* (2010), the TSA will be abolished by the middle of 2011 and its functions lodged mainly with the HCA. Arising from the review, quite a wide range of the regulatory functions being developed by the TSA have been abandoned in favour of a more local and flexible system operated by housing associations themselves and similarly complaints procedures have been devolved to localised systems, changes that have generally been welcomed by the associations.

The budget for building affordable social housing was cut by about 60% in the 2010 Comprehensive Spending Review (CSR), although a pledge was subsequently made to build 150,000 affordable properties over the term of the government. This was seen by most commentators as a drastic decline in the required rate of building, not even adequate to keep up with existing demand, let alone meet newly occurring needs – set against social housing waiting lists in the order of 4 million applicants. As outlined in Chapter One, public-sector housing programmes are always vulnerable to being axed in periods of spending cutbacks because it is *capital* spending and therefore relatively easy to reduce. In this case, the government have indicated that they plan to increase rents in social housing to about 80% of local private market equivalents in order to fill the funding gap on their capital programme. This also seems somewhat implausible given that, in a different set of announcements in the CSR, a major reform of housing benefit capped rent payments to fixed amounts dependent on dwelling type at lower thresholds than currently operate. The likely outcome of this is that very few social and affordable houses and flats will be built, particularly in London and the South-East where demand is greatest due to high house prices. It also seems likely that existing tenants will have a strong incentive not to move because the increased rents only apply to new lettings. Moreover, many tenants will be drawn into the housing benefit net as rents increase, causing disincentives to work, which is completely at odds with the government's aim of making the tenure more flexible and 'fair'.

Already a residual housing tenure containing a high proportion of disadvantaged and workless households – less than a quarter of tenants in social housing are active in the labour market – social housing has shrunk to only 15% of households. The high turnover of tenancies was observed many years ago now by Murie, who called council housing a 'transitional tenure' (Murie, 1997, p 457), but even this may change in the short term as existing tenants stay put, fearful of facing rent increases as tenants of either public or private landlords. There seems little doubt that in the big picture of housing and social change in the UK the historic stock of council housing that once provided secure, permanent accommodation for millions of families in good-quality and decent housing or flats, often new, has gone. The end of council housing comes as the poet T.S. Eliot described the end of the world, 'not with a bang but a whimper' (Eliot, 1925).

There is a significant degree of complexity involved here, but what happened to British council housing from the mid-1970s onwards was a combination of the working through a long-term 'maturation' of the stock (Kemeny referred to it as the 'maturation crisis') and the impact that globalisation had on the UK economy, forcing it to be reinvented as a services economy in a very short space of time, with the loss of core manufacturing and mining, so that council housing's purpose declined. In theory, it could have been different. The options were to run a low-rent or regulated rental system that competed with the private sector or to make the opposite move, which was to 'marketise' state housing, to draw it into the logic of the private rental system, with income support for low-income tenants unable to afford fully market rents. The Right to Buy council houses was a clear signal by the Thatcher governments that, in an archetypal market economy such as the UK's, a 'social market' solution to the maturation of council housing was an unlikely scenario. Home-ownership was far too entrenched and its pursuit was the default position.

Despite the sheer size and long history of council housing, it was always going to be trumped by the even more powerful social and economic forces that played the home-ownership card at a very early stage. As we saw earlier in the book, the cultural and social foundations of the home-owning society were already established before the Second World War. The economic and ideational foundations that supported the home-owning society were unshakeable and so there never was a 'housing debate' about the maturing stock of state housing, which at its peak served a third of the population, more than most East and Central European communist societies in their heyday.

Conclusion

Although quite a large part of this chapter has not been directly about 'housing', the aim here has been to show the complementarities between the big picture of economic restructuring under the impact of globalisation and how this connected to the maturing of the UK as a home-owning society. This is rather a complex analysis involving both place and time. At the macro-level of analysis, globalisation compelled the country formerly known as the 'workshop of the world' to undergo a period of rapid economic restructuring resulting in the emergence of an economy based around services (70% of GDP). As a result, the old-fashioned Beveridgean welfare state came under increasing pressure, and under Thatcher and Blair the 'competition state' took hold with new policies and institutional structures geared towards supporting economic performance. Finally, at the lowest level of analysis, individual households were drawn into this complex reconfiguration. In particular, the growth of (mainly) part-time female work reshaped the labour market, giving rise to new relationships between the sexes, within households and in the housing market, especially the ability of two-earner households to access home-ownership despite the high cost of housing. This in turn fed into the changing geography of the country as counter-urbanisation kicked in and a home-owning suburban landscape became a familiar feature of the 1980s and 1990s.

Finally, a temporal dimension cut across this scenario because not only was home-ownership the default housing tenure built up from the interwar story as we have seen, but the rise and maturation of the council housing stock led to a new narrative of how to respond to the historic value of state housing, with a potential to run a popular low-rent housing system rather akin to the integrated rental markets in some Continental nations (Kemeny, 1995). The home-owning society was too ingrained and these were fertile conditions for its further expansion and ultimately domination of the housing system. At the same time, the collapse of manufacturing also acted to undercut the social purpose of council housing so that it was squeezed both by economic restructuring and by the long timeline of the historic value of the stock. The coup de grâce was the Right to Buy policy enshrined in the Housing Act 1980 and subsequent amendments to its terms. This much smaller 'social' housing sector had become a residual part of a new welfare state settlement in which social citizenship gave way to new ideas about asset-based welfare built on an 'opportunity' culture.

In other words, there was a confluence of factors in time, place and ideas ranging from the global scale and yet also connecting to individual households. Here is the secret of a new connection between the competition state shaped around the needs of the labour market, with a residential form of capitalism built around two-earner households. The 'home-owning society' narrative unlocked new ways of thinking about welfare needs and their provision not only by the state, but increasingly by individual households calculating that their interest was potentially best served by their principal asset, their housing wealth, and as a consequence by a low tax environment and a low inflation economy. Women going out to work was connected to sustaining the growth of home-ownership because household budgets required two incomes to support mortgages. Home-ownership created a direct incentive towards female labour force participation. This story also had ballot box and intergenerational implications, as will be seen in Chapter Six.

SUMMARY

- Globalisation compelled the British economy to restructure towards a services-based labour market. Meanwhile, the 'old' industries built on manufacturing and mining declined sharply in the 1980s and 1990s and the institutions of the state were reconfigured in order to cope with the much faster-moving and intensely competitive global economy.

- The old-fashioned Beveridgean welfare state began to give way to a 'competition state' in which workfare programmes became the main emphasis so that welfare expenditure supported the wider economy. The breakdown of the state-managed and -regulated services economy (from after the war) into private and more marketised forms in the 1980s opened the door for an influx of female workers.

- A high proportion of the jobs in the services economy were taken up by part-time female workers. Millions of full-time male jobs in manufacturing were lost to China, the Asian/Pacific nations and other low-cost production centres.

- The new services tended to be located in suburban areas and smaller towns where swathes of new owner-occupied housing was built creating a new wave of suburbanisation based on two-earner households directly connected to female labour force participation. Indeed, home-ownership created an incentive for women to go to work.

- Large cities, formerly the hub of the manufacturing industry, lost population as these industries were closed and in the process the social purpose of council housing in these areas was undermined. A crisis of low demand led to tens of thousands of council properties being demolished.

- At the same time, the maturation of council housing posed questions about its future, but there was no hope of creating an integrated rental market similar to some European countries. This factor and the loss of social purpose were complementary processes that caused council housing to degenerate.

> • The 'home-owning society' narrative unlocked new ways of thinking about welfare needs and their provision not only by the state, but increasingly by individual households. Housing wealth began to buttress the competition state model, meaning that 'housing' became more important to welfare state change.

Reading guide

There are literally hundreds of books on the topic of globalisation. Standard reading is P. Hirst and G. Thompson (1999) *Globalization in Question*. Also, Will Hutton and Anthony Giddens' book (2001) *On the Edge: Living with Global Capitalism* is a clear analysis of the implications of globalisation processes for the modern world. Hudson and Lowe's (2009) *Understanding the Policy Process: Analysing Welfare Policy and Practice*, 2nd edn, contains a more detailed account of the issues discussed in this chapter. Low demand is extensively documented. The main research paper is contained in Bramley et al (2000) *Low Demand Housing and Unpopular Neighbourhoods*, produced for the DETR. There are many papers on the residualisation of council housing in the journal *Housing Studies*. A good recent text on social housing in Britain is Suzanne Fitzpatrick and Mark Stephens' (2009) Shelter publication *The Future of Social Housing*. Jim Kemeny's (1995) *From Public Housing to the Social Market* is the source of the debate on the maturation crisis.

6

Housing and welfare states

OVERVIEW

Housing was neglected in the comparative welfare state literature until very recently. The reason for this appears to relate to some of 'housing's' characteristics, particularly that it is found mostly in the private sector unlike other welfare services. The significance of housing and its critical connection to welfare states was first recognised and explained by Kemeny. Discoveries made by Esping-Andersen showed that there were different types of welfare state in modern capitalist societies. Kemeny's analysis suggests that different housing systems can also be identified, especially either those that promote open, liberal housing markets in which home-ownership predominates or conversely 'social market' economies, such as Germany, where housing is not thought of as a commodity, but as a social right. The creation of 'deep' mortgage markets following the deregulation of banking in the 1980s has connected home-owners to the flow of global capital and impacted on voters' attitudes to taxation and spending on public services. Through the advances made in this work, housing has taken its rightful place as a key feature of how we think about and define 21st-century welfare states.

Key concepts:

corporatism, dual rental/integrated rental markets, globalisation, mortgage markets, social market economies, varieties of residential capitalism, welfare state regimes

Introduction

The recent banking crisis revealed in a very alarming way the extent to which the global financial markets are integrated, particularly through the securities market and the international banking system.

The trigger to the banking crisis of 2007–09 was the massive scale of bad debts accumulated in the US sub-prime mortgage market and serious errors made by credit-rating agencies about the price of risky loans (Muellbauer and Murphy, 2008). These 'toxic assets' were bundled into so-called 'securities' in the form of bonds that were sold on through the global money markets to investors imagining these were secure, long-term investments, ideal, for example, for pension funds. This example – of housing debts finding their way into pension funds in other countries – is a glimpse at some of the factors influencing contemporary public policy and welfare states.

The bursting of the global financial bubble followed a period of unprecedented growth in house prices across most, but not all, of the OECD countries underpinned by the invention of new forms of financial trading, principally the process known as 'securitisation', which unleashed a massive flow of capital that spread through the global financial system (see Box 7.1 in Chapter Seven). It was the context in which this happened and the sheer scale of it that has impacted on how we need to think about the relationship between housing and welfare states. It was the new mortgage markets, truly global in reach, which acted as a conduit for the flow of capital into household domestic budgets. This, in turn, meant that owner-occupiers began to think very directly about their properties as commodities rather than only as homes. People began to literally 'bank' on housing for consumption and welfare services in a way that was unimaginable before the liberalisation of the financial markets during the 1980s. In many OECD countries, the attitudes and voting behaviour of home-owners was strongly influenced towards low tax/low interest rate policies and less support for public spending in areas where private assets provide good-quality alternatives. Of course, there was a great deal of variation in this depending on long-term, culturally embedded attitudes to welfare provision and risk, but nowhere was immune from the impact of what happened. One consequence of this, particularly in societies dominated by home-ownership, was to enable home-owners to access housing equity (the value stored in their property) in exchange for increasing mortgage debt, with major impacts on consumption and, in the context of the concerns of this chapter, significant changes to welfare states and attitudes to welfare provision. Alan Greenspan, formerly for many years Chairman of the US Federal Reserve, considered equity withdrawal so significant to assessing the performance of the US economy that he conducted private research on the impact of the transmission of housing 'wealth' into the macroeconomy (Greenspan and Kennedy, 2008).

The core argument in this chapter is that we cannot make sense of welfare state change unless we understand, at least in outline, this global institutional–financial nexus. Deregulation of banks, surging house prices (in most, but not all, countries) and huge flows of new capital that have washed across the globe like a financial tsunami have impacted everywhere. This is a big agenda and has to be spread over two chapters. The starting point for the analysis, taking up most of this chapter, is to discuss what might now seem obvious, but until recently was almost unknown – research on the relationship between housing and welfare states. Housing was neglected in the comparative welfare state literature, but recent work and the realities of the financial crisis that began in 2007 have given housing a much stronger profile, to the extent that, far from a sideline in the story any more, it is increasingly a key player. Indeed, the argument here is that some of the basic welfare state types, even those with a strong 'statist'/collective system, have been shaken and changed by the housing nexus, a potent mixture of global capital flows, mortgage institutions (whether liberal and 'open' or repressed/regulated) and the type of housing system in a society, which generally reflects welfare state traditions. As we saw in Chapter One, there are broadly speaking two types of 'housing' system: societies dominated by 'home-owning' (most of the English-speaking nations and a raft of post-communist nations fall into this category); and systems where renting and owning are more integrated (typical of the social market/corporatist economies of Northern Europe, such as Germany and Sweden).

This chapter is about the relationship between housing and the welfare state. It begins by exploring why housing was for many years not written about (with one very notable exception) in the comparative welfare state literature. What was it about 'housing' compared to the other pillars of the welfare state – health, social security, education, employment policy – that made it apparently difficult to analyse? One of the answers is the problem social scientists had in deciding whether housing was a social right or a commodity bought and sold in a market. But this is not the whole story, and unravelling this issue requires a detailed conceptual outline of welfare state types and how housing fits into these. This leads us to the rather astonishing idea that since the deregulation of the banking system in the 1980s, welfare states have been sculpted in new ways by the globalisation of capital flows and that 'housing' is a central part of this process. We begin by wondering why housing was neglected and end by showing that it has become a central player.

Chapters Six and Seven are a two-part drama. In Chapter Seven, we explore in more detail this process of change – especially looking at global house prices – and the erosion of the old welfare state landscape, and begin to sketch the new welfare state terrain that is emerging.

The neglect of housing in the welfare state literature

Reading back through the comparative welfare state literature, one of the more puzzling questions is why housing was almost never mentioned as a key dimension and certainly never thought of in the studies that sought to discover the differences between 'capitalist' welfare states. This seems all the more strange when, as we saw in the British case in Chapters Two and Three, the state had to intervene to address the huge imbalance of households to dwellings after both the 20th-century world wars. All post-war European welfare states were developed in the context of acute housing shortages and so for a time the wider welfare state agenda and housing policy coincided.

In the British case, as we saw in the earlier chapters, there was a clear division between state-built 'council housing' for rent at subsidised prices and what was always spoken of as the 'normal' housing market, dominated even before the Second World War by home-ownership. One of the great tectonic plates of 20th- and 21st-century Britain had been substantially laid down in the country's social and economic 'geology' during the interwar period. This is an illustration of the importance mentioned at several places in the book of thinking through the nature of social change and especially the idea of timing: when and in what order ('sequence') events occur matters a great deal in our analysis. As we saw, in many ways the British case was unusual here, with the Continental, corporatist states operating a more open, less centralised system in which a wider constellation of interests were represented, notably private landlords, who entered the state-managed integrated market in which rent-setting and tenancy rights were overseen and mediated by the wider state in exchange for access to state subsidy. As will be shown later, these differences have significant implications for how we need to think about welfare state change in the early decades of the 21st century.

Why was housing neglected in social policy research?

The reason why housing has been neglected in the welfare state literature requires some explanation. Most obviously, as Torgersen points out, from the point of view of the state, housing is mainly a capital form of expenditure. Most of the cost arises from building the 'bricks and mortar' and buying land. When the state does provide housing, it is normally for a minority of households who cannot afford to be in the market. Note, however, that this view is less relevant to the 'social market' nations of Central and Northern Europe, which, as we will see, have housing systems that are focused on renting and provide housing for a wide cross-section of society. Torgersen also argued that the other core welfare state functions of education and health services are normally universal – provided for everyone – (at least in European countries) and much of the ongoing cost in these services goes towards paying staff – doctors, nurses, teachers, managers and administrators – and so the funding system is more about revenue costs (paying salaries) rather than capital investment. Torgersen called housing a 'wobbly' welfare state pillar because capital programmes are much easier to cut in periods of financial austerity than salaries

(Torgersen, 1987). It should not come as a surprise that within days of being elected in May 2010 the Conservative–Liberal Democrat Coalition government announced as an early demonstration of its 'cuts' agenda a significant reduction in capital spending on social housing, the abolition of security of tenure for council house tenants and downgrading of the regional house-building targets.

Kemeny suggests a more subtle argument for the neglect of housing in comparative welfare state research. He argues that this oversight resulted from the degree to which housing was 'embedded' in society, making it an elusive subject. He argues that it impacts on lifestyles, in a way similar to Giddens' idea of 'individualisation' – that being 'at home' is where we create our identity as people, where we are able to be most 'ourselves' and where gender roles and stereotypes are shaped (Giddens, 1989). The point is that housing is such a familiar part of everyday life that it is easy to overlook its significance. Kemeny argues that housing and especially housing tenure (see Chapter One) also influence the shape of urban built environments (cities where rental housing dominates tend to a preponderance of flats, whereas home-owning-dominated societies tend towards sprawling suburbs) and social structure (collective forms of living such as high-rise flats against more individual forms in detached houses). He was the earliest of the social scientists to recognise the connection between housing systems and the wider welfare state – that housing in a sense can come also to shape, if not actually define, different types of welfare system (Kemeny, 1980). His key point is that different housing systems and how these influence welfare states are the outcome of political processes and choices and not predetermined preferences, for example, the common idea that people prefer to be home-owners rather than tenants. We return to this line of thought later on because Kemeny revised his position, but for now we can take from this work the idea that we need to see the big picture of influences that shape the connection between housing and welfare states. Kemeny's idea is further outlined in Box 6.1.

So far we have noted some key features of housing that allegedly make it 'different' and even difficult to incorporate into ideas about welfare state development:

- Housing is a capital form of expenditure requiring large amounts of initial investment in land and construction, which makes it prone to cuts in spending.
- State intervention in housing is usually only for the support of a minority of low-income households, but note that this applies mainly to 'home-owning' types of society.
- Most households buy their own home in the housing market and think of their home as a financial asset as well as a place to live.
- Housing is socially embedded. It is such a familiar, everyday experience that its impact can easily be overlooked.

Box 6.1: Kemeny's discovery of why different housing types shape attitudes to welfare

The essence of Kemeny's argument is that owner-occupiers come to have a specific outlook towards taxation and spending on public services arising from the financial logic of buying into residential property. This trade-off arises because the costs of buying a house are normally very front-loaded over the lifecycle. Home-owners have to save up for a deposit and the mortgage payments are expensive at a time when income tends to be low at the beginning of careers. This compression of costs at the beginning of a housing career eases after the mortgage is paid off, usually over 20–25 years. This predisposes home-owners to support a low tax/low spend welfare state. They oppose high levels of public spending with a risk of increasing interest rates that inevitably make monthly mortgage payments more expensive.

On the other hand, renters pay their housing costs out in a much more even way, but over the whole of their lifetime. Their housing costs tend to peak during the middle years when the arrival of children pushes up rent payments, but this coincides with peak earnings capacity in the middle of the life course, with housing costs diminishing again when children leave home in later life. Housing costs for renters continue more or less evenly throughout their life and so housing payments are more evenly spread than the heavily front-loaded costs of home-owners. Once their mortgages are paid off, home-owners' housing costs are much lower and this has implications for attitudes towards pensions planning, as we will see in the next chapter. Kemeny argues that this logic predisposes home-owners to support residual, low tax welfare states especially in relation to pensions planning because home-owners have low housing costs once mortgages have been paid off in later life. The idea that housing shapes attitudes towards welfare and public spending as a matter of political preference is the key to Kemeny's work.

It seems, therefore, that the neglect of housing can be accounted for by its somewhat complex and potentially wide-ranging impact on society, and it is this that made it difficult to capture in the comparative welfare state literature compared to social security, health or education, which are all more clearly state–managed services. Rather more mundanely, it might also be added that a quantitative analysis of housing is made even more difficult because the meaning of different housing tenures varies from country to country. The legal foundations of 'owning' and 'renting' are very varied, making it difficult to 'count' housing beyond rather crude comparisons of housing types, of

standards and commonly of size (how many rooms and square metres of space are available to a family). It was typical of early comparative studies to use indicators that could easily be quantified. These studies tended to the view that modern welfare states were more or less similar and were responding to the same issues. According to Wilensky, for example, it was the demographic imperative of ageing populations that drove welfare state change, and that all welfare states were converging around the need to provide pensions and care support. The differences, he argues, were mainly a matter of timing, what he called welfare state 'leaders' and 'laggards'. In his study, Wilensky specifically excludes housing as an indicator in his quantitative analysis of the OECD countries, saying that 'the comparative analysis of public spending in this area [is] nearly impossible' (Wilensky, 1975, p 7).

Comparative studies that looked at housing were almost non-existent until the 1980s. In one piece of pioneering research, Donnison (1967) identified three types of housing system using a narrow definition of housing policy as public/state housing. Rather like Wilensky, he regarded countries as passing through various stages – 'haphazard', 'residual' and 'comprehensive' – basically a 'leaders and laggards' thesis. He cited Turkey and Portugal as being at the haphazard end of the spectrum, and Sweden and the Netherlands at the opposite extreme. The idea behind Donnison's work was that these stages of development were governed not by political choices, but by the level of economic development of a country. A similar 'convergence' idea surfaced later on in the work of Harloe in which he argued that countries pass through phases of what he called 'commodification' (the dominance of private housing systems), 'decommodification' (state intervention) and 'recommodification' (privatisation of state housing) in response to periodic crises in market economies (Harloe, 1985). For a while, Harloe's work was influential and there followed a number of one-country studies that showed how countries in the post-war period had indeed passed through these stages (on Sweden, see Lundquist et al, 1990; on the Netherlands, see Priemus, 1995).

All these studies basically had in common the idea that there was a single overarching factor that drove welfare states or housing systems to converge on a common outcome, whether it was the ageing population, crises of capitalism or stages of economic development. There was also very little engagement with the connection between 'housing' and welfare states, other than the unproblematic, narrow idea of housing as 'state housing'.

From convergence to divergence

However, during the 1980s, studies of single countries or of clusters of countries pointed in a rather different direction, particularly that countries with similarly advanced types of economy and economic development had quite different types of welfare states and housing systems (Kemeny and Lowe, 1998). The idea of divergence was like a tide turning against the dominant flow of research based mainly on quantitative data-driven studies and was soon to lead to easily the most influential comparative study of welfare states, Esping-Andersen's *The Three Worlds of Welfare Capitalism* (1990).

Starting from a theory of political power and the relationship between different social classes, Esping-Andersen identified three quite distinct welfare state 'regimes' (see Box 6.2 for more detail). How this worked out in practice was that different societies responded to the provision of core welfare needs in different ways. There were key differences in the way resources were deployed through either state provision, the market, the community/voluntary sectors, families or individuals. For example, in some countries health-care services were provided mainly by the state, in others through the market, and in yet others by a mixture of the state and market. Basically, Esping-Andersen sought to show that the degree to which a society relied on state or market solutions to welfare needs told us a great deal about the type of welfare system in any one place and crucially that these systems created different opportunities and disadvantages in society. Wealthier households tended to do well in market-dominated health-care systems, whereas the less well-off fared better in more state-managed health services. Welfare states, Esping Andersen argued, had an important role in what he referred to as the 'stratification' of society.

Box 6.2: Esping-Andersen's (1990) *The Three Worlds of Welfare Capitalism*

Esping Andersen began his famous book *The Three Worlds of Welfare Capitalism* with a theory. He argued that welfare states were the outcome of how power struggles between different social classes were resolved. These inter-class alliances or conflicts created what he called 'regimes', emphasising the idea of his class theory of power. The three 'worlds' are:

- The **social democratic welfare regime** – results from the success of working-class movements in creating alliances with middle-class political parties and groups, keeping conservative interests divided and so over time becoming the dominant force in shaping society. These welfare states, typically those of the Nordic countries such as Sweden and Norway, base their welfare provision around a decommodified system – meaning an emphasis on state provision and collective solutions, in other words detached from the open market. Here, there is an emphasis on the social entitlement to high-quality welfare. This approach has an important impact on stratification, on how wealth and opportunities are distributed in society.

- The **corporatist welfare regime** – results in effect from a deadlocked power struggle in which no one interest dominates. As a result each element of the social structure is provided with its own subsystem of welfare. The emphasis here is on maintaining traditional social hierarchies, and social policy becomes a means of securing social order. Governments, trade unions and employers combine to develop social insurance schemes with fairly generous benefits. The historical sources of this regime are a strong state, a corporatist economic order and an important role for religion, especially Catholicism (promoting traditional family values). Sometimes this regime is referred to as being conservative because its aim is to stabilise and not to change society.

- The **liberal welfare regime** – emerges from societies in which the working class is divided and conservative forces dominate, creating a residual approach to welfare with an emphasis on individual responsibility with a high degree of commodification. Here the aim of welfare states is the opposite of the corporatist stability and preservation of social order so that individuals should be free to realise their potential and hierarchies are replaced by merit. The welfare state is geared towards private and market-led solutions with the aim of encouraging links into the market for the provision of care needs, health and social insurance. The archetypal case is clearly the USA.

It should be noted that having defined these types of welfare state Esping-Andersen then sought empirical evidence to support his concepts. He aimed to measure the impact of social policies on the stratification of society. Using pensions policy, health and social security he devised a series of statistical tests to build up his classification. There have been major criticisms of this methodology, not least because it is all based on data from one year, 1980, and that his data were chosen quite carefully to match his theory. It is interesting to note for our purpose that 'housing' was not part of his empirical work, and in this his was typical of comparative welfare state research up to then. This work has also been criticised for errors in the analysis of the data, but it is more important to note that it is not the flaws in the empirical work, but problems with Esping-Andersen's theory, that matter most. The emphasis on class and on power as the factors shaping his 'three worlds' arguably excludes other wider cultural issues and influences that are not related to class. Indeed, the pursuit of ever more types and varieties of capitalism might now be considered rather fruitless.

Esping-Andersen admitted that his 'three worlds' are not pure and many countries do not fit neatly into any one of them. The UK, for example, with its large-scale welfare state is nevertheless usually thought of as closest to the liberal regime.

Esping-Andersen's study had an enormous resonance across the social sciences. 'Housing' was not part of the 'Three Worlds' study. Once again, however, there seems to be no particular reason for this except that the housing data did not seem to fit with his model. However, in previous work, Kemeny (1981) had compared the housing systems of three countries in which he had lived and worked: Australia, the UK and Sweden. He showed that government policy, using housing subsidies in different ways, favoured either the growth of home-ownership (as in Australia and the UK) or a non-profit system in which renting was equally a mainstream option and home-owning did not dominate the housing system. These very different approaches to housing were not the result of a preference for owning as against renting, but were the products of political choices made in different societies. Building on this idea and starting with an evaluation of Esping-Andersen's study, Kemeny showed that in the housing domain there were in essence not three types of housing system, but two.

Kemeny's housing regimes

The reason why Kemeny's conceptual discovery is important is that for the first time it enabled a direct connection between 'housing' and comparisons of welfare states. Instead of being mysteriously difficult to incorporate into cross-national work or separated out as a special case, housing became much more central to characterising how and why welfare states change. Kemeny went on to show that housing has an enormous resonance in how people think about their retirement pensions and by extension other aspects of welfare provision. At the very least, this theoretical breakthrough at long last made the connection between housing and welfare states. Housing, Kemeny prophetically argued, far from being marginal to welfare state research, might well come to be seen as central to it.

The core of his thesis is that there are basically two housing types or systems, although within each type there is considerable variation. First, associated with the liberal welfare regime, Kemeny described a 'dualist rental market' in which the state takes charge of the provision of rental housing for low-income households who cannot afford to buy in the open market. This housing is heavily subsidised, usually from central funds, and is allocated on the basis of need. The private rental system operates completely differently, without subsidy and with rents that reflect the current capital value of the property. In this 'dual rental market' renting purely for profit operates separately from social housing, which Kemeny calls 'non-profit renting' and which has quite different functions. Both are generally thought of as 'second class' forms of housing. By limiting access to state housing only to low-income households as a matter of social policy, a wedge is driven between the public and private rental sectors. The general tendency is that the smaller the non-profit sector is, the more deprived and disadvantaged are the tenants. In this context, home-ownership is the default, 'normal' form of housing for most people and governments encourage this perception and support it with tax breaks on capital gains and sometimes tax relief on mortgage payments.

The English-speaking countries – the USA, the UK, Canada, Australia and New Zealand – are all typical of this basic housing system, which includes the high home-owning societies such as Ireland, Spain, Portugal and Greece. There are of course wide variations in each case, but the logic is clear to see. In dual rental societies, home-ownership is more or less unopposed as the dominant housing form. For historical reasons, there are considerable variations in the size of the non-profit rental sector (as we have outlined in earlier chapters, the UK had an exceptionally high proportion of public housing, accommodating nearly one third of the whole population at its peak in the 1970s), and generally the more targeted on low-income households 'social housing' is, the more deprived are the families that live there. Although, of course, not part of his analysis, the idea of 'the home-owning society' connects closely to Esping-Andersen's liberal welfare regime.

The other housing type is what Kemeny calls a 'unitary rental market' or 'integrated market' and is closely associated with the corporatist political systems typified by the 'social market economies'. Here, housing subsidies are provided to all types of landlord, with the central state not usually being the source of housing per se. This system has a range of different providers: housing cooperatives, housing associations, independent housing providers, as well as some limited provision by local authorities. These agencies compete on an equal footing with private landlords. It is a common misconception that cost rental housing is always public or quasi-public, but very often, such as in Germany, a high proportion of cost rental housing is provided by private landlords. Because they all receive subsidy, the state can ensure an equality of standards, and here it is the public sector that tends to determine rent levels in any one area because housing subsidies have been shared across all the providers. Maximising profit from rents is as a result constrained, and rental housing in this integrated market is much less stigmatised and open to people of all social strata. Owner-occupation is therefore less desirable and does not dominate.

Households choose home-ownership for 'housing' reasons – type of property, particular locational needs, access to a garden – rather than as part of a home-owning imperative due to lack of alternative choices, where 'getting on the housing ladder at all costs' dominates and where access to public rental housing is barred to most people. The key countries with this system are Germany, Sweden, Denmark, the Netherlands, Austria and Switzerland.

Box 6.3: Integrated rental markets

Because much of the housing discourse in the UK works on the basis that 'the home-owning society' is the default housing system, much less is known about the cluster of integrated rental markets of Sweden, Germany, Austria, the Netherlands, Denmark and Switzerland. As with the home-owning society cases, there is considerable variety among the core integrated rental nations. This diversity reflects the form of corporatism that lies at the heart of these states (ie the balance of power between the various key social actors – trade unions, employers, governments). One of the ways to differentiate integrated rental markets is the degree to which pressure groups can lobby for particular interests – of tenants, private landlords, building companies, housing cooperatives and so on. These interests can exert significant influence because these states have multi-party political systems in which governments almost always are made up of coalitions that must seek support from different parties and the interests they represent. Corporatist power systems tend to induce compromise. In the home-owning societies, it is often the case that two-party adversarial political systems squeeze out smaller interests. We must take note, therefore, of the balance of power and the strength of housing interests in assessing each case. In Sweden and Denmark, for example, housing cooperatives and tenant-managed organisations are about as large as the private landlords. In Sweden, it is the local authorities who manage the system, but in Denmark, the non-profit sector is privately owned by housing cooperatives/trusts with a strong element of tenant control. In Germany and Switzerland, the non-profit sectors are much smaller with a large assortment of private landlords, making the influence of the non-profit sector much weaker. So, in the integrated rental market housing systems, there are very different 'strengths' to the influence that the non-profit sector has in shaping the rental market.

It is worth recalling from Chapter Two that the historical roots of this idea can be traced back to Bismarck in the 1880s when the German Social Democrats refused to participate in governments that seemed to so strongly favour the elite social strata. As outlined in Box 2.1, Bismarck's social insurance scheme was a carrot to the German working class and was designed to create social stability by buying off the socialists. This was underpinned by the three-class voting system that gave a massive bias in favour of the small wealthy elite, including large-scale landlords, with a third share of the votes for parliamentary and federal government elections. The social and political compromises that emerged from this nexus were the basis of the German corporatist model of social organisation. In the very different circumstances of the 1930s, these ideas were redefined into the 'social market' by the Ordoliberals, a group of philosophers and economists who were influential towards the end of the German Weimar Republic (which governed in Germany after the First World War and up to when Hitler's Nazi Party hijacked the republic in 1933). Ordoliberals argued that the state needed to take a strong interest in managing and regulating the capitalist economy in order to foster competition and stop monopolies subverting good government and coming to dominate society. These ideas became central features of the 'social market' system that was responsible for the post-Second World War reconstruction of Germany (the so-called *Wirtschaftswunder* – 'economic miracle'). It created a very specific 'variety' of capitalism in which there was a division of functions in managing the economy:

- the Central Bank is responsible for planning monetary policy – keeping inflation in check and the currency stable with all these functions insulated from political interference;

- the government of the day is responsible for fiscal policy – deciding on the balance between public spending on, for example, defence and the welfare state, including 'state' pensions and other transfer payments such as unemployment benefit; and
- the employers and the trade unions take on the main responsibility for delivering the foundation of the entire domain of the macroeconomy – the wealth-creating industrial sector, including the nation's industrial investment, international trade and the long-run foundation of economic activity.

The idea of the state directing economic and social policy and harnessing the differing interests in society is the foundation of the corporatist model of society and matches closely Esping-Andersen's 'conservative' regime, and the same social conditions created the integrated rental market (see Box 6.3) as part of the same social settlement.

Because state-managed social housing was blocked off by powerful private landlords, what happened instead was that the German trade unions and other workers' organisations were allowed to borrow from the social insurance fund (created by the Invalidity and Old Age Insurance Fund Act 1890) to build their own, independent housing cooperatives over which they had management control, including the selection of tenants. A subsidised housing system developed with a mixture of landlords using this funding source so that there was a plurality of landlords, a situation very different from the British case where social housing was provided almost exclusively by local authorities, our familiar 'council housing'. Already, at the end of the 19th century, two 'varieties of capitalism' were clearly defined: on the one hand, the corporatist model typified by the German case and, on the other, the market economy of which late-Victorian Britain was the archetype. And it is in this context that we also find the seeds of Kemeny's two housing regimes:

- a plural system in which public and private landlords received subsidies so that they competed on an equal footing (and hence the idea of this system as a 'unitary' or 'integrated' market) and in which home-ownership did not become a dominant influence because there was so much choice already; and

• the market-dominated system in which state housing always existed separately from the housing market, separated both from unsubsidised private landlords and, as we saw in the 1920s and 1930s in Britain, from home-ownership, which became the dominant, default tenure even while still a minority of households lived in it because the two rental systems were separated (hence the idea of the 'dual rental' market, the one with restricted access based on a means test for low-income households and the other a declining market provided by private landlords who found it impossible to compete with the other two housing tenures in the absence of subsidy).

Varieties of capitalism

Research into the ideas and methods that underpinned modern capitalism in the 1980s began to clarify its different forms and one influential stream of work pointed towards the idea that there were two fundamental types of system. Crouch, for example, in a study of industrial relations, argued that there were several methods for dealing with labour and management disputes (Crouch, 1977). He showed that there was a corporatist model (in a 'strong' and 'weak' version) – in which labour movements were more or less influential – and 'contestational bargaining' (such as in the UK or Italy) and 'pluralistic bargaining' (eg Spain and France), again with different strengths of labour movement influence.

More recently, political economists working on comparative themes have identified two core types of capitalism and, very much as Kemeny argued, have conflated the social democratic and corporatist types into one overarching system. The motivation behind this work was variously to understand the differences and similarities between societies in the face of globalisation, European integration and the Euro currency and the shift in the 1980s and 1990s towards a neoliberal ideological agenda.

A key debate developed under the umbrella title of 'varieties of capitalism' (VOC) (see Box 6.4) and, rather like Crouch, focused attention on the way that different national economies were organised, especially in relation to the manufacturing industry. Hall and Soskice (2001) argue that the core institution by which the challenge of globalisation is met and filtered is the industrial firm, acting as a 'key agent of adjustment'. A company's relative success or failure depends on its ability to manage its industrial relations, production systems, staff training and external relations – with suppliers, customers, trade unions, other business associates, banks and through to the government itself. It is the integration of this complex network and the building of 'institutional complementarities' – the idea that there is an interconnection between these elements. It comes as no surprise that this research identified two dominant forms of political economy, the liberal market model familiar to the open capitalist economies of the UK and the US and a coordinated market economy, which is that found in Esping-Andersen's corporatist nations, the typical 'social market' societies.

Box 6.4: Varieties of capitalism

This approach to understanding the differences and similarities between advanced industrial economies emphasises the way in which economic institutions are coordinated:

- In **liberal market economies** (LMEs) firms operate principally through hierarchies and competitive markets based around classical supply and demand. Manufacturing tends to be at the low-skill end of the spectrum. The financial institutions are not coordinated, but operate through a classical economic model.

- In **coordinated market economies** (CMEs) systems are required to have more cooperative approaches that are much less based on market signals and more on networks to coordinate a more socially responsive economic model. What characterises these societies is the operation of high-skilled, high-wage industries with long-standing connections to banks, generous (but expensive) welfare states and publicly funded education and training.

The VOC approach has been criticised for being too rigid and giving too much emphasis to 'the firm' and not enough to other sources of influence on how an economy is managed, particularly the weak role assigned to the state and wider governance. It might also be noted that manufacturing industries are much less important in Western economies than they used to be, so that the affiliation between high-skill manufacturing (in CMEs) and low-skill manufacturing, which is said to be a characteristic of LMEs, is considerably less relevant, in both cases, but especially in those LMEs in which the core economic activity is built around the knowledge economy and services. The VOC literature limits its research horizon to discussing the extent to which global financial markets impact on investment planning and the stabilisation of companies, but only those engaged in manufacturing. The shape of this debate is, as a result, blinkered to the wider impact that the global financial markets have had on a specific area of the economy. Indeed, the VOC research tends to engage in national comparisons and so underplays the inherently global nature of recent shifts in the structure of the world economy. Although there is some institutional complementarity with welfare states through the focus on unemployment and social protection, the VOC approach inevitably neglects our 'housing' domain and has no empathy with the macroeconomic impact arising from personal assets, most of which are held in the form of property. It is not surprising to find housing once again on the margins of a key theoretical school.

This major flaw was, however, identified by Schwartz and Seabrooke (2008), who argued that it was 'odd' that the VOC approach neglected residential property markets given the significance they have recently had first of all in driving consumption over at least the 10 years up to 2007 and, secondly, with international institutions agreeing on the centrality of residential property to macroeconomic stability. Here, the point is not that the VOC position is wrong, but that its focus is too narrow. Its method and analytical tools are useful when carried into the residential property market. Schwartz and Seabrooke's work brings us right back to our 'housing' theme and begins to build the case for a connection between housing and contemporary welfare states. The key point is that the liberalisation of the financial markets during the 1980s has created a new set of institutional structures built around global financial markets. As Schwartz and Seabrooke (2008, p 242) argue: 'housing finance systems can connect people to global financial capital flows and interest rates in a more direct way than tax systems, public debt or employment'.

Varieties of residential capitalism

Schwartz and Seabrooke retain from the VOC literature the idea of key institutional 'complementarities' – connections and spin-offs between firms, agencies, banks, government programmes and so on. What they argue is that during the period of huge global financial flows in the 1980s and up to about 2006, housing finance systems connected households to this vast quantity of global capital in a very direct way and, because of the significance of housing to people's domestic budgets, this impacted on political attitudes and also how they thought about their welfare needs. The difference from the VOC approach, with its focus essentially on national industrial structures, was that these financial flows were global and had to be understood as a worldwide phenomenon. Home-owners in very liberal, commodified housing systems were particularly open to taking on mortgage debt (and so converting their housing equity into goods and services), and this was bound to shape political attitudes – resisting taxation that pays for welfare state provisions, preferring to pay by cash for services, and supporting political parties that favour and protect property. Schwartz and Seabrooke suggest, in the same vein as the VOC idea, that there are a 'variety of residential capitalisms'.

Schwartz and Seabrooke build their typology around two dimensions in a national housing system; how many home-owners there are compared to renters – our familiar idea of housing tenure – which gives a fix on the degree of decommodification, of how privately geared it is. The second dimension is a measure of how 'liberal' or 'controlled' a country's mortgage market is, which reflects the extent of mortgage debt in an economy and also the degree of mortgage securitisation. If the mortgage market is open, fully functioning and built around key institutional structures – banks and building societies, estate agents, mortgage brokers and crucially the degree to which mortgages are hooked into the flows of global capital – home-owners can increase their levels of debt by borrowing bigger mortgages without moving. A household's property becomes in effect a form of bank against which it can draw periodically, especially when house prices have geared up the value of the asset and when interest rates are low (enabling home-owners to increase their debt at lower costs or to move to more expensive houses relative to their income). As Muellbauer argued, home-ownership does not inherently lead to 'housing wealth', but the keys to unlocking equity are the institutions and products available in the mortgage market, leading rather more accurately to consideration not of a 'housing wealth' effect, but a 'housing collateral' effect (Muellbauer, 2008). Housing equity is unlocked mainly by new borrowing, taking on bigger mortgages. The degree of indebtedness of home-owners is clearly a measure of the decommodification of a housing system (because this debt is paid out of private household income).

On the other hand, where mortgage market regulations and institutional structures are more limiting and/or where there are fewer owner-occupiers in a housing market with stable prices, the degree of exposure to global capital markets is much less. Based around these two key elements – proportion of home-owners in a society and the type of mortgage market (whether open/liberal or controlled/regulated) and measured by the quantity of mortgage debt in a society against GDP – Schwartz and Seabrooke devised a typology of 'residential capitalisms' (see Box 6.5 and Figure 6.1).

The most interesting result of the Schwartz and Seabrooke typology for our purpose is the emergence of the 'corporatist-market' quadrant, countries where stratification is less, the non-profit sector is a weaker player in the integrated rental market and, moreover, where the mortgage market is less regulated. This sits uneasily with the culture of housing as a social right, which has long been the story of these cases – Denmark, the Netherlands, Germany, Sweden and also Switzerland – the core of the corporatist nations with integrated rental markets. In effect, what Schwartz and Seabrooke have done is to highlight the more market-sensitive end of the integrated rental market spectrum. Adding to the core housing regimes the influence of the structure of mortgage markets has brought into much sharper relief the vulnerability of some of the integrated rental market societies to significant change, even to the point where they are on the threshold of losing their identity as integrated rental markets. Denmark and the Netherlands in particular have become much closer to the dual rental/home–owning model.

Figure 6.1: Varieties of residential capitalism

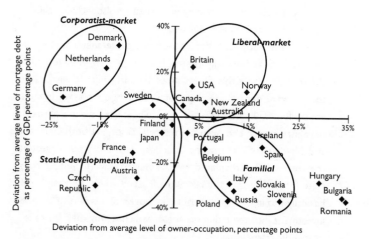

Source: Schwartz and Seabrooke (2008, p 24)

Box 6.5: Varieties of residential capitalism

Schwartz and Seabrooke's typology incorporates both the VOC 'liberal' and 'corporatist' economic systems and mirrors Esping-Andersen's welfare state regimes. Averaged out over the decade 1992–2002, their dimensions of proportion of home-owners against proportion of mortgage debt to GDP produces four different housing finance systems:

- **Corporatist-market** – here, owner-occupation rates are relatively low (47% on average), but mortgage regulation is relatively weak and there is as a result a significant exposure to the global financial markets. Social renting is relatively high (20.7% on average), but these are societies typically associated with Kemeny's 'regulated rental market' so that there is rather little distinction between public and private renting. Denmark and the Netherlands are the archetypal cases, but Germany and Sweden are also included, though with lower rates of mortgage debt.

- **Statist-developmentalist** – here, home-ownership is moderately high at 58% and socially rented housing is also relatively high. What distinguishes this cluster, however, is the quite low exposure to mortgage debt, suggesting that the mortgage market is quite controlled/regulated and relatively insulated from the global circuit of capital. France and Austria are typical cases, but both Germany and Sweden are close to the boundary with this type, suggesting the logic of the 'regulated rental' system – with quite strong state management of the rental market and where housing is still basically thought of as a social right. Governments aim to channel investment into the industrial sector, which is why they are called 'statist developmentalist'.

- **Liberal-market** – here, home-ownership averages over 70% with low levels of social rented housing in which people regard housing as a commodity. The ratio of mortgage debt to GDP is quite high, similar to the corporatist market, suggesting a fairly 'complete' set of mortgage institutions and, until 2007, a large number of products available. In these societies, home-ownership is the default form of housing tenure and first-time buyers tend to be young, 'getting on the housing ladder'. All of the 'English-speaking' cluster belong to this group.

- **Familial** – here, home-ownership rates are among the highest anywhere in developed societies, often with little or no social housing. The mortgage market is also very weak and undeveloped because households in this type tend to have relatively low incomes. In the absence of social housing and a developed mortgage institutional structure, access to housing is very dependent on families to 'look after their own', with children sharing with parents, inheritance and self-build all features of these countries. The post-communist states figure highly in this group. Italy, Spain and Belgium are included because the rules for mortgage lending are restrictive and/or mortgage securitisation is disallowed.

In Denmark, for example, the consequence of an open mortgage market, shaped by government, ignited an unprecedented property boom in the 10 years up to 2006 (Mortensen and Seabrook, 2008). In a country once famous for its strong welfare state and risk-averse attitudes, there has been a significant ideational shift from viewing housing as a social right to a discourse favouring property as a means to wealth. Party politics has decisively shifted to the right so that tax reforms favouring tenants, urban renewal programmes and so on have all been constrained in favour of housing market policies. The extent of the institutional change is most dramatically illustrated in the abandonment of the historic system of cooperative housing that once was the toast of the social democratic model. Once upon a time, these housing cooperatives – providing about one third of housing in most large towns and cities – offered a right for moderate-income households (often public-sector workers) to buy a share in an apartment that was mutually owned. The European Union competition rules have played a significant role here in undermining the integrated rental markets, as Doling (2006) predicted they would. Rules permitting market pricing of these flats created incentives for cooperatives to break from the traditional system, causing significant inflation in the prices of flats (over 110% between 2000 and 2005). This move from deliberately holding down prices to the complete opposite has incentivised cooperative-owners to move out into the freehold market, but closed the door to the idea of housing as a social right. Furthermore, at a stroke this change created major intergenerational inequalities as first-time buyers and modest-income households can no longer access large parts of the housing cooperative sector. To an extent, the generous welfare state cushions this shock, but first-time buyers are compelled to take out risky high-interest, interest-only loans to afford any access to the market. This is a story more typical of 'home-owning societies' than an integrated rental market (see Box 6.6 for the case of the Netherlands).

Indeed, the transformation of housing systems in this way is not only confined to the integrated rental market systems. As will be outlined in the next chapter, the home-owning societies were dramatically impacted by the new global financial regime and by demographic changes, rising housing demand due to rising incomes (and planning controls in some cases) and an economic environment of low interest rates. In Spain, a classic South European home-owning society with almost no social housing, for example, mortgage rates dropped from 17% in 1991 to 4% in 2005 and loan maturities went up from 10 to 25 years. As a result, annual house-building grew from 200,000 to over 600,000 units per annum. At the same time, gross household debt rose from 42% of disposable income in 1995 to 140% in 2006, although house prices rose by a staggering 170% in the decade between 1996 and 2006. The impact on affordability for the younger generation of first-time buyers has been equally dramatic, and has not been eased by the banking crisis despite sharp falls in house prices in recent years.

These snapshots from around Europe suggest that all the housing regimes have felt the force of the global financial tsunami and, critical to 'the housing debate', have responded according to their characteristics, particularly how open or repressed the institutions of their mortgage markets were. House prices have risen everywhere (with a few notable exceptions), and home-owners have accumulated mortgage debt and consumed goods and services at a rate without precedent until the housing bubble burst and the banking crisis beginning in August 2007 brought closure, at least for the time being.

Hints about intergenerational inequalities that have emerged on the back of these housing market developments and changes in the number of women working reflecting the rise in two-earner households in home-owning societies are commonplace. In other words, these housing market identities bring with them significant impacts in terms of attitudes to taxation/public spending, towards risk, intergenerational politics, relations between men and women, consumption, and welfare state change. This is quite a complex nexus of historical/institutional, economic and social factors and, as we will see in the next chapter, has some significant outcomes. The key point is that the financial markets, as they developed in the late 1980s, 1990s and beyond, were truly global. Key to this whole scenario has been the major structural changes to global finance, especially the invention of mortgage securitisation that has created a massive additional source of funding to the traditional deposit-based system of lending. The consequences of this for welfare state change and the relationship between housing and welfare states are explored in the next chapter.

Box 6.6: Challenges to the Dutch integrated rental housing market

Along with the UK, the Netherlands has one of the largest social housing sectors with long historical roots based on Dutch social interests, notably around Catholic–Protestant religious divisions. This stock accounts for over a third of households and is currently owned by some 500 non-profit housing associations. Following rulings on competition within the European Union, the purely 'social' functions of the associations have been separated from their other activities (eg in regeneration) where they have to compete on the open market to prevent government-sourced money from 'leaking' into commercial contracts.

Elsinga et al (2008) point to three possible threats to the Dutch integrated market system:

1   the imposition of EU competition rules, which has the effect of separating off the social housing sector;
2   that the high level of equity (housing wealth) stored in the social housing sector could become the target for governments needing to find sources of capital for spending programmes and to solve budget deficits; and
3   that home-ownership has become popular with higher-income households as it has been encouraged by governments through tax relief on mortgage payments.

Home-ownership grew from 45% to 55% of households between 1995 and 2007. In the same period, house prices nearly doubled and mortgage debt outstanding as a proportion of GDP rose sharply to 111.9%, the highest in Europe (Kim and Renaud, 2009). Local housing supply elasticity is also a factor here due to planning constraints in a relatively small country. creating inelastic housing supply and consequently pressure on house prices. Although not yet clear, the outcome of these changes over the last decade or so clearly marks a significant threat and likely breakdown of the integrated rental market, squeezed from within by the EU competition rules (leading to the separating out of the purely 'social' housing functions) and from without by the global financial markets through relatively open/liberal mortgage institutional structures. Home-ownership is now the majority tenure and clear social divisions in housing between low-income renters and better-off owners are apparent, a typical characteristic of a 'home-owning society'.

Conclusion

Housing studies used to be a much-neglected backwater, familiar only to specialist scholars living in a rather narrow 'social policy' world and cut off from the wider social sciences. Housing was almost completely ignored in the comparative welfare state literature and, as we have seen, by comparative political economists intent on designing their 'varieties of capitalism' around the 'hard realities' of the industrial economy. The most influential book in this genre, Esping-Andersen's (1990) famous *The Three Worlds of Welfare Capitalism*, failed even to reference the word in its index. Following the crash of the US housing market and the scandal of the massive scale of mis-selling of sub-prime mortgages, arguably triggering the near meltdown of global banking (Schwartz and Seabrooke, 2008; Kim and Renaud, 2009) and creating the worst economic recession in living memory, who now can doubt the significance of housing in how we think about the nature of our society?

This chapter has sketched some of the foundations of this long debate because it was necessary to see that 'housing' has for too long been overlooked in the central debates about the welfare state and to put it right. Housing always was important to the pattern of society, political discourse and the nature of welfare states. More than anyone, Jim Kemeny recognised this and over many decades has nurtured the case for bringing housing back into the mainstream. The events of the last few years have vindicated what sometimes must have felt like a lone voice in a wilderness. Housing, of course, is not the only factor at work here, but its impact in shaping society and the wider welfare state can no longer be ignored. As we have seen in this chapter, modifications to some of the seminal writing on welfare states, notably *The Three Worlds of Welfare Capitalism*, have already taken place because power relations have shifted, new forces have entered the arena and, above all, the global political economy has decisively shifted, becoming more integrated than could ever have been imagined before the invention of the internet.

The key point in all this is that housing markets and housing's other institutional structures have to some extent become important factors in shaping welfare state change. This is because mortgage markets have become a conduit through which new global capital has come to be connected to individual households, and not just in the home-owning societies. Even the rugged social market economies have been shaken by the power of the global financial tsunami. This raises questions about how we should think about the connections between housing and the welfare state in the next phase of the 21st century. Has global finance, channelled through to individual households, changed even the meaning of 'home'? Home as a place to live, but also the much riskier idea of home as a resource, a bank that from time to time one can draw on. And home, as a result, shapes political attitudes and preferences. Remembering that we know that welfare state institutions are quite 'sticky' and resistant to change, how much of the glue that holds them together has come unstuck because of this? Evidence will be reviewed in the next chapter.

SUMMARY

- Housing was a much-neglected area of international and comparative welfare state research and generally was not considered to be a major pillar of the welfare state. For example, housing was not included in Esping-Andersen's (1990) path-breaking *The Three Worlds of Welfare Capitalism* study.

- This neglect resulted from housing having specific characteristics, such as the high level of capital investment, the extent to which housing is socially embedded in society and also misunderstanding among social scientists about whether housing should be considered a commodity or a social right. In fact, it can and should be considered as both.

- Kemeny's pioneering work showed that housing is influential in shaping political attitudes to welfare provision because home-ownership is a very front-loaded financial commitment, leading voters to support low tax, low interest rate and low spend social policies.

- Corporatist societies in Central and Northern Europe have evolved an integrated rental housing market in which home-owning has not been the default housing tenure and renting from a plurality of landlords has been the norm.

- The deregulation of the banking system in the 1980s created a new context for the housing–welfare state debate because the new institutional structures of the mortgage market began to connect home-owners to the flows of global capital.

- Schwartz and Seabrooke linked the degree of owner-occupation in a society with the amount of mortgage indebtedness to create a typology of 'varieties of residential capitalism'. This work shows that in some of the 'social market' countries such as Denmark and the Netherlands, the integrated rental market is breaking down.

- From being a neglected backwater in the social sciences, housing is now widely researched for its impact on the macroeconomy and social stratification, and there is an increasing amount of evidence of its impact in shaping 21st-century welfare states. Its profile was significantly increased as a result of the crisis in the sub-prime mortgage market in the US that triggered the global banking crisis.

- Home-owners have come to think of their property as a 'bank' and have taken on masses of mortgage debt to sponsor access to consumer goods and private welfare services such as pensions, access to fee-paying education and private health care. It is within the complex nexus of housing market institutions that new ideas about household welfare strategies have emerged.

Reading guide

Jim Kemeny's (1992) book *Housing and Social Theory*, where he describes the foundation of his ideas, is the most accessible of his books. His ideas on the integrated rental market are discussed in *From Public Housing to the Social Market* (1995). The debate with Castles is well aired in a special edition of *Housing Theory and Society*. Esping-Andersen's (1990) famous book *The Three Worlds of Welfare Capitalism* has been much criticised, but is still a classic text and is a reasonably accessible read. Peter Malpass's (2005) book *Housing and the Welfare State* has a useful historical background to the UK case, but is limited because of its ethnocentric focus – only on Britain. Frank Castles' (1998) book *Comparative Public Policy* is essential reading for anyone following up the debate about comparative welfare states. The source for the Schwartz and Seabrooke material is their (2008) paper 'Varieties of Residential Capitalism in the International Political Economy: Old Welfare States and the new Politics of Housing'. All the papers in that edition of *Comparative European Politics* have been published as H.M. Schwartz and L. Seabrooke (2010) *The Politics of Housing Booms and Busts*. The 'Varieties of Capitalism' debate is explored in detail in P. A. Hall and D. Soskice (eds) (2001) *Varieties of Capitalism*.

7

The globalisation of the mortgage market

OVERVIEW

A revolution in global finance following bank liberalisation in the 1980s and the invention of new methods of bundling debts into bonds – through the process of securitisation – enabled banks to separate the origination of mortgages from the long-term investment of these debts. In this new global financial system, a tsunami of capital was created that washed across the planet, creating a surge in house prices almost everywhere, especially in the house price bubble of 2000–05. There were, however, many variations in the institutional structure of mortgage systems, so the economic and social outcomes of people's access to new forms of lending at a national level were very varied. Societies with open/liberal markets benefited most as innumerable new mortgage products connected households to these global flows of capital. But even some of the social market economies were impacted by this new era of global finance and integrated rental markets came under pressure. The process of housing equity withdrawal enabled home-owners to access accruing property values in ways previously impossible.

Key concepts:

house price bubbles, housing equity withdrawal, offset mortgages, secondary mortgage markets, securitisation

Introduction

The situation that has propelled housing into the mainstream of debate about macroeconomics, social change and, for our somewhat narrower purpose, welfare state change is the dramatic and rapid consequences of the liberalisation of the banking system in the 1980s and, through the allied process of globalisation, the release into the worldwide economy of a huge wave of new capital. In the housing context, this meant that the old ways of conducting business were consigned to the dustbin of history. In the old system, banks and building societies gave loans to new house-buyers from the deposits of their investors and basically held these mortgages until they matured, typically over 25 years. In the new era, banks could raise capital from the international wholesale money markets, refreshing their capital as needed in an apparently unending supply of credit. The invention of 'securitisation' – a way of bundling up mortgages into bonds that are then sold to investors – allowed banks to offload the long-term risk of these debts to others and so create a supply of new capital. In this process, mortgage markets stopped being basically national institutions and became truly global actors. For almost three decades, the planet was immersed in a financial revolution that changed people's lives everywhere because 'housing' was the conduit through which ordinary families were connected to this surge of new capital with massive implications for consumption and, as will be discussed more fully in Chapter Eight, how we need to think about welfare states. If public welfare systems began to falter or break down, then at least there was the surety of the private asset, people's own homes, to fall back on if needs be. The globalisation of the capital markets was matched by an equally dramatic shift in attitudes, not just political preferences for low tax and low interest rate environments and parties that supported this direction of public policy, but more so because housing generated assets that opened up new choices: consumption spending ahead of income, planning major financial commitments within families, having private capital to fall back on in a crisis. Home-owners began to think of their house as a financial resource. As Susan Smith and Beverley Searle put it, people began 'banking on housing', to think of their home literally as an institutional resource from which from time to time they could draw (Smith and Searle, 2010). The idea that housing was becoming integral to how households thought about welfare provision was identified as far back as the 1980s as the liberalisation of the mortgage market began to bite. At this time, the focus was on welfare choices arising from equity withdrawal either during a move or as a 'last-time sale' by elderly owners moving into residential care. Lowe pointed out that welfare choices and welfare state restructuring was significantly impacted by equity withdrawal from the housing market (Lowe, 1992a). He argued that this brought into play a range of new opportunities for a wide cross-section of society as home-owning filtered down the social class spectrum: 'It is the ability to move flexibly between the public and private sectors that is in part sponsored by decisions on debt and equity in home ownership' (Lowe, 1990, p 58). The globalisation of the mortgage market since then has enabled families to extract large amounts of equity from their homes by remortgaging *in situ*, and has moved the argument up by several gears as a result.

The first part of this chapter continues the explanation of the wave of capital that swept across the planet in the decade before August 2007 when the banking crisis struck and the housing bubble burst (or, in some cases, began to deflate). This involves touching briefly on the structures of the US mortgage market because it is here that the process of securitisation became so important to the globalisation of the housing finance markets. A key consequence of this was an unprecedented surge in house prices that swept the advanced economies (with a few notable exceptions) from about 1995 to 2006/07 together with associated mortgage debt that households everywhere built up. Although it is still a very raw experience, some discussion of the bursting of this super-inflated house price bubble is required, particularly in the US because the falling apart of the mighty American housing market was the trigger that unleashed the global banking crisis.

The globalisation of the mortgage market

Here is not the place to unravel the complex web of the global capital markets, but basically most of this finance was sourced from the US. The mighty American economy was like an engine fuelled by money borrowed short-term and often at quite low interest rates from economies in which there were massive amounts of savings looking for a return, particularly from China (Seabrooke, 2006). The American banks like the ill-fated investment bank Lehman Brothers then reinvested this capital in longer-term and quite often much riskier business, but with potentially high rates of return. One of the main outlets for this capital was the American housing market, which was given a significant boost. Later, however, the capital also fed into the sub-prime market in which a range of tempting, low-interest loans were made to low-income households, but which soon required the loan to be renewed at a much higher rate of interest, so-called 'teaser mortgages'.

The US housing market

The huge scale of home mortgages in the US housing market is the result of what Green and Wachter call a mortgage revolution dating from the 1930s, but becoming a unique phenomenon in recent decades, and unlike any other housing/mortgage market in the world (Green and Wachter, 2010). Mortgage debt grew from 20% of household balance sheets in 1949 to 46% in 1979, reaching 71% in 1981 (Mishel et al, 2003). Against the value of assets, with a high proportion in housing, mortgage debt had grown to 41% of household assets in 1981. One of the key features of this situation was the institutional organisation of the American mortgage market, which has been very concentrated around a few hugely influential organisations, notably the Federal National Mortgage Association (FNMA). The FNMA was founded in 1938 during the Great Depression as part of Roosevelt's 'New Deal' because the Federal government wanted to establish a mechanism for making mortgages more easily available to low-income families. Basically the model was that the FNMA, popularly known as *Fannie Mae*, guaranteed the mortgages originated by other lenders, so reducing the risk if borrowers defaulted on their loan. The organisation was privatised in 1968 in order to remove its by now huge annual balance sheet from the Federal budget. In 1970, the government created the

Federal Home Loan Mortgage Corporation (*Freddie Mac*) in order to compete with *Fannie Mae*. Between them, they regulated the process for originating new loans and were the conduit through which a very large part of the secondary mortgage market operated (see Box 7.1). This part of the business involved (until 2005) the packaging of these loans into bundles of mortgages of various types, a process known as 'securitisation'.

The core idea behind securitisation was that the process of originating loans and holding them as long-term investments were two quite separate functions. As Renaud and Kim suggest, 'Securitization is now a major pillar of the structured debt finance revolution in modern finance' (Renaud and Kim, 2007, p 6). The reason for doing this is to spread the risk of defaults and to shelter the originating businesses and banks from the unpredictability of interest rate changes and to move mortgage debt off their balance sheets, allowing them to refresh their capital and originate more loans. The bundles of mortgages can also be more or less risky depending on the original source of the loans, such as the so-called sub-prime market that developed strongly in the US housing market in the 1980s and 1990s in which low-income households were drawn into borrowing that eventually proved unaffordable. In the prime market for *Fannie Mae* and *Freddie Mac*, as the intermediaries between the originating business and the purchaser of the mortgage bundles, the incentive was the creation of very lucrative transaction fees.

Box 7.1: Secondary mortgage market and securitisation

A secondary mortgage market separates the act of making mortgage loans – usually referred to as 'originating' – from the act of holding mortgage loans. The reason for this is that the long-term investment value of these loans when bundled together is more effectively dealt with by investors in the capital market, such as pension funds or insurance companies who need investments that give a good return and are secure over long periods. The business of originating loans – done in the UK mainly by high-street building societies and banks – is very different to the management of the bundles of loans, referred to as 'mortgage-backed securities' (MBS).

The process of bundling up mortgages into MBS is called 'securitisation'. These bonds, in theory, are secure forms of investment ('securities') because they are backed by the value of the property that is gradually 'amortising' (being paid off as the home-owner pays off their loan and interest typically over 20 to 25 years). If the owner cannot make their payments, then the property can be sold and the debt redeemed. Any asset can be securitised in this way.

By buying bundles of mortgages, investors considerably reduce their exposure to the risk of defaulting on individual loans. The quality of the bonds depends very much on their original source. A huge amount of very poor loans were made in the US sub-prime housing market. These loans were made at the riskier end of the mortgage business mostly to low-income households. Sub-prime loans are sold differently from the 'prime' market because the conditions of the loan do not meet *Fannie Mae*'s underwriting guidelines for prime lending (creditworthiness of the borrower, the size of the loan in relation to the borrower's income, the interest rate deals, the size of the loan in relation to the value of the property).

The fraudulent selling of sub-prime loans was the root cause of the crisis that broke across the global financial markets in the summer of 2007 because the value of bonds that originated in the sub-prime housing market deteriorated very rapidly and because these risk-laden bonds had contaminated the derivatives market. As bonds were sold on and became more and more detached from their source, investors simply did not know where the toxic debts had come from.

Mortgage-backed securities (MBS) are one of the mechanisms through which mortgage debt began to circulate round the global financial markets. As the bundles of more or less secure bonds were sold on through the bond markets, so the degree of risk attached to them became less clear. International banks, pension funds and insurance companies all clamoured for their share of what appeared to be secure debt. MBS and similar bonds enabled these huge financial enterprises to acquire long-term forms of capital. These long-term investments are precisely the products that are needed by pension funds – long-term and secure assets that involve the amortisation of the debts (gradually paid off over the term of the loan) – and so there is an institutional connection between the housing market and pensions, a key complementary trade-off (Schwartz and Seabrooke, 2008).

The institutional nexus in this housing market became exceedingly complex in the 1980s, but the most important development was the growth of private companies trading in the MBS market in which borrowers did not conform to the prime mortgage rules. This 'private-label' market grew dramatically as US house prices surged, rising from $586 billion in 2003 to $1.2 trillion in 2005, a very large proportion of which was accounted for by sub-prime mortgages (England, 2006).

The bubble bursts

By 2008, it was clear that the decline in US house prices was more than normal cyclical boom-and-bust adjustments. New house-building and the second-hand market ground to a halt and the huge US housing market came under severe pressure with national data showing that prices fell from their peak in 2007 by nearly 20% and in some places by very much more. Millions of loan defaults and property repossessions followed the unwinding particularly of the sub-prime market. The scale of this was such that its shock waves triggered the crisis in the global financial system with trillions of dollars' worth of 'toxic' debt – once thought of as safe investments – wiped out in a very short space of time. A major problem was that the normal risk-based underwriting information was not adhered to by the private-label companies during the period of the unprecedented boom years in the market when home-owners with no or poor credit records were offered loans with so-called 'teaser rates' – tempting low-interest loans at the start, but soon rising to much higher rates. In essence, there was a problem in assessing risks in a market in the throes of an unprecedented boom. Basically lenders tried, and succeeded, in expanding the mortgage market to low-income families not served by the prime market. This industry grew rapidly and became very competitive (Green and Wachter, 2010).

The prime market was also exceedingly overheated in the early years of the 2000s. By the end of 2003, annual house-building starts had risen from 1.52 million in the 12 months to October 2001 to well over 2 million. Meanwhile there was a huge increase in remortgaging, households taking on new mortgage debt in order to release some of their rapidly accumulating housing wealth. At is peak in the third quarter of 2003, a staggering $952 billion of refinancing was originated (Case and Quigley, 2010). Indeed, during the boom in the years leading up to the bubble bursting in 2006, three quarters of mortgage lending was for refinancing *in situ*, which was pouring money into the American consumer market and to a large extent was sustaining it. How we account for the elements that created this house price surge and the tsunami of debt that was created is beyond the scope of this book, but it seems almost certain that householders became caught up in a psychological net that encouraged normally conservative behaviours to be overtaken by more risky strategies. People had come to expect house prices to rise and, indeed, had been made wealthier over these decades as a result of prices generally rising year on year. Anticipation of price increases also influenced the behaviour of lenders because objections to riskier loans with high loan-to-value ratios could easily be explained away by future increases in property values. Sub-prime borrowers on short-term teaser interest rates could also anticipate that they could refinance the loan once the short period at low rates expired.

It seemed too good to be true, but for almost three decades the US housing market had produced an era of almost continuous boom – with blips and downturns on the way – and finally surging towards what was an inevitable bursting of the massively inflated house price and mortgage bonanza in 2006. The problem was that this model was inherently unstable, with oversupply in the market, and once price signals indicated slowing and then decrease the pack of cards fell with alarming speed. Anything might have triggered it, but it would seem that the historically unprecedented bubble was bound at some stage to implode. The market has begun in recent months to clear itself of excess supply through auctions and the normal market has slowly recovered in some places, but in the worst-affected places, so-called 'glut cities' (Miami, Las Vegas) or where the industrial base of the local economy has collapsed (such as in Detroit), prices continue to fall and show no signs of recovery.

The US mortgage market, securitisation and global capital

Because the sheer size of the US housing market, its role in recycling global capital and the invention in the US mortgage market of the idea of securitisation, the story begins in America. However, for our purpose it is what happened across the rest of the globe in the wake of the new processes of lending and selling on of MBS into the global circuit of capital that is crucial. Like a great earthquake, what happened in the US echoed across the planet and came to shake the foundations of even quite stable and different housing and mortgage markets.

For now, it should be noted that the process of securitisation is how the housing market connects to the global capital markets and is the reason why huge amounts of new debt were created as banks were able to underwrite new capital, which then chased new lending outlets. This circuit of securitised debt fuelled the creation during the 1990s and up to 2006 of the massive indebtedness of owner-occupiers in many, but not all, of the OECD countries, and was the principal reason for the surge in house prices across much of the developed world (see Figure 7.1), and is a primary source of the funding of new family welfare opportunities and choices that are at the root of the case for the emergence of the so-called asset-based welfare state (see Chapter Eight).

The other key condition in which home-ownership grew and became a major household financial asset across large swathes of the industrial world came from the economic stability created by central banks focusing on low inflation strategies, which in turn created a low interest rate environment ideal for home-owners. Figure 7.1 shows the linkage between declining interest rates for the main industrialised nations over a 25-year period. Interest rates declined on average from 15% in 1980 to 4.4% in 2005 and it is this fall that provided a long period of much cheaper mortgage lending across the nations, and as governments deregulated their finance systems and moved towards market-based finance, these policies connected home-owners to the flows of global capital. The major consequence of this combination of cheap debt and access to global capital was the surge in house prices almost everywhere lasting for nearly three decades, rising sharply after 1995 and peaking, as can be seen in Figure 7.1, in 2000–05 (Green and Wachter, 2010).

Figure 7.1: Global average interest rates and house price index

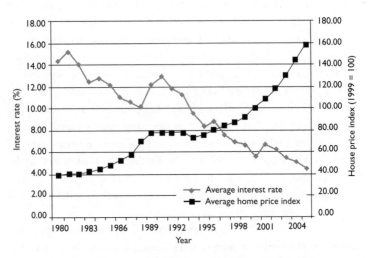

Source: UN Statistical Database, cited in Green and Wachter (2010, p 419)

The global house price surge and mortgage debt

Real house prices (ie adjusted for inflation) rose sharply from about 1995 in most of the OECD countries. In Ireland, house prices rose by 180% in little more than a decade, in the UK by 133%, Spain by 105%, France 99%, Sweden 93% and the Netherlands 69%. Only in Germany, Japan and Switzerland did prices remain stable or fall slightly. These global house price rises were unprecedented in history. Albeit that the world economy was growing rapidly, it is clear that house price increases across so many of the advanced industrial economies were synchronised and closely tied to the global expansion of credit (Kim and Renaud, 2009).

Figure 7.2: Changes in house prices in OECD countries, 1995–2006

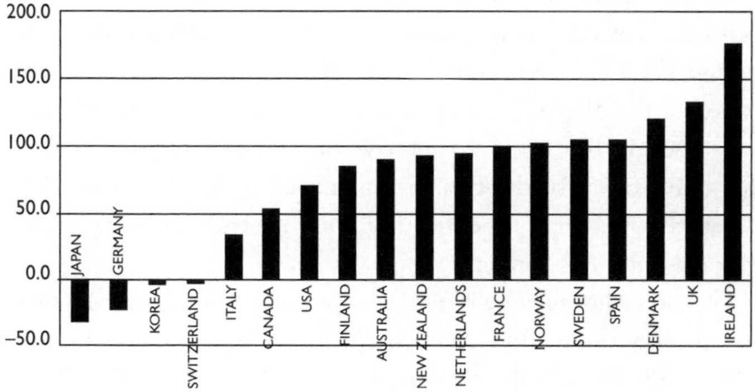

Source: Hennigan (2008)

It is apparent from Figure 7.2 that house prices have increased significantly in most OECD countries, but not all. A longer time series would show that the scale of house price increases across so many countries in the 1990s and up to the end of the boom period in 2007 is unprecedented, with a notable surge after 2002. The range of increase for the OECD countries was between 50% and 120%. Evidence suggests that this growth in house prices was also a feature of the so-called 'emerging economies' of China, India and Brazil, countries less affected by the global recession and undergoing rapid urbanisation. In Beijing and Shanghai, for example, there was no sign of a slowdown in the property market into 2011 because the Chinese economy continued to grow, albeit at a slower pace.

A key feature of the housing market boom was the high degree of synchronisation across the globe. Both the rate of increase and its spread across many nations would suggest very strongly that the reason for it cuts across normal domestic housing market systems. Despite the complexity involved, it is clear that the key impetus behind the surge in house prices almost everywhere from 1995 onwards and especially in the house price bubble between 2000 and 2006 was the massive scale of credit that circulated through the global financial markets in the context of a low interest rate environment. Evidence for this has been suggested from a number of sources. Girouard (2010), for example, showed that the history of rising and falling house prices across the OECD nations had previously tracked the general business cycle, but that this was not the case for the house price bubble in the recent period, from 2000 to 2006. What came into play this time was the globalisation of the financial circuit of credit (Girouard, 2010). What we have seen for the first time, then, is a truly global rather than national housing boom and bust.

The global house price boom was a response to the generally strong condition of the worldwide economy for about two decades starting in the early 1980s as the result particularly of the rise of the Chinese economy both as a source of low-cost manufacturing and opening up to foreign direct investment. Trade liberalisation leading to a huge increase in trade, new technologies and especially the invention of the internet were key features of this acceleration in the world economy. According to the Bank of England, global Gross Domestic Product (GDP) – that is, the total value of all the goods and services available – grew from $10 trillion in 1980 to $48.2 trillion in 2006, with a very large part of this growth accounted for by financial assets, most of which were owned by the high-income countries (Bank of England, 2007). The scale of financial assets within worldwide GDP has about tripled since the early 1980s, and this increase in financial globalisation and an associated explosion of new capital enabled a global house price boom.

The drivers of the global house price boom were thus:

* financial liberalisation in the 1980s;
* trade liberalisation, including the invention of the internet and massive trading in 'weightless' products, all creating a huge increase in global trading;
* a low inflation environment engineered in large part by central banks; and
* access to new forms and sources of funding for mortgage markets, especially through the process of securitisation.

National variations

Looked at from a national perspective, house prices are affected by a number of fundamentals and these too need to be accounted for. Data on household income showed that the surge in house prices in the early 2000s was connected to increases in disposable income. In Ireland, Norway and Spain, all cases where prices surged, income growth was high. Population growth was also quite strong and the proportion of adults of household-forming age was rising strongly from the mid-1990s. Demographic changes – natural population growth, immigration policy and increases in the number of households in populations – are key fundamentals and differ, of course, between countries. Economists explain that house prices can also reflect the responsiveness of the building industry to demand, although with a considerable lag in supply because it normally takes several years to build a house starting from purchasing land, then the construction and finally to the sale. However, if production does not increase in response to demand, then prices will surely increase. Very inelastic housing supply in the UK was one of the key findings of a Treasury Report by Kate Barker. Planning restrictions, shortages of good building sites and an over-abundance of mortgage products collided, causing house prices to become unsustainably high and unaffordable especially for younger, first-time buyers (Barker, 2004). Malpezzi and Wachter (2005) similarly showed that countries with inelastic supply – such as the UK or the Netherlands – tended to have an underlying pattern of higher prices and were more volatile compared to countries where supply is easier and more responsive to demand pressures, such as Germany and France. In both Spain and Ireland, the rapid growth in house prices stimulated a large increase in supply, indeed oversupply.

Box 7.2: The German housing system

Over the years, the German housing market has been relatively stable because, as we saw in Chapter Six, attention has focused on developing an integrated rental market as well as supporting home-ownership. Most finance for owner-occupiers is organised through local banks and savings institutions, the Bausparkassen. The Bausparkassen originated after the First World War in a period of dire economic distress and high unemployment. They enabled lower-income households to gain access to mortgages, but under very strict conditions. The model was similar to UK building societies with savings deposits providing funds for borrowers at favourable interest rates. This is still the main system and over the years it has ensured that there has been a stable supply of finance. The market is held in check compared to the US or UK models because loans are given on fixed-interest deals over 10 years and are not redeemable. Since the global liberalisation of finance, the mortgage market has become more open to commercial alternatives, but building costs in Germany are high and there have been major problems in the market following the reunification between East and West Germany at the end of the Cold War era.

Although very challenged by flows of global capital, the German housing market has remained stable and house prices have not increased, even though about €100 billion of new lending is originated annually. This, however, is in the context of strict planning rules (but available land) and the continuing support by governments for the production of multi-family rental flats. Thus, the integrated rental market, high building costs, strict building regulations, problems arising from reunification and, above all, the continued influence of the Bausparkassen system, all contribute to a relatively stable market, which is very distinct from the 'Anglo-Saxon' home-owning society model.

Another key factor at the national level is the structure of the mortgage systems in different countries and this clearly relates back to the 'varieties of residential capitalism' outlined in Chapter Six. Variations in house prices between nations are bound to reflect how liberal/open their financial structures are compared to the more controlled/closed state-managed institutions. When the massive wave of global capital was launched into the global economy it was like a tsunami crashing into whatever structures were in its way. The liberal systems rapidly changed their character, creating highly competitive markets with thousands of mortgage products enabling low-income households to enter the housing market, sometimes with mortgages at more than 100% of the value of the property and with little or no deposit. Securitisation and developments in mortgage markets created more risk-based lending and this was intensified by competition between lenders. Interest rates were lowered as margins were squeezed.

These developments were behind the easier access to loans, albeit at high interest rates, to households of marginal creditworthiness. The US sub-prime market developed a massive amount of 'toxic' debt by originating unregulated mortgages from among the poorest households who unwittingly became tied into contracts that were unsustainable. Sub-prime lending certainly contributed to the expansion of home-ownership in the US, but also the debacle that we know triggered the global banking crisis and all that followed in its wake.

Table 7.1 summarises some of the key housing indicators of the corporatist states and the liberal-market economies. What stands out is the quite varied pattern between the countries as we might expect. There is some consistency between the English-speaking cluster. The 'corporatist/market' economies of Denmark and the Netherlands have seen significant house price inflation, seemingly responding to

Table 7.1: Key 'housing' indicators of selected corporatist and liberal states, 2004/05

	Integrated rental market	% Home-owners	Mortgage debt as % GDP	Securitisation possible	% House price increases, 1995–2006
CORPORATIST STATES					
Austria	Yes	56	22	No	1
Sweden	Yes	41	40	Yes	56
Germany	Yes	43	41	Yes, as covered bonds	0
Denmark	Yes	51	98	Yes	102
Netherlands	Yes	53	65	Yes	97
LIBERAL/MARKET STATE					
UK	No	69	80	Yes	152
USA	No	68	70	Yes	55
New Zealand	No	70	78	Yes	102
Australia	No	72	74	Yes	100
Spain	No	85	48	Yes (recently)	180
Italy	No	69	18	No	24
France	No	54	30	Yes (limited)	50

Source: Derived from Schwartz and Seabrooke (2008, Table 1); Kim and Renaud (2009, Table 3)

fairly open mortgage markets, but we should not forget that planning constraints and house-building in crowded/small countries might impact here. Italy and France might be considered closer to the more fully corporatist cases and both have significant constraints on the openness of their mortgage markets, leading to lower levels of mortgage debt and less inflationary push in their housing markets. Each case has its own narrative. Indeed, housing market structures differ very considerably across the OECD countries, largely reflecting the openness of the mortgage market and the tax regimes that support or repress home-owning.

Box 7.3: The Italian mortgage market

Italy illustrates the case where the banking system is very limited in exposure to the open market and there is a much more limited scope for borrowers to take on debt. Banks have to put the onus for repayment of loans squarely onto the borrowers and are unable to pass the balance sheet risk to the purchasers of MBS through securitisation. Interest rates are high and loan-to-income ratios are much lower than the European average. As a result, mortgages in Italy tend to be small and families use their own resources (often in a 'cash economy') to build extensions and/or extended families live together for much longer than in countries with more open mortgage markets. The effect of this is that mortgage debt is very low by international standards and there is, of course, a very weak housing market because a relatively small amount of property appears on the open market. Mortgage debt as a proportion of GDP is less than 20% and although nearly 70% of Italians are owner-occupiers, their house prices were only marginally affected by the 1995–2005 global surge. The low degree of liberalisation and high transaction costs means that much less equity is withdrawn from housing and there are fewer opportunities for smoothing consumption for households with few other assets.

The impact of this massive shift in global capital on welfare states will be examined in Chapter Eight, but before that some explanation is needed of the structure of national mortgage institutions because these are critical in shaping how different countries have responded to the new financial era and how we interpret the welfare state consequences.

The global house price boom and debt

One of the consequences of the huge amount of capital that was released onto the global financial markets was a sharp rise almost everywhere in mortgage debt. This indebtedness enabled owner-occupiers to 'gear up' their finances by borrowing larger amounts in a low interest rate environment and assuming a smoothly functioning housing market with an upward trajectory of house prices gradually and sometimes quite quickly increasing their household's assets. As we have seen, housing is by far and away the largest and most valuable asset held by most people. There seems little doubt that the success of the 'liberal' economies in the 1980s and 1990s was built to a considerable extent on the increase in the consumption of goods and services facilitated by the massive indebtedness of home-owners (Schwartz and Seabrooke, 2008). Housing wealth effects in the two decades before the slump in prices, in most countries from about the middle of 2007, were strongest in the most open and liberal mortgage markets, which had in any case a long-run tendency to use housing assets for consumption and, as we will see later in the chapter, for creating a platform of assets together with new ways of thinking about welfare needs, as Smith and Searle call it 'banking on housing' (see Chapter Eight). Indeed, it is the point made in several places in the book that housing – at any rate owner-occupied housing – became the conduit that connected these huge financial flows to how households think about and plan their welfare needs. More so than this is the point that their political attitudes – on taxation of property, on having a low interest rate environment, on general taxation to support public spending on welfare – are all shaped in the context of housing debt and equity.

Figure 7.3: Mortgage debt outstanding as a percentage of GDP, 2005/06

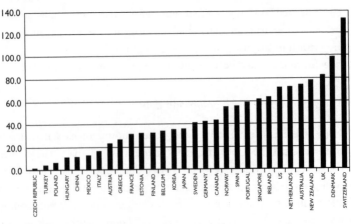

Source: Miles and Pillonca (2007)

Figure 7.3 shows the considerable variation in indebtedness, and compared with the increase in property values in the boom years shows the household balance sheet of increasing housing wealth, and the large scale of mortgage debt in some countries on the liability side. What is striking about this chart is the sheer size of the indebtedness of home-owners in some countries in many cases amounting to more the 50% of GDP. This is one of the ways in which housing impacts on a country's macroeconomics, on the operation of the economy as a whole (the interrelationship between inflation, national income, unemployment, prices and so on). So many households with such a load of debt become vulnerable in periods of house price declines because their debt is secured against the value of the property. Although the evidence shows that most households are very well aware of this and keep their budgets under control, circumstances sometime cause problems. A job loss in the family can be catastrophic for keeping up repayments.

The second feature of the chart is the considerable variation in the amount of indebtedness in different countries. This takes us back to the 'varieties of residential capitalism' outlined in Chapter Six. The key point here is that it is the different institutional structures of the mortgage markets and the extent to which, in some cases, there is an established market at all. As we saw in Chapter Six, some of the countries with the highest rates of home-ownership – notably, some of Europe's post-communist nations – do not have properly functioning, open access mortgage markets because, apart from a super-wealthy elite, incomes are far too low to repay commercial mortgages funded from the global financial markets. Inter-family lending, self-help building and inheritance are the characteristics of this 'familial' situation: home-ownership but with no housing market to speak of (see Box 7.4 for the case of Russia).

Box 7.4: Post-communist Russian housing – private housing without a market

Following the collapse of the USSR in 1990 and its satellite states in East and Central Europe, large parts of state rental housing were sold because local councils and state enterprises who owned this housing stock – typically flats in large blocks – could not afford to keep them. This rapid privatisation took place, however, in the absence of normally functioning mortgage markets, private construction industries or properly functioning legal foundations to property transactions.

In the 'old system', state-built, low-rent flats were often allocated on a rewards-based system to Communist Party functionaries, skilled workers or professionals who were needed around the country. In effect, housing was an inducement to move as rents were negligible. The 'Stalin model' of housing was common across the communist states (Szelenyi, 1983). There was, however, a large-scale black economy in the sale of these flats, usually in cash deals for foreign currency. People outside the state housing system either lived with relatives or had to self-build on city outskirts or in the country. In the USSR, after Stalin's death in 1953, Khruschev ordered the construction of millions of flats, promising housing for every family. With an emphasis on quantity over quality, these flats were built in enormous high-rise blocks and were cramped and of very poor quality (only 5% of flats had more than three rooms). Massive shortages persisted despite Khruschev's housing campaign. In 1985, the Russian state estimated that a further 40 million flats, more than twice the existing stock, would be needed to redeem Khruschev's promise.

After the collapse of the Berlin Wall and the demise of communism, the state engineered a mass (free) privatisation of housing, imagining that an open market economy would thereby be kick-started. This line was encouraged by the International Monetary Fund, the World Bank and others who supported the 'Washington Consensus' and there was a popular belief in privatisation as a solution. The fact is that the state was bankrupt and unable to function as a landlord. People living in the best flats (the most privileged under the old system) and young families particularly welcomed this move, but a large segment of households were fearful of giving up their entitlements – which under the communist system were very strong, almost equivalent to owning. State housing construction ground almost to a halt, so privatisation intensified existing inequalities and exacerbated shortages. Free privatisation ended in 2010 followed by a state-managed plan to support first-time buyers (Young Families programme) in the hope of stimulating the drastically declining birth rate.

The mortgage market supported by the three main government banks grew rapidly from 2006, but mortgage debt remains very low (about 2% of GDP) because few people can afford either deposits or to fund the repayments. Even then President Putin admitted that less than 10% of the population can afford mortgages (cited in Zavisca, 2008, p 380) and the situation is no better following the crisis in the global banking system. This means that a few wealthy Russians have benefited from privatisation and the construction industry caters for their needs. House prices in Moscow have rocketed and are equal to or even above those in many of the great capital cities around the world. Outside the few big cities, people are basically on their own with little or no state support. The mortgage market is funded internally and has slowed in recent years from a very low base.

The Russian case illustrates what has happened across much of the post-communist world. Privatisation did not kick-start a housing market because none of the institutional structures had been established and the overwhelming majority of Russian families could not afford to be in such a market. As Zavisca puts it, 'housing is largely a frozen asset' (Zavisca, 2008, p 383). Russia is a nation of home-owners, one of the highest rates of owner-occupation in any of the developed nations, but there is no housing market to speak of outside a few big cities. Instead, housing is almost entirely a family affair through self-building, inheritance and overcrowding, with several generations living cheek by jowl. Small amounts of property are exchanged through informal cash deals, but little otherwise happens. This situation puts these post-communist

states – notably Bulgaria, Romania and Hungary – into our 'familial'
form of residential capitalism, the only difference being that Russians
still imagine and are told by the state managers that somehow all will
be well in the end. It is a story familiar to people who lived through the
deceits of communism.

The ranking of countries does not always follow the varieties of
residential capitalism clusters or even the basic division into the liberal
mortgage markets and the more financially repressed systems.

The variety of mortgage products

It cannot be emphasised too much that global economic growth
and the rise of the new mortgage market structures produced, up to
2007, a huge new effective demand for home-ownership because of
much easier access to credit. In many countries, the mortgage market
amounted to a new form of financial industry with new and much
greater variety of products including the choice of either fixed-rate
or floating-rate mortgages. Although there are exceptions, notably
Germany and Japan, the gradual and sustained integration of the global
markets has reduced the variability of the costs of mortgage finance,
especially with the Eurozone currencies (Kim and Renaud, 2009). As
can be seen in Figure 7.3, the range of mortgage debt across the wider
spectrum of countries is considerable and, as Kim and Renaud (2009,
p 15) suggest, is essentially 'a measure of the depth of the mortgage
market'. The factors shaping the equity–debt equation reflect country-
specific circumstances, but crucially the policy responses made in
the face of the wave of global finance, and the extent to which the
institutional structures blocked or enabled access to credit through a
variety of mortgage products.

In the early stages of banking liberalisation, this took the form of
relaxing controls on banks and building societies so that they could raise
capital externally instead of relying on deposits from their customers.
Access to the wholesale money markets brought in new competition,

and the invention of mortgage-backed bonds and the process of securitisation allowed access, as we have seen, to new sources of investor capital. New products were created by the thousands in order to attract borrowers. In Australia, flexible mortgages with variable repayments became common, often originated through a new breed of brokers. In the UK, there were literally hundreds of flexible mortgages. 'Offset' mortgages were particularly significant because they linked savings, current accounts and mortgage debt into one product. Calculations of mortgage debt (including making estimates of the value of the house) against savings and regular income produced a calculation of the amount of lending the bank would allow. 'Pre-agreed reserves' even appear on bank statements. The Treasury-commissioned Miles Review of the mortgage market (Miles, 2004) identified over 4,000 different products in the prime market, very similar in many cases, but this glut of options revealed how very highly developed the UK market had become.

In short, what happened after bank liberalisation in the 1980s and the creation of securitised bonds – originating in their modern form in US in the 1970s – was the creation of an entirely new system for funding home purchasing and remortgaging. New technologies combined with the elimination of government fund regulation, the opening up of a truly global financial market and almost everywhere a decline in interest rates created a worldwide housing finance system. It was these factors that drove the impact on households of the global financial tsunami and the mechanisms that enabled access to the equity stored in property, and when and how much to withdraw. We look at this in more detail in the case of the UK, one of the most complete mortgage markets in the world. The first stage, however, is to define the equity 'leakage' process.

The rise of equity withdrawal

As we saw earlier in the chapter, there is very strong evidence of a correlation between house price increases and household consumption. There are strong 'housing wealth' effects in countries such as the US, the UK, Australia and the Netherlands, but much weaker linkages in France, Germany and Italy. These differences are basically a function of the 'completeness' of the mortgage market, in other words how easily households can access equity stored in their property through housing equity withdrawal. This is the principal mechanism by which the bank of housing wealth is transmitted into the wider economy.

Box 7.5: Types of equity withdrawal

Housing (or Home) Equity Withdrawal (HEW) is a general term describing the process by which home-owners reduce the stored-up value of their property by converting this 'wealth' into cash to spend, referred to by economists as 'liquidity'. HEW involves either taking money out during a move or by increasing the amount of mortgage debt *in situ*, without moving. It is the latter opportunity that has massively grown since the revolution in global finance. The most common situations when HEW occurs are:

- When there is a 'last-time sale' of the property of a home-owner who has died and the house/flat is sold by the beneficiaries who inherit the proceeds of the sale. A last-time sale may also result in an elderly owner moving into nursing care and using the proceeds of the sale to fund their care costs.

- Households moving on may opt to trade down to a cheaper house and keep the difference in value (assuming there is no outstanding mortgage debt that will be the first call on the proceeds). This typically happens on retirement.

- When a home-owner takes out a home equity plan (in effect a second mortgage), which provides regular income using the property as collateral. This is most commonly done by people in retirement who need additional income.

- When selling a house or flat and moving into rental accommodation.

- When remortgaging, which involves existing owners taking out a further loan against the value of the property without moving. This 'further advance' can be used to pay off existing debts (worth doing

---

because the new loan may be cheaper), buy a car or access privately funded medical treatment or education (pay school fees). In every country where there is a reasonably deep mortgage market, this *in situ* borrowing escalated for nearly three decades up to 2007.

It should be noted that trading against the value of a home enables new spending, but of course creates new debt. There is no 'free lunch', but it does allow people to advance consumption plans and pay for immediate necessities at any stage of life. Increasing house prices erodes these debts and opens up the possibility of further borrowing. In a housing market crash, however, it can leave families vulnerable to negative equity and even repossession if for some reason they cannot keep up with the monthly payments. This balance of risk against gain made by home-owners is typical of societies with liberal mortgage markets.

As Girouard argued based on her analysis of OECD countries, 'These large country differences in the link between housing wealth, mortgage debt and consumption are mainly explained by financial market characteristics, together with housing transaction costs and exemptions from capital gains taxes and high rates of owner-occupation' (Girouard, 2010, p 47). Her analysis of the completeness of mortgage markets suggests the following features of 'complete markets':

- a range of mortgage products available;
- serving a broad range of borrowers;
- using low loan-to-value calculations;
- providing second mortgages; and
- a wide range of mortgage equity release products.

Another key feature of mortgage markets is the use of fixed and variable interest rates with the more open markets offering a range of options. In Germany, for example, rates are typically fixed for 10 years and it is very difficult and costly to pay off before the full term or to refinance. In the US, by contrast, most loans are fixed, but penalty-free prepayment options are readily available because most loans are funded through MBS. In the UK and Finland, most loans are on a variable rate and monthly payments respond almost immediately to interest rate changes. With mostly very open, complete mortgage markets, most of the English-speaking home-owning nations have had very easy access to equity withdrawal until the banking crisis.

In order to tap into their home's equity, owners have to either downsize and keep the difference between the value of the properties or, without moving, borrow against the existing home, using it as collateral (see Box 7.5). It seems likely, therefore, that equity will be 'leaked' either when moving or when house prices are rising or, indeed surging, as we have seen was the case during 2000–05. A significant leakage also occurs during so-called 'last-time sales' when an owner sells up and moves to residential care or dies (usually leaving their property as an inheritance – see Hamnett, 1991). The first two of these imply that the timing of the impact of equity withdrawal on consumer spending, and hence the significance of the macroeconomic impact of housing wealth, is likely to correlate to when there is a lot of moving going on or when home-owners can 'smooth' their consumption of goods and services (and, within reason, irrespective of incomes increasing, remembering that increased borrowing brings higher monthly payments).

In the UK, equity withdrawal began to become significant in the national accounts in the early 1980s, arising from the deregulation of the money markets. Net withdrawals leapt from £407 million in 1980 to £1,596 million in 1981 and peaked prior to the slump in house prices in the 1990s at over £16 billion in 1988, a sum equivalent to over 7% of consumer spending (Wilcox, 2000, p 50). The surge in house prices in 1999 and the sustained recovery has meant that massive new resources have become available through new lending products and remortgaging, notably, that large amounts of housing equity can be extracted without moving house. The amount of equity taken out in the UK rose to around £63 billion in 2003, which was equivalent to nearly 9% of consumer spending (Wilcox, 2010a). As pointed out earlier, Alan Greenspan, former Chairman of the Federal Reserve

Board (the US's central bank), considered this issue so important that he conducted private research and published his findings in a number of papers. For US home-owners, Greenspan discovered that home equity withdrawal by the middle of the 2000s had reached an epic scale with home equity loans and refinancing during a move amounting to $1,880 for every adult and child in the USA. An increasing volume of home sales in the early 2000s unlocked an additional store of home equity. When sales reached a peak in 2005, the capital gain was valued at almost $1 trillion dollars. Survey data suggested that 18% of these proceeds did not go towards buying a new property, meaning that there was a net equity withdrawal on these transactions alone of nearly $180 billion (Greenspan and Kennedy, 2007). Although this was an exceptional year and rapidly declined after the banking crisis, for several decades home equity had played a major role in financing household consumption, paying for home improvements, financing small businesses and paying off medical bills.

Belsky points out that we need to question this as a real 'housing wealth' effect because households can borrow in other ways or finance consumption by saving less from current income. His conclusion from a survey of studies is that housing wealth is very widespread, not just in the US, and is much more important than wealth generated in other ways, for example, from stock market investments. A much greater spread of people, particularly lower-income households with few other assets, appear to use housing equity for consumption and would not otherwise spend. Housing wealth lifts consumption especially when prices are increasing (Belsky, 2010).

The fact is that housing equity for most people is by far the biggest form of financial asset they possess and, given the revolution in mortgage markets, it has become extremely accessible, at least until the banking crisis. Equity withdrawal is very closely associated with the house price cycle and in the current, probably quite prolonged, trough, households are paying off debt rather than spending. Steve Wilcox's data for 2009 show that over £24 billion was added to equity, a considerable reversal of the scale of 'leakage' from housing equity for most of the previous three decades (Wilcox, 2010b). As the recession unwinds, it is not unreasonable to suppose that lessons will have been learnt, but the fundamentals of housing as fungible wealth remain. Home-owners will be able to spend from this asset when mortgage markets return. In the longer story, it is this fact that has radically transformed spending and consumption patterns, intergenerational transfers of wealth and increasingly the welfare state landscape. In a nutshell, housing equity has become a 'buffer' that can be relied on in a crisis and increasingly as core state functions continue to be eroded. The problem, of course, is that just when this cushion is most needed, it has become much less accessible. Clearly, domestic welfare strategies built around housing equity are vulnerable when prices are declining.

Conclusion

An unprecedented surge in house prices in many of the leading industrial nations between 1997 and 2006 is almost certainly a consequence of the wave of new capital that spread out across the planet, impacting everywhere. This was not a separate, autonomous process, but part of an upswing in the global economy due to 'weightless' trading on the internet, a low interest economic environment arising from the intervention of central banks to control inflation, and the rise of East Asian economies, especially China, as major centres of manufacturing and latterly becoming an open and integral part of global trading. Above all have been the massive amounts of capital produced by securitised asset-backed bond markets, particularly mortgage-backed bonds. These assets packaged into a variety of products have been valued at several trillion dollars, $600 billion arising from the US sub-prime mortgage market alone. This uninsured debt was, to use Schwartz and Seabooke's analogy, an iceberg that nearly sank modern capitalism in August 2007.

But from the liberalisation of the banks in the 1980s through to 2007, the new institutional structures of the national mortgage markets all responded to the tsunami of global capital that drove house price increases in many countries and created massive amounts of mortgage debt as households geared up their assets and began to trade on their home equity. The key point from this chapter is that these new institutions, both national and global, created a nexus in which individual households became enmeshed in the nets of global finance. Key complementarities were forged in this new world of global finance, notably, that mortgage-backed securities were attractive investments for insurance companies and pension funds seeking long-term, amortising investments. The 'trade-off' between pension savings and inducements to home-ownership returns us to the debate between Kemeny and Castles.

Not every country was the same – as was shown in Boxes 7.2, 7.3 and 7.4 – and it should be reiterated that there are a variety of 'residential capitalisms' ranging from the open liberal markets to 'repressed' mortgage markets, including the cases of some of the post-communist states, notably Russia, where privatisation and mass home-ownership exists without functional housing or mortgage markets. For many households, especially those in the liberal regimes, the effect of these new mortgage institutions was to make homes an apparently liquid cash-generating 'bank'. Governments also sought to cash in on this revolution in global finance with housing at its heart, especially as welfare states came under pressure. The next chapter explores in more detail what happened in this new world of housing equity for households, for governments and for welfare states.

SUMMARY

- Following the liberalisation of the banks in the 1980s, new flows of capital were created, notably through the invention of mortgage-backed securities.

- Through the process of securitisation, mortgages and other tradeable assets were bundled into bonds that were sold into the global financial markets and in this way the process of originating mortgages and their long-term investment was separated.

- The stability of the global economy, an economic environment of low interest rates and increasing affluence provided a context in which global mortgage markets were able to flourish and home-ownership grew in most of the industrialised nations.

- The wave of global capital that swept across the planet in the 1990s and 2000s created a synchronised surge in house prices between 1995 and 2006 and a boom towards the end of this period buoyed up by expectations of rising prices.
- The scale of debt built up in the sub-prime mortgage market in the US was massive and the collapse of this investment bubble triggered the global banking crisis.
- Mortgage markets differ very considerably. In some countries, these were very open and 'complete', with hundreds if not thousands of mortgage products available in a competitive market. In other countries, these markets were very regulated and limited in scope, and, in yet other cases, functioning housing and mortgage markets are almost non-existent and housing is a luxury enjoyed by a few privileged wealthy households.
- Mortgage debt as a proportion of GDP has grown massively and is basically a measure of how open or repressed a nation's mortgage market is.
- Access to housing equity is principally achieved through the process of Housing (or Home) Equity Withdrawal (HEW), which normally happens during a move or by remortgaging *in situ* (ie taking on new lending without moving).
- The scale of HEW across the home-owning societies is massive and contributes considerably to consumption, but also potentially to a household's welfare needs and opportunities, especially access to privately financed services and as a buffer against bad times or times of exceptional financial need.

Reading guide

Two key papers on the global house price boom and the growth of the international mortgage markets are R. Renaud and K. Kim (2007) 'The Global Housing Price Boom and its Aftermath' and K. Kim and B. Renaud (2009) 'The Global House Price Boom and its Unwinding: an Analysis and a Commentary'. Together these papers give an excellent insight into the house price boom, its connection to the new mortgage markets, the flows of global capital and some of the social and political consequences of these. A number of chapters in S. Smith and B. Searle (eds) (2010) *The Blackwell Companion to The Economics of Housing* are useful in providing economic analysis of these trends and some of the contributions are usefully embedded into case studies that make this material accessible and intelligible to non-economists. It is a rare economics book that deals exclusively with 'housing'. The significance of the US housing market in growing and recycling global capital is discussed in L. Seabrooke (2006) *The Social Sources of Financial Power*. Herman Schwartz's (2009) book *Subprime Nation: American Economic Power, Global Capital Flows and Housing* is a detailed account of the international context of the US sub-prime housing market disaster.

8

Towards asset-based welfare states

OVERVIEW

In the UK, the Beveridge-inspired welfare state began to break down in the 1970s under the impact of globalisation and was partially replaced with a 'competition state', or at least a model that promoted economic efficiency as the principal goal of the welfare effort. Within this paradigm shift, there was a strong emphasis on the 'financialisation' of everyday life in which citizenship became associated with the garnering of personal assets. Gordon Brown explicitly associated this policy shift with an imperative towards home-ownership, which is the source of access to a substantial (and often the only) household asset. In a debate between Castles and Kemeny, it became apparent that there was an incentive towards home-ownership in many countries as populations aged and pensions spending came under pressure. This 'really big trade-off' debate did not go far enough in exploring the whole of the life cycle of opportunities for home-owners to unlock housing equity through remortgaging so that there has become a 'really, really big trade-off'. Evidence that owner-occupiers were using their properties as 'banks' to buffer or cushion their welfare needs emerged in path-breaking research. The attitudinal shifts that went with this strongly suggest that asset-based welfare has been commonly practised for several decades and is part of how families normally think about their welfare strategies.

Key concepts:

asset-based welfare, financialisation, mortgage equity withdrawal, the competition state, the really big trade-off

Introduction

It cannot be stressed too much that housing markets, the growth of home-ownership and the institutions of global capital, particularly mortgage-backed securities (MBS), formed a nexus that became increasingly significant in reconfiguring welfare states across the OECD nations, even impacting on the social market economies. 'Housing' and the financial institutions that were built around it have together been key elements shaping a new paradigm and new political attitudes to welfare. What was happening here was, in the language of political science, a key juncture, a moment when there was a shift in established paradigms and when the time came to rethink the nature of welfare states. Of course, other complementary processes were at work, notably, the ageing of populations, and not everything changed, because welfare state institutions are famously hard-wired into society – as institutionalist scholars describe it, welfare states are highly path-dependent and 'sticky'. It is, however, much clearer now to see the role housing had come to play in this new world and its significance and influence over several decades before the credit crunch era. To revert to Paul Pierson's geological metaphor, the tectonic plate of housing had been strengthening for some time before the financial earthquake let loose by the global financial markets caused considerable shocks and fissures in the old welfare states. Many features of the old system remain, but the welfare state landscape now appears quite significantly different.

The impact of 'housing' on welfare state change

Chapter Six introduced the idea that housing had been a neglected corner of comparative welfare state research, and, after some analytical firefighting, it was shown that this neglect was unjustified and more so now following the sub-prime debacle in the US housing market and its connection to the global banking crisis. The focus there was mainly on the damage that was happening to the integrated rental housing systems in Europe and that this was an indicator of an even wider potential crisis in welfare states more generally. 'Housing' was in fact so important in this debate, especially the privatisation of significant parts of what had been previously social housing projects and the growth of home-ownership in almost all the wider group of OECD countries, that it was impacting on quite stable and secure welfare state regimes. In other words, the power bases of some of the social market welfare states have been challenged and in some important aspects have already crumbled. For example, we saw in the case of the privatisation of Dutch non-profit housing associations that they have been forced to split their commercial work from their role as providers of social housing largely due to EU competition law. Home-owners have become a majority in the Netherlands in recent years, house prices rocketed over the last decade and the mortgage debt-to-GDP ratio (the measure of how deep the mortgage market has become) has escalated.

Before going on to look at the specific evidence for the impact housing policy and housing markets are having on welfare states and people's attitudes to planning for their welfare and care needs, it is important that we remind ourselves that there is a wider debate in the social sciences about theorising the nature of the modern state and welfare state. It is against this research that our 'housing debate' needs to be tested. Having established that housing is a central and key player in welfare state development and that this role has been heightened since the 1980s' banking deregulation, we need now to make a more nuanced assessment of the welfare state–housing interface. Arguably, a new welfare state paradigm has emerged, which a housing asset-based welfare state may be shaping and influencing.

A new welfare state paradigm

In the social and public policy literature, a new paradigm based around a more entrepreneurial welfare state style has been discussed for some time. The idea of the 'competition state', for example, argued that in the UK the old-fashioned, post-Second World War welfare state modelled on the Beveridge Report (the Keynesian plan of full employment, economic demand management and welfare rights) has given way to a much more market-sensitive system under the impact of globalisation.

In short, this means an emphasis on individual responsibilities in social policy (through workfare programmes and active labour-market retraining), the marketisation and privatisation of public services, and the general replacement of insurance-style unemployment benefits. In short, this meant an emphasis on individual responsibilities in social policy (through workfare programmes and active labour-market retraining), the marketisation and privatisation of public services, and the general replacement of insurance-style unemployment benefits. As we saw in Chapter Five the academic research literature began to experiment with a range of new ideas and new thinking about the nature of post-modern welfare and welfare states. For example, Cerny and Evans' notion of 'the competition state' (Evans and Cerny, 2003) and Jessop's 'Schumpeterian workfare postnational regime' (Jessop, 2000) both expressed the 'productivist' idea that welfare states had become subordinate to the requirements of macro-economic management in the face of an increasingly competitive global economy. Jessop argued that this change forced a downward pressure on social rights and that the shift to an open economy made it difficult to sustain high tax/high spend welfare states. This meant not only a change of direction but also new modes of delivering social policies using the private and voluntary sectors.

In the UK case, Watson argued that during the period of the New Labour government from 1997, the influence of the Treasury on this agenda became significant with their case for replacing state-provided welfare services with a more individualised system built around citizens as asset managers. The idea of an asset-based welfare state was inherent in this idea and in the creation of 'financialised economic agents' (Watson, 2009). In other words, people have to become much more self-aware as active savers from income and investments, including housing, in the provision of welfare needs at any stage in life. This issue, he argued, arose partly from the difficulties of fulfilling traditional minimum income guarantees and particularly following the Myners report on future pension provision (Myners showed that the current trajectory of state pension provision was unsustainable) (Myners, 2001). Watson argued that the Treasury under the political leadership of Gordon Brown came to the view that sustaining house price increases was key to this agenda of facilitating households to save through their housing so that it became more than a home, a place to live, but also a key part of a responsible citizen's asset base. New Labour came behind 'the Treasury's preference for using the housing market as a means of social reform' (Watson, 2009, p 49). Evidence of such an attitudinal shift, towards people thinking about their home as an asset, is presented below.

Meanwhile, we should be careful not to overstate the case for an asset-based welfare system. The competition state and Jessop's notion of the Schumpeterian workfare post-national regime do not mean that welfare states automatically converge on a common neoliberal model. As was outlined in Chapter Six, the basic 'worlds of welfare capitalism' are very much intact, but with significant variations inside the models. Nevertheless, ideas such as Evans and Cerny's and Jessop's strongly suggest that there has been, or rather we are in the process of, a significant paradigm shift in the political economy of the Western capitalist economies. Paradigms are what Hall calls an 'interpretative framework', that is to say, an accepted set of ideas and core beliefs that sets the agenda and provides policymakers with 'a compass [although] not necessarily a road map' (Heffernan, 2002, p 743). This is not to say that the old paradigm is necessarily broken because, as Hudson and Lowe suggest, 'One reason why policy paradigms are so important is they display immense stability and only change periodically' (Hudson and Lowe, 2009, p 57).

And so it is important to realise that even though a new set of ideas has surfaced and become prominent – indeed, a new paradigm based around a post-globalisation open society – how this translates into the real world and into policy is not straightforward. As Heffernan (2002, p 749) argues, 'ideas explain the form of change that is enacted, but actors, institutions and environments provide the opportunity for change to be effected'. As we saw above, Watson shows how the UK Treasury undoubtedly moved their thinking under Gordon Brown towards an asset-based system of welfare, which incorporated 'the financialization of everyday life' (Watson, 2009, p 49). When key political institutions begin to rethink and act on their new ideas, then core paradigms are being significantly challenged. New ideas become layered into existing models and processes. On the broader international canvass, it is important not to jump to the conclusion that the neoliberal agenda is taking over. Indeed, in a more recent study following up his 'three worlds of welfare capitalism', Esping-Andersen argued that there has been little or no movement away from his three core regimes. As he suggested, 'in most countries what we see is not radical change, but rather a "frozen" welfare state landscape' (Esping-Andersen, 1996, p 24). This position would seem to be dating quite rapidly and is at odds with some of the findings outlined in the last two chapters. Albeit that we need to proceed with some caution, by the same token, we should not ignore evidence of how a paradigm might be overturned, of how apparently immovable tectonic plates shift, indeed, as we know, ice-caps and frozen landscapes do melt, even if the evidence is in dispute.

And so the question to be discussed here is the degree to which our 'housing' agenda has begun to melt Esping-Andersen's core regimes. Schwartz and Seabrooke's 'varieties of residential capitalism' suggest some significant cracks in the ice and in the cases of a number of the corporatist states, core housing institutional structures have come adrift from the main ice sheet: members of housing cooperatives have voted to realise the market value of their homes, house prices rocketed and mortgage debt mounted. The search for new policy and a new direction for welfare states in the face of the post-globalisation economy has, in the view outlined here, been significantly impacted by the continued rise of home-ownership – even in core social market economies, owner-occupation has become the main housing form and seriously challenged the integrated rental market model – and above all by the new and evolving institutional structures of the mortgage markets and their connection to global flows of capital. This is a completely new phenomenon. Homes until the liberalisation of the banks in the 1980s were just that, places where people lived, and rents and mortgages were the price.

Box 8.1: The 'financialisation' of everyday life

When the Treasury signalled the need for a different approach to pensions planning (HM Treasury, 2001a), the message was, as Watson describes it, 'encoded with covert moralizing' (Watson, 2009, p 43) in which the relationship between state and citizen is fundamental shifted. This type of citizen has aspirations to be asset-rich by saving and forgoing current consumption for the sake of future consumption and access to welfare services later in life. This way of smoothing consumption over the life cycle means that people save during the phases of life when income is high so that this stored-up wealth can be unlocked later. This form of asset-based welfare breaks the bond between citizens and the state because the state no longer guarantees a minimum income level, but instead guarantees equal opportunity to build up private assets in a culture in which a savings habit is a normal feature of life (HM Treasury, 2001b). More than this, citizenship carries no automatic right to support from the state and individuals must prove their willingness to engage in the savings culture if they want to be supported. As Watson suggests, 'Acting in this way, everyday life is reduced to an ongoing series of financial decisions' (Watson, 2009, p 45).

Since then, as we have seen in Chapter Seven, the invention of MBS and the globalisation of capital have introduced a powerful new set of institutional structures and new key players into the debate on welfare state change. The question is to work out how much the new housing asset base impacted on the post-globalisation welfare states. How much did it contribute to shifting the existing paradigm? It seems quite probable that in the liberal market societies with open mortgage institutions and high home-ownership rates, its role was indeed much more significant than has generally been acknowledged. Kemeny's intuition about the importance of housing in defining welfare states has become much more transparent because of the new institutional formation of the mortgage market and how this works into the different worlds of the capitalist welfare states. The bottom line here is that home-ownership creates incentives to think of one's housing in relation to household welfare choices. Daily life, in Watson's rather ugly word, has become 'financialised' (see Box 8.1). As has been discussed before, one key question here focuses on the relationship between pensions planning and the growth of home-ownership. This was, as Castles described it, the 'big trade-off', but in the era of global capital flows, house price inflation and the new institutions of the mortgage market, what we will find is that housing wealth is not just confined to mature home-owners planning for retirement. What is happening is the 'really, really big trade-off'.

The really big trade-off debate

One of the first signs of this changed paradigm, or at least a symptom of how housing became more than a place to live, can be found in Kemeny's work on the trade-off between savings for pensions and the growth of home-ownership, which developed into a full-blown debate with Frank Castles. As we saw in Chapter Seven, Kemeny had argued for some time that home-owners are predisposed to support 'low tax' public policy and that this is a matter of political preference arising from a life cycle of housing expenditure, especially the compression of costs in the early stages of housing careers. The corollary of this argument is that once mortgages are paid off after 20 or 30 years, housing costs in later life are considerably reduced, taking pressure off retirement income. Castles' research came to broadly the same conclusion:

> By the time of retirement, for a large percentage of owners, the process of home purchase is likely to be complete, leaving them with a net benefit equivalent to the rent they would otherwise have to pay on the property minus outgoings for maintenance and property taxes. In other words, when individuals own their own homes, they can get by on smaller pensions. (Castles, 1998, p 18)

This was the first time that Kemeny's ideas had been rigorously tested. Although previous work had suggested that the trade-off did not apply to all countries (Castles and Ferrera, 1996) and there clearly is a necessity to consolidate the argument by looking both at rates of home-owning and the complex structure of pension markets and other retirement funding sources across a wide spectrum of countries (Dewilde and Raeymaeckers, 2008), the connection between the assets accruing in privately owned property and how people plan their long-term welfare needs seems now to be well established. Kemeny, indeed, accepts many of the criticisms of his work, particularly Castles' point that the trade-off might be caused not by the growth of home-owning, but through weak, and weakening, welfare states providing an incentive to owner-occupation as a means of life-cycle saving. And, on the other hand, the strong, high tax/high spend welfare states crowd out savings for deposits and paying expensive mortgage bills. Kemeny concedes that what is important here is the fact of the trade-off and not its origin, which is a rather 'chicken and egg' argument. There is perhaps a lack of evidence as yet to clarify which is the chicken and which the egg.

Direct evidence of the trade-off effect surfaced in interviews with home-owners in a sample of European countries with many respondents saying that they thought about their property (usually reluctantly) as a potential resource for care needs in older age or to enhance retirement income. In Germany and the UK, decreasing welfare entitlements and the poor quality of private pension provision were frequently cited as reasons why housing equity was a useful failsafe resource (Quilgars and Jones, 2010).

The idea that welfare cuts might encourage home-ownership rates to grow as renters look for ways of avoiding poverty in retirement, which could well undermine the purpose and logic of the integrated rental markets, is certainly a defensible case (and as Kemeny originally argued). Recent collapses in bond market values and stock exchange valuations show the risks of any form of privatised protection against 'grey poverty'. As Kemeny argues, home-ownership is a flexible means of providing for housing needs in older age. Assets accrued over time can in later life provide options for releasing equity, such as trading down to cheaper housing, and at any rate housing costs tend to be low and can be 'cut to the bone' (Kemeny, 2005, p 66).

The Kemeny–Castles debate and the research it has triggered is important in its own right, but the earlier argument, especially in Chapter Six with the intervention of Schwartz and Seabrooke's ideas on 'residential capitalism', is that the globalisation of the financial markets and the creation of entirely new forms and sources of capital – that are truly worldwide in their reach – have changed the nature of this debate to something much bigger and more significant. Securitisation, MBS, the synchronised house price boom and bust, and the huge consequential scale of mortgage debt are all indicating something much more than the focus on a particular trade-off, albeit important, between home-ownership and pensions. Something of the much bigger picture of the relationship between housing and welfare states has been overshadowed. In a sense, this concern takes us back to Kemeny's original, broader understanding of the connection. This, however, is a new chapter in the debate about housing's role in society – in shaping consumption and macroeconomic policy, impacting on female labour-market participation, creating intergenerational wealth tensions, defining voting behaviours that support low tax regimes and so on. In other words, there is a 'really, really big trade-off' at stake here that shifts the debate into a new, higher gear (see Lowe et al, 2011).

The really, really big trade-off

As was outlined in Chapter Six and further explained earlier in this chapter, what has changed the tempo of this debate about the connection between welfare states and housing is the globalisation of the financial markets. As was suggested, the huge flows of capital that have circulated the planet through a complex nexus of institutional structures and financial products have rewritten the scale and nature of the debate because of the way these flows connect directly to household budgets, impacting very directly on decision-making about consumption, debt, long-term welfare and, increasingly, short-term welfare choices. This is what is new and what the Castles–Kemeny pensions debate overlooked, for the 'really, really big trade-off' is indeed what Kemeny originally argued, but in the much more intensified circumstances of the early decades of the 21st century: that the combination of growing rates of home-ownership – whether by policy choice or increasing affluence – together with a globalised mortgage market has created quite new conditions in which the housing–welfare state debate is significantly heightened.

The pace of this change is rather startling. We have already seen that some of the integrated rental market societies have come under serious pressure, with increasing rates of home-ownership, growing political interest in promoting the home-owning model as governments come under pressure to reduce public spending, and ballot box responses to support low tax policy programmes. How this feeds into wider welfare state change remains to be seen and we must be cautious here because the process of change is not straightforward. And, as we have seen in Chapter Six, the political economies of the welfare state are well defined and remarkably stable. The most clear-cut evidence for a reconfiguration of these core welfare states is going to be found in the most open liberal-market nations, the 'home-owning society' cluster. The UK is a good example of what happened.

Box 8.2: The idea of asset-based welfare

The idea that households should be encouraged to self-provide for their welfare needs can be traced in literature back to Victorian values of self-help, so that well before modern welfare states were invented, people had no option other than to build up assets that would be used when needed. In Chapter Two, it was noted that this was the main motivation of many small-scale private landlords in the 19th century who owned a few properties as an insurance against old age. In the recent debates, the phrase 'asset-based welfare' was introduced by Sherraden (1991), who argued that means-tested benefits created a culture of dependency. He argued that if households could be encouraged to build up personal assets, then this would liberate them and give them long-term goals and,

---

moreover, this would underpin an enterprise culture with a wider impact on society. His idea was that all levels of society should be included in this focus on asset accumulation.

Sherraden was criticised because he drew much of his inspiration from research on home-ownership that was known to be flawed. For example, Saunders' argument that home-owning is a natural instinct and created ontological security was shown to be unsound by research suggesting that it can be a cause of stress and financial liability especially for low-income households. More recent work on asset-based welfare has shown that it is already quite commonly practised in East Asian societies. In Singapore, the government sponsors and manages a mandatory Central Provident Fund, originally to support pensions, but latterly for many other welfare needs. Groves et al (2007), reviewing these welfare models, argue that there are increasing similarities between these ideas and those of European nations, especially as home-ownership has become the majority tenure in almost every country, with the UK being the principal example. However, as was shown in Chapter Six, such convergence of policy does not sit very well with the complexity of how home-owning has impacted on the wider welfare state regimes, especially after the liberalisation of the banks in the 1980s. Toussaint and Elsinga (2009) show from qualitative comparative research of eight countries that many Europeans think of their home as a 'nest egg', but apart from in the UK, few people actually trade their housing equity for welfare services. European governments often encourage home-ownership as a means to secure an asset base that might secure retirement income in the manner argued by Castles and Kemeny.

The key, however, is not to confuse government policy with wider household strategies, particularly the surge in equity withdrawal that has been common across the OECD countries, as was shown in Chapter Seven. The globalisation of mortgage markets has changed the tempo of how we need to think about asset-based welfare.

The UK as an emerging asset-based welfare state

The UK is a particularly interesting case because, as was shown in Chapters Two and Three, the country was a nation of renters, making up over 90% of households up to the 1920s. It was a gradual and quiet social revolution beginning in the interwar period that transformed initially England and then the rest of the country into a nation of home-owners. In fact, as was argued in the earlier chapters, home-ownership was already the default housing tenure in England well before becoming a majority tenure in the early 1970s and stabilising at about 70% by 1990. The latter stages of this process coincided with a low interest rate era, and despite the slump in prices in the 1990s, owner-occupied housing accounted for nearly 50% of personal disposable assets by the turn of the century. Housing was by far the largest element in personal disposable assets far exceeding other financial holdings (stocks and shares, insurance policies, etc) and was the most widely spread across the social class spectrum.

This was a major change from the long-term story. Atkinson and his colleagues (1989), for example, showed that in the pre-Second World War era, the vast majority of wealth, measured by property, stocks and shares and so on, was owned by a tiny fraction of the population. But the share of wealth among the top 5% of wealth-holders fell from 82% in 1923 to less than 60% in 1960, a significant part of this change being attributed to the expansion of home-ownership and house price inflation. In the early 1970s, private pensions and net housing accounted for about 30% of personal wealth and grew to nearly 60% by the late 1980s (Lowe, 1988). This figure continued to increase though the 1990s and up to 2006–08 when it had grown to 78%, split evenly between net housing wealth and private pensions, at £3.5 trillion each (ONS, 2009). It is also clear from the Office of National Statistics *Wealth in Great Britain* report that housing wealth is the most evenly distributed form of wealth. The net mean value of home-owners' wealth in 2006–08 was £205,500, although a quarter of these households had net property wealth of £85,000 or less. Nevertheless, it is quite clear that millions of home-owners possess a housing asset base of very considerable proportions (ONS, 2009). While clearly there were and remain major inequalities – tenants of course share none of this – the net effect of the growth of property as an asset has been to redistribute wealth rather than to polarise it further, bringing the possession of a sizeable asset to a majority of the population for the first time in history (Hamnett, 1999; Lowe, 2004).

As Britain matured as a home-owning society, so there were very distinct shifts in both attitudes towards housing as an accruing asset – house prices in the UK started to accelerate faster than rising incomes in the mid-1960s and this was followed by classic boom-and-bust house price cycles – and the realisation that this was fungible wealth, that is to say, that this store of finance could be unlocked and used. Governments, too, began to realise the potential of personal assets, which chimed with Thatcherite ideology. Thatcher thought of private property as the basis of social formation, if not of 'society' as such. This was a rehearsal of the classic Conservative view as described in Chapter Three. The property-owning democracy was a lifeblood tenet of 20th-century Conservative thinking. Home-ownership is not just another housing tenure encouraged by government policy, but is much more deeply ingrained in society because it is replete with moral overtones. As Gurney shows, even the language resonates with aphorisms about owning a home in contrast to renting. And so phrases such as 'an Englishman's home is his castle', 'it's yours at the end of the day' and 'renting's just money down the drain' trip off the tongue almost without thinking. Even the idea of 'home' imperceptibly defines the superiority of owner-occupation over renting through what Gurney identifies as 'normalising discourses' (Gurney, 1999a). He shows how the growing use of the word 'home' has come to differentiate between owners and renters (see Box 8.3). In England, indeed, there is a deep culture of 'possessive individualism' that can be traced back at least to the period of the 17th-century civil wars and arguably before that (Macpherson, 1962), which established the conditions in which the 'Industrial Revolution' forged very new ideas about property ownership and in which new social classes were invented. This takes us beyond our brief, but it is important always to seek out the deep cultural supports that are embedded in societies, or, as described here, the 'tectonic plates', which are the superstructures of social formation.

Box 8.3: Gurney's normalising discourse

Normalisation refers to the idea that a concept becomes a default, internalised in everyday speech and usage. In the case of the 'home-owning' societies, Gurney identifies three 'normalising discourses' of the word 'home':

- New forms of homelessness – this refers to the growing use of the word 'home' to differentiate between owner-occupiers and renters.

In the Conservative White Paper, *Our Future Homes* (Department of the Environment and Welsh Office, 1995) the chapter on home-ownership cited the word 'home' 35 times, the chapter on private renting 10 times and the chapter on social housing only seven times. The idea of being at home is, therefore, much more strongly associated with owner-occupation, with nearly five times more references than social housing. Gurney cites an interview with a tenant who grew up in a council house: 'even though it was a council house it was a happy loving home'. Living as a tenant in social housing is thus subtly associated with a kind of homelessness as though being really at home would only be possible in another tenure.

- Being a good citizen – this associates home-ownership with a set of desirable values such as pride, self-esteem, responsibility, citizenship and so on.

As *Our Future Homes* puts it, '80 per cent of people favour home ownership over other forms of tenure. They value independence and control over their own home' (Department of the Environment and Welsh Office, 1995, p 173). Renters, especially social renters, are stigmatised as somehow uncaring and lacking in self-respect.

213

> • Being natural – this is the most powerful of the normalising discourses and promotes the idea that home-owning is normal and taken for granted as the best choice of tenure.
>
> Thus, affluent middle-class families who rent are thought of as being 'strange' or even 'stupid'. 'Being natural' suggests a completely internalised set of values and responses. As Gurney suggests, 'At the heart of Foucault's definition of power is the idea that mechanisms of power represent themselves as natural and common sense' (Gurney, 1999b, p 179).

Early evidence of the impact that housing equity was having on British social policy began to emerge in the literature towards the end of the 1980s in studies concerned with the scale of capital accumulation in housing and how this might impact on family welfare across the life course (Lowe, 1990) and in several studies of housing inheritance (Morgan Grenfell, 1987; Hamnett et al, 1991). As Lowe argued in the context of the increasing scale of owner-occupation in the UK and growing evidence of equity leakage, 'living standards and welfare choices for families are increasingly influenced by their housing options and choices; housing careers and family life-cycles are subject to important interdependencies' (Lowe, 1990, pp 58–9).

A case in point was Lowe and Watson's estimate that as far back as 1984 – and in that year alone – 51,000 elderly home-owners sold up, releasing £1.8 billion of equity that was used to move into private sheltered housing or private residential care (Lowe and Watson, 1989). Studies by Holmans and Frosztega (1994) and Hamnett (1999) came to broadly similar conclusions, that private-sector sheltered housing and private residential care were largely sponsored through equity withdrawn from the mainstream housing market. Other work also focusing on elderly home-owners investigated how 'home equity' might be unlocked to support retirement incomes and/or pay for essential repairs on the property. The idea that housing wealth could be a resource to spend from rather than accumulate for future generations spread rapidly and was one of the symptoms of the attitudinal shift towards housing equity and debt that began to accelerate as the liberalisation of the banks took hold in the mid-1980s, literally opening the floodgates to what had previously been but a relative trickle, almost exclusively focusing on elderly home-owners with little or no mortgage debt. Lowe, for example, extended the argument to suggest that the process of equity leakage – by moving house ('trading down'), through housing inheritances and by remortgaging – might sponsor services for families of all ages and not just the elderly, so that housing equity was 'increasingly sponsoring the wider shape and pace of welfare state restructuring' (Lowe, 1990, p 59).

This, of course, was made possible by the more open mortgage market, but crucially what was happening here was a change in outlook in which people began to think about their homes as a source of funding for a variety of needs: consumption, paying off credit card debts and providing a financial store to be unlocked if needs arose. As Lowe argued, 'In this context it is the ability to move flexibly between the public and private sectors of provision that is partly sustained or improved by home equity' (Lowe, 1992b, p 88). At first, during the early 1980s, the idea of 'equity leakage' from homes was rather cautiously developed and was mostly associated with care needs of the elderly, people often described in social policy research at the time as 'income poor but equity rich', people who had paid off their mortgages and lived on small pensions, but in increasingly valuable homes. There was a flurry of research concerning housing inheritance and what happened to legacies from euphemistically named 'last-time sales' (Morgan Grenfell, 1987; Hamnett, 1991). As have more recent studies, these concluded that because of increasing life expectancy, inheritance although large scale was not likely to feed through as a major issue for some time to come and the evidence suggested that, even as it was, housing-based inheritances tended to compound existing wealth inequalities.

More recently, evidence of an extraordinary attitudinal and cultural shift in the way housing was thought about surfaced in a joint Department for Work and Pensions/Her Majesty's Revenue and Customs study, which found that nearly two thirds of home-owners 'would consider' using their home to help fund retirement, and the strategy most likely to be used for this would be to trade down in the market and release equity (Clery et al, 2007). Asked in this survey about their pension planning, a clear majority of home-owners indicated that they thought investment in a property was the best means to secure retirement income (Table 8.1).

Table 8.1: Which option would make the most of your money (home-owners)?

Age	Employer pension	Personal pension	Stocks and shares	Property invest-ment	High-rate savings	ISA (or other tax-free savings)	Prem-ium bonds	Others
18–34	7%	4%	10%	56%	10%	13%	–	–
35–49	13%	5%	8%	57%	7%	10%	–	–
50–69	12%	6%	8%	49%	7%	14%	1%	1%

Source: Clery et al (2007, Table 7.9, p 134).

The idea of investing in a pension fund was the least attractive of the range of alternatives, with younger respondents highly sceptical about this form of long-term saving strategy. This is a very good illustration of the phrase coined by Smith and Searle that people had come literally to 'bank on housing' (Smith and Searle, 2007). Indeed, as more and more flexible mortgage products became available and more affordable as competition in the market intensified, and as interest rates fell, the idea of housing equity withdrawal *in situ* became more commonplace and widely discussed. The huge scale of equity withdrawal was outlined earlier. Here, the debate moves on to discuss the two related empirical issues: what people did with these resources, and the evidence of how households' attitudes to their welfare needs were shaped by this new sense that homes had become 'banks'.

Banking on housing

In a series of studies, Susan Smith, and later on with her colleague Beverley Searle, mounted a number of inquiries into the phenomenon of housing equity withdrawal, focusing particularly on the social outcomes of this new behaviour. They were interested in what they referred to as the growing 'fungibility of housing wealth', of this as a channel that converted housing assets into consumption. Their studies were based on a series of qualitative interviews with owner–occupiers about whether, under what circumstances and how equity withdrawn from homes was used (Smith and Searle, 2008).

Smith and Searle's interrogation of the British Household Panel Survey (BHPS) – a representative sample of the population – showed that nearly one third of home-owners with mortgages (by far the majority) in any one year withdrew equity and that the mean amount borrowed peaked in 2007 at £22,600 (although the median amount was £8,500). As they argue from this evidence:

> It confirms that equity borrowing is not a trivial undertaking
> … it also suggests that by the early 2000s equity borrowing
> had become an every-day occurrence – part of the routine of
> mortgage holding; a phenomenon which cannot be reduced
> to the irrational exuberance of borrowers stacking up debts
> against a property bubble. (Smith and Searle, 2010, p 344)

They found that the common explanation of what borrowers use this money for had shifted away from explanations mainly connected to improving their property and building extensions (which in a sense is not really 'equity withdrawal' but a form of investment by adding value to the house) to a large but much less-specified usage called 'other reasons'. They found that people were not drawing down money to buy cars and other consumables – by 2007 this explanation accounted for less than 10% of the reasons for borrowing – and that nearly half the explanations fell into the catch-all category, a figure that had doubled over the 17 years of the existence of the BHPS. Smith and

Searle explain this as follows: 'the more flexible mortgages become, the more likely it is they are used to fund non-housing expenditure' (Smith and Searle, 2010, p 345).

The interrogation of the BHPS data came also to a counter-intuitive result that equity released via *in situ* mortgage products is most frequently used not by elderly people on the classic 'life-cycle' model, but by younger people. The study found that 25- to 34-year-olds were four times as likely to be involved in withdrawing equity and this correlates to the period of family formation and not impending or actual retirement. In fact, the detailed analysis showed that the circumstances that triggered equity release were divorces, redundancy and changing jobs, with having a child heading the list. Their conclusion, which is mirrored in parallel work conducted in Australia, is that mortgage equity withdrawal has much less to do with consumerism ('high days and holidays') than it is about 'the role of mortgage debt in the repositioning of housing wealth as an asset base for welfare' (Smith and Searle, 2010, p 349).

This conclusion was further underscored by a subsequent round of in-depth interviews with home-owners in which it became clear that people have come to think about their housing wealth as an insurance against life's problems and necessities, a resource available at any stage and not just after years of saving. The idea of housing as a 'shield', a 'blanket' or a 'comfort zone' suggests strongly the idea of people thinking about their housing in very much the manner envisaged by Kemeny (2005), Lowe (2004) and others that there might well be a trade-off between pensions and tolerance of lower state welfare provision on the one hand and home-ownership as a financial buffer against adversity on the other. This safety net idea 'suggests that home occupiers as much as governments recognize that housing wealth has acquired a de facto role as an asset base for welfare' (Smith and Searle, 2010, p 351). In the light of these findings, the 'other uses' category discovered in the BHPS analysis begins to make more sense.

Indeed, there are the stirrings of the 'really, really big trade-off' buried in this evidence, but we have arrived at the brink of current knowledge. Given the scale of equity withdrawn by various means, especially *in situ* remortgaging, and the significance of housing in household asset-holdings and what we now know about this as a 'financial buffer' (described earlier), it seems quite plausible that a significant element of the 'competition state' – especially those services particularly amenable to purchase from the private sector – might be sponsored by housing-sourced finance. Or, at least, the rather subtle balance of household budgets that incorporates thinking about homes as banks – as a financial resource to be drawn on when needs must – might well connect up to the BHPS's huge home equity 'other uses' category via the sponsorship of expensive and otherwise unobtainable privately supplied services and welfare needs. For example, in 2009, 80% of first-time buyers borrowed some or all of the deposit for their mortgage from family and sometimes friends (Wilcox, 2010b). These are very considerable sums indeed and almost certainly a significant part of this will be as a result of parents remortgaging their own properties to service their children's housing needs. As we have seen throughout, there are important intergenerational issues here, in this case as 'baby-boom' parents, the main beneficiaries of the house price surges from the 1980s onwards, trickle down housing wealth to their children. It seems quite likely – and there is anecdotal evidence of this – that funding for school fees has been sourced through remortgaging by some families, especially for the quite common switch of children from the state sector into the independent sector at sixth-form level (nearly 20% of sixth-form students), involving very considerable bills. It seems not unreasonable that paying for non-NHS dental care, private operations for people without private health insurance, access to expensive drug treatments and so on might be sponsored if not directly from, then almost certainly against the housing equity failsafe 'buffer'. Given the weight of theoretical argument, the absence of empirical evidence is a real gap, but there would seem to be a prima facie case for this sort of connection: household budgets can be geared to support the private purchasing of services, and housing equity is the means.

This means that the 'really, really big trade-off' comprises two key elements. First of all, set against the evidence for pensions planning and the incentives to home-ownership in the Castles–Kemeny debate is the even more significant case that across the life course, indeed, well before retirement, home-owners are using their housing equity as a welfare buffer and, second, this repositioning of welfare towards an asset-based system – especially the ability to purchase private services – is very likely to be sponsored by equity borrowing. 'Housing' is, therefore, significantly implicated in welfare state change in the UK, indeed, in all its totality – from shaping ballot-box behaviours through to the microeconomy of purchasing private services – it turns out to be a major player and not at all the neglected welfare 'pillar'. What we seem to have unearthed here is not just a nascent 'asset-based welfare state', but an active system that has become literally the lifeblood of domestic welfare decision-making for millions of home-owners over several decades. Of course, as has been emphasised at several points, this is not the end of the old Beveridgean welfare state, but the process of transition to a new paradigm is already in full flood. In the language of institutionalist scholars, housing equity withdrawal and the processes around it have layered into the existing welfare state quite new and distinct opportunities and critically ideas about how 21st-century UK citizens think, and are made to think, about their welfare needs.

Conclusion

The idea of asset-based welfare has been discussed for some time. Sherraden wrote a seminal paper as far back as 1991 in which he distinguished between welfare delivered through direct social transfers and by less visible means through the tax system that contribute towards the accumulation of assets (Sherraden, 1991). His controversial idea to develop individual development accounts for low-income households in the US provoked a debate and his idea was taken up in 1997 when individual asset bonds for low-income families were matched by government contributions. The nearest policy initiative in the UK context, Child Trust Funds, set up by the Blair government to provide every child in the UK with a small endowment from the state, was quietly dropped by the Coalition government and axed in the spending cuts in the autumn of 2010. The idea of asset-building for welfare is common in the East Asian models of welfare (Holliday and Wilding, 2003) and the key role housing plays in these systems has been discussed by Doling (2002) and Groves et al (2007). In the UK case, it is clear that the debate about asset-based welfare is about housing equity because it is by far and away the largest and most widely spread household asset.

Thought about in the way outlined in this chapter, housing enters into the debate about welfare state change as a key element in the structuring of the 21st-century competition state. In this model, citizenship becomes defined by responsibilities to secure a savings and asset base and this becomes much more central to family welfare provision as it evolves. This financialisation of citizenship became explicit under the premiership of Gordon Brown. A central part of this strategy was saving through housing, thinking about it as a cushion or buffer against adversity or when needed for the purchase of beneficial services. This significant element in the paradigm shift away from the Beveridgean model and towards the competition state clearly binds in home-ownership as a key part of the strategy. The revolution in mortgage markets and people's access to the flows of global capital was the mechanism that unlocked the nascent asset-based welfare model. For three decades up to 2007, millions of home-owners, building their strategies around the two-earner household, converted housing equity into private welfare as and when needed (and brought forward spending decisions on large items). This was not an either/or position, but enabled most home-owners to make a flexible response to welfare planning – in education, health care, sports and culture, pensions provision and so on – to choose a 'mixed economy of welfare' through access to public or private service provision. There is a gathering weight of evidence that this strategic response had a major impact on how UK home-owners began to think about their properties. Home became much more than merely a place to live.

SUMMARY

- A paradigm shift began to change the old-fashioned Beveridgean welfare state towards a 'competition state' in which the main welfare effort has been to enhance the country's economic performance in the face of an increasingly competitive global marketplace.

- There was a 'financialisation' of everyday life in which citizenship became associated with responsible savings and garnering of assets, at the heart of which was the accruing value of housing equity.

- Different welfare state regimes, such as Esping-Andersen's 'three worlds' – which he claimed were very stable 'frozen landscapes' – began to be challenged, and to an extent melted, by the growth of home-ownership everywhere and the spread of liberal/open mortgage markets.

- Kemeny and Castles argued that cuts in welfare state spending create an incentive towards home-ownership as people look for ways of avoiding poverty in retirement. This 'really big trade-off' was widely debated.

- The scale and nature of this debate has, however, been changed because of the impact of global mortgage markets on home-owners enabling them to access equity rather than having to save for years. The 'really, really big trade-off' occurs at any stage with increased mortgage debt traded for goods and services.

- Housing equity withdrawal became common in the 1980s, but was mainly associated with moving house and inheritance. This quickly changed, however, with the liberalisation of the mortgage market, which until 2007 enabled UK home-owners to withdraw equity by remortgaging *in situ*.

- Research evidence has shown that home-owners have come to think of their property as a form of 'bank' that acts as a buffer against unforeseen needs, a cushion to be used to buy welfare services if needs be. In this way, modern home-ownership has become central to the reconfiguration of the UK's welfare state.

Reading guide

M. Evans and P. Cerny's (2003) 'Globalization and Social Policy' in N. Ellison and C. Pierson (eds) *Developments in British Social Policy 2* is a straightforward outline of the competition state thesis. An early statement of the link between how home-owners connected their housing wealth to welfare needs was made in S. Lowe (1990) 'Capital Accumulation in Home Ownership and Family Welfare', in N. Manning and C. Ungerson (eds) *Social Policy Review 1989–90*. The debate between Kemeny and Castles on the 'really big trade-off' between pensions and home-owning is captured neatly in a single special edition of *Housing, Theory and Society* (2005), vol 22, no 2. The research by Susan Smith and Beverley Searle on the theme of 'banking on housing' is outlined in S.J. Smith and B.A. Searle (eds) (2010) *The Blackwell Companion to the Economics of Housing; The Housing Wealth of Nations*.

9

Conclusion

OVERVIEW

This chapter sums up and reflects on some of the key themes discussed in the book. Its purpose has been to contribute to the reconnection of housing to comparative welfare state scholarship and to provide a narrative account of the development of the home-owning society in the UK. Council housing, by contrast, grew in parallel with home-ownership, but entered a phase of terminal decline in the late 1970s. The chapter reflects the theme of the relationship between housing and welfare states and finishes with a discussion of the nature and significance of asset-based welfare

Introduction

The purpose of these chapters has been to provide students and practitioners working in housing with a broad-brush approach to thinking about the connection between housing and welfare state change. For far too long, 'housing' has languished in the backwaters of the comparative welfare state literature, hardly even mentioned in its key texts. As was argued at the outset of the book, the reason for this is probably connected to some confusion about whether housing is a social right or a commodity because housing for most people is provided through markets, albeit encouraged and supported by governments, and this would seem to have put it outside the compass of 'normal', state-centred social policy. The book is built up from a political science perspective, particularly the new institutionalist approach as outlined in Chapter One. Going back to basics about 'housing' from this standpoint, Chapter One also defined the key parameters and concepts for thinking about housing as a distinct

225

field of public policy: the underlying demographic structure of populations in relation to numbers and types of dwellings; the nature of the housing stock; and how the alignment of housing tenures and their institutional structures come to define different housing regimes, especially the difference between home-owning societies and social market/rental systems.

The urgency of this agenda arises from the liberalisation and then globalisation of the banking system in the 1980s. Reality changed very abruptly. Almost everywhere in the developed world, certainly in the OECD countries, house prices rocketed and mortgage debt burgeoned in the context of a low interest rate environment. This means that we have to change up several gears in assessing housing's significance because, although not the only consequence, most commentators of the recent near-meltdown of the global banking system lay the blame for triggering the crisis at the door of the US housing market, especially corrupt sub-prime mortgage dealing. Seeing this opened eyes to what had really been happening for some time: that a globally structured mortgage market fuelled by trillions of dollars of new capital had surged across the globe and impacted everywhere. The key here was that mortgage products became the conduit for global capital to reach down to people's homes and domestic budgets. As a result, new ways of thinking about housing emerged from exposure to this financial tsunami that lasted for nearly three decades up to 2007.

And so the first purpose of the book was to explain what was going on here, particularly the impact on how students of social and public policy needed to think about the relationship between housing and welfare state change. This had two dimensions: first, explaining and debating how this global financial market was challenging what were once seen as quite stable welfare state regimes – Esping-Andersen's 'frozen landscape'. Political science showed us that welfare state regimes are resistant to change, they are institutionally sticky, and yet here was evidence that some of them were coming unstuck because of the globalisation of mortgage markets and how this was impacting on home-owners and even changing basic regime types because of this disturbance to core housing systems. If nothing else, this situation proves that the days when 'housing' could be ignored or neglected in thinking about welfare state change have finally been binned. What remains to be done is to continue the research agenda following perhaps Schwartz and Seabrooke's 'varieties of residential capitalism' – to see how much damage has been done to the three worlds of welfare capitalism, but perhaps also thinking about welfare state change in rather different ways.

The *longue durée* and housing

The second mission of the book has been, somewhat counter-intuitively, to focus on the long story of how the British home-owning society evolved, leading to an exploration of how this has impacted on welfare state change. In a world that produces and consumes 'news' 24/7, the expectation in books such as this is to outline the very latest developments in policy and in society. The problem with short-term mainly descriptive accounts, however, is that it is often not possible to make sense of what is *really* happening in a snapshot of time. All we see is the surface detail and little or nothing of the fault lines and structures. Even the periods covered by the span of governments, usually over four or five years, can be misleading, although institutionalists point to these periods as a factor that potentially create junctures and policy change as governments come and go. The 'legislative attention span' is part and parcel of the political round, but often conceals deeper and longer-term forces that shape policy.

In the book, various themes emerged as a result of reading the long story. First, the point made at the outset, that origins and 'birth moments' are tremendously important to what happens over long periods of time. Institutionalists discuss this under the heading of 'path dependency', meaning that once a decision is made to follow a particular route, the benefits (and the ease) of travelling down that route tend to increase (unlike the law of *diminishing* returns in economics) as do the costs of switching to a new direction. This is partly because once a social right has been conferred it is bound to be difficult to reverse the decision. This is why welfare state institutions are 'sticky' and tend to be resistant to change. It was argued in the early chapters that the 'early start' to housing policy with quite strong state intervention into the housing market caused it to have a rather different timeline to other areas of social policy, being generally several decades ahead. This difference resulted from the institutional structure of 19th-century private landlordism because it was always run by small-scale investors, a cottage garden industry of amateurs. This *petit bourgeois* class could never have spearheaded a national housing programme, even if there had been a mechanism for subsidising them. Council housing was the alternative route. By the 1970s, even in the midst of a default idea of home-owning as 'normal', state housing accounted for very nearly a third of all households. Home-owning, however, had been culturally and socially embedded into British society in the 1920s and 1930s. The pattern and direction of British housing was clear-cut before 1939 – a declining private rental sector with virtually no supply at the middle and bottom end of the market, a major state rental sector driven by municipal authorities and the slum clearance effort, and a surging demand for home-ownership from the new white-collar classes. It was all there before 1939 and to which the war was but an interruption.

The effect of the massive scale of housing shortages produced during the war period was to sustain and build the council house sector for much longer than might have been the case, creating a state housing sector surpassed in scale only by some of the European communist states and in many cases even outperforming them in production of rental housing. One supposes that had the war not intervened, the situation might have been very different. During the mid- to late 1930s, private builders were adding to the owner-occupied housing stock at record speed, including 900,000 properties built for private landlords (not far short of the whole of the interwar council house programme). So there was a powerful impetus behind private house-building and who knows what the outcome of this may have been had it continued. Slum clearance would certainly have continued as a key task of local authorities. It seems quite likely that private landlords would have sold properties at the middle and lower end of the market more quickly   *
than they did, perhaps causing a surge in investment/improvement in

this stock by a new generation of home-owners. Of course, this was not what happened, but it is worth a moment's reflection on what might have been, for it informs our interpretation of the impact made by the Second World War on housing policy. Could it be that we have ended up in the early decades of the 21st century with a not dissimilar outcome – the 'home-owning society' – and is it just that the route to it was rather different than it might have been and perhaps rather more tortuous and messy?

What then happened to the vast implant of council housing in this context? We saw that it continued to be built because of the failure to revive private renting and its special role in dealing with the worst of the Victorian slums. But as globalisation kicked in and manufacturing declined, so its key social purpose in providing housing for 'male breadwinner' households in manufacturing and mining became redundant. Kemeny's 'maturation crisis' (see Chapter Six) was also part of the story and dovetails into the home-owning society agenda, for it could never have been allowed that state housing – bringing to the table its historic cost subsidy, low and declining debt, and, as a result, a potentially very appealing *declining* rent structure – would exist in this form. British housing could never have followed the course of the integrated rental market societies such as Germany and Sweden despite having one of the largest and most financially mature state rental sectors in Europe. In those countries, it was precisely the absorption of the historic cost subsidies into the housing system that created a more harmonised public and private rent structure *with the public sector setting the ceiling for rents and driving the rental market, not the current capital value of the private sector as in Britain*. In Britain, the home-owning society narrative was too deeply ingrained.

The long story tells us that there was always going to be a path down which Britain travelled diverging from comparable nations, especially the social market economies such as Germany. Both nations, Britain and Germany, started with the same question at the end of the 19th century, standing as it were at the foot of the tree and looking up to the branches above: who was going to house workers' families? To begin with, the answer started to be worked through with quite subtly different solutions, but the branches soon diverged and in the end led to very different housing regimes. Beginnings matter a great deal. To have followed the European 'social market' route would have meant climbing back down the tree of history and up a different branch. The British branch generated a question that our European neighbours did not have to face or at least not in the same way. What was to be done with the huge state rental sector in a society long-since committed to the home-owning society narrative? As ever, events intervened, so the answer is partly one connected to globalisation and the economic restructuring that this brought to the UK and partly is a working-through of the ideas and ideologies of dominant political interests, particularly those supporting the completion of the home-owning society project.

The slow death of council housing

The first part of the narrative concerns globalisation. The demise of council housing and its reinvention as 'social housing' was to a large extent an issue of economic restructuring and not a 'welfare state' issue or particularly one to do with 'housing policy' *per se*. The studies of 'low demand' for housing all point in this direction (Lowe et al, 1998; Mumford and Power, 1999; Bramley et al, 2000). Tens of thousands of houses and flats were demolished in the 1990s and 2000s because populations had moved out of the 'old' industrial cities, leaving only a residual shell of the historic ideal as outlined in Chapter Five. Of course, the lack of political support for council housing, especially the consequences of the Right to Buy, were devastating for the sector. But deindustrialisation undermined its social purpose and it was not long before the debate turned to discuss the residualisation of council housing and its transformation into 'social' housing. Once again, we face a 'timing issue'. Globalisation was reshaping the UK economy at the peak of council housing's spread.

The process of residualisation has been well documented elsewhere (Forrest and Murie, 1988; Murie and Jones, 2006; Hills, 2007), with the sector shrinking in size, the housing stock became more focused on peripheral estates and in high-rise flats, with an increasing concentration of the nation's poorest, most deprived and vulnerable families. The government's regular *Survey of English Housing* has charted this decline over many years; the composition of the estates changed from a mixture of ages and family types to a disproportionate over-representation of the elderly (nearly a quarter of heads of households are elderly widows) and younger, small families and single parents. Most startlingly, more than two thirds of social housing tenants are economically inactive and those who do work are mostly in very low-paid jobs. About half of Britain's poorest people live in a tenure that now accounts for less than 15% of the population. One of the main consequences of residualisation is the high rate of tenancy turnover, with households moving into and out of this stock with no perception of it as a long-term solution to their housing needs, a process known as 'churning'. Social housing in the 21st century is very different from how it used to be through much of its history – a desirable, stable, affordable, socially mixed and attractive housing option (Ravetz, 2001).

As Figure 9.1 illustrates, since 2007, local councils own less housing than housing associations so that council housing is no longer even the dominant partner in the social housing stock. This is due to the process of Large Scale Voluntary Stock Transfer, (LSVT) which was initially an officer-led idea to move stock out of the restrictive financial regime imposed by the Conservative government in the mid-1980s. Section 32 of the Housing Act 1985 enabled authorities to dispose of land and buildings, raising billions in capital receipts and transferring council tenants to specially set up housing associations and Arm's Length Management Organisations (ALMOs). The Private Finance Initiatives for transferring council stock were less successful, but largely because of the injection of private finance in this process, a large percentage of the social housing stock has been brought up to the Decent Homes Standard (see DETR, 2000), although the target to finish the programme by 2010 was not met. This programme focused on the thermal and comfort levels of properties and, although rather unheralded, was one of the most successful reform programmes of the New Labour period. Social housing tenants complain in quite large numbers about overcrowding and also about their neighbourhoods, but Hill's research found that 40% of social tenants said that social housing would be their preferred tenure given a free choice (including owner-occupation), while only 8% of private tenants say the same of private renting (Hills, 2007).

Figure 9.1: Council housing stock and Right to Buy sales, 1999–2009

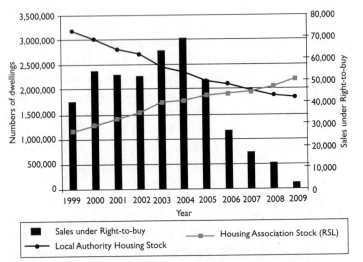

Source: Gilson (2011); data from Department for Communities and Local Government statistics.

Figure 9.1 shows that Right to Buy sales have slumped over the five years to 2004, although they increased in 2009/10 to over 8,500 due to an increase in housing association sales (so-called Registered Providers) and sales under various schemes run by these providers, including Right to Acquire, Social HomeBuy and other outright or shared equity sales to sitting tenants (which are counted in government data on sales). Only a third of Right to Buy sales were 'traditional' sales of local authority properties. The 70,000 sales in 2004 were at the height of the house price boom, when tenants could secure good mortgage deals, and were mostly of council-owned properties. The slump is due to a number of factors. The rules for purchasing under the scheme were changed in 2005 so that a five-year tenancy is now required for new tenants to qualify, and properties purchased after October 2004 can no longer immediately be placed on the open market, but must be offered back to the original landlord. Right to Buy discounts were capped at £16,000 so that in many places the discount is such a small part of the property's market value that it puts the scheme out of reach of low-income tenants (the average market value of local authority properties purchased in 2009/10 was £101,260). The slowdown in the housing market, the lack of availability of credit, rising unemployment, changing government attitudes to sales and the general economic decline have all added to this slowdown in the Right to Buy. There are few tenants able or willing to buy in a tenure that is much less stable, with a high concentration of social problems and low-income households.

The death knell of social housing

In 2011 and 2012, the final nails in the coffin were driven into the great visionary project of council housing espoused by politicians, social reformers and some architects across the course of the 20th century. Death was administered by the Coalition government whose Localism Act 2011 ended the core foundational idea present from the beginning of 'council housing' that municipalities should provide 'tenancies for life', or at least 'permanent, secure accommodation'. Although existing tenants retain this right, new tenants do not. The new 'flexible tenancy' could be offered for as little as two years. The idea behind this is that providers should make the best use of their housing stock.

In the new system, local authorities have been given the freedom to design and administer their own waiting lists for applicants. This comes in response to the 1.8 million households currently on waiting lists in early 2011 and, as Figure 9.2 shows, this figure has increased over the decade from 1999 while the size of the social housing stock decreased by over 300,000 properties. The figure of 1.8 million was inflated partly as a result of the 'open' waiting lists introduced by the

Homelessness Act 2002. Coalition government ministers have argued that this created an oversupply of people who knew they would never be housed. These new 'devolved' waiting lists could be quite tightly defined in stress areas or looser in areas of lower demand, perhaps continuing with the open lists where suitable. The bottom line in the Localism Act is that authorities have to retain a 'reasonable preference' category for the most needy and also homeless families. Moreover, what these figures show is that there is a huge latent and actual demand for affordable social housing, suggesting that the historic problem of the deficit of dwellings to households that so blighted the story of 20th-century housing has not in fact gone away.

Figure 9.2: Social housing stock and waiting lists, 1999–2000

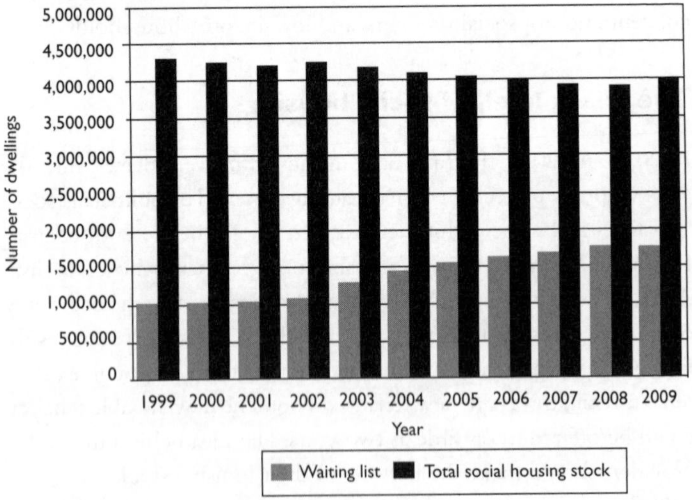

Source: Department of Communities and Local Government housing statistics.

Flexible tenancies

As in the private rented sector with its 'shorthold assured' tenancies, so in the social housing sector the new 'flexible' tenancy is a misnomer. Neither is the one 'assured' nor the other 'flexible' *from the point of view of tenants*. Local authorities, however, have discretion over the introduction of the new tenancies and a recent survey suggested that 42% of authorities plan to reject the two-year tenancy regime and and in many cases not offer a fixed-term tenancy at all, or at least significantly lengthen the term of the tenancy beyond two years. The 'rebel' authorities include a large number of Liberal Democrat controlled councils, including Sheffield, which contains the parliamentary constituency of Deputy Prime Minister Nick Clegg (Hardman, 2011).

There remain many unanswered issues here, particularly the criteria that local authorities will use for reviewing flexible tenancies. In areas of high demand, especially in the London boroughs, quite large numbers of movers might be involved. The government announced in February 2011 a sum of £5 million to support local authorities to pay court fees in cases where tenants refuse to leave, suggesting an expectation of trouble ahead. The ending of tenancies for life opens up a range of uncertainties in practice and symbolically is the end of 'council housing', in its historic role and is further evidence of its withering away as T.S. Eliot wrote in his famous 1925 poem *The Hollow Men*:

> This is the way the world ends
> This is the way the world ends
> This is the way the world ends
> Not with a bang but a whimper.

One further final nail in the coffin of social housing is that the budget for building new affordable homes was slashed by 60% from £8.4 billion to only £4.4 billion. in the Comprehensive Spending Review announced in October 2010. This should come as no surprise because, as we saw in Chapter One, Torgersen showed how vulnerable housing is to large-scale public spending cuts because capital programmes are easy targets. Once houses already in the building programme have been completed, there will be no more construction of 'social houses'. Instead, housing associations will be able to charge rents for new tenancies of up to 80% of local markets and plough these surpluses back into supporting their development plans. In fact, in many areas of the country, housing associations already charge 75% of market values and this change will have little impact on income streams in low-rent areas. In short, the idea to self-fund a programme of so-called 'affordable' housing might have very perverse consequences, especially in high house price localities. On the face of it, homes available for lower-income households might decline as housing associations let available tenancies at higher rents to push forward their development programmes.

In the second decade of the 21st century, after nearly a century of achievement, 'social housing' is becoming a form of quasi-private rental sector, still managed by a variety of 'social landlords', but in reality an increasingly market-conforming tenure with low-income households sheltered by a reduced housing benefit and sometimes shovelled off into the private rented sector. This is precisely *not* secure or permanent accommodation as it was always designed and envisaged by governments of all political types – from pragmatic right-wing Tory Prime Minister Baldwin through to left-wing radical Nye Bevan. In this, Britain has been rather an exceptional case, for nowhere else in Europe (outside the USSR) have local authorities built and managed such an extensive stock of rental housing. This is something of a valedictory note to end the book. In public policy there are endings as well as beginnings. They are usually long, drawn-out and messy. Such is the case with council housing.

And so, the home-owning society

Despite the fact that owner-occupiers were still a minority, less than 40% of households, by 1945 home-ownership was already the default housing tenure, layered in to British society socially, ideationally and culturally. Critical to this part of the narrative was the one-off entry of women into the labour market as the economy recreated itself as a services-based enterprise beginning in the 1970s. Of new jobs in the 1980s, 80% were taken up by part-time female employees, not replacing full-time male factory workers and miners, but filling the labour force in retailing, insurance and banking, and the expanding public-sector services. In addition, the expansion of higher education was by now producing highly qualified female graduates in equal numbers to their male counterparts. As we saw, the services economy was not in the main created in the great northern industrial cities, but in smaller towns and the new out-of-town suburbs. Here, almost all the new housing was provided by the home-owning market. Indeed, one of the main incentives for women's labour-market participation was to afford mortgages and furnishings for their homes. The two-earner household was a creation of the services economy built around suburbanisation and the home-owning society. Those families that could fled from council housing and made new lives elsewhere.

Outside the UK and the comparable home-owning societies with deep mortgage markets, the stratifying impact of home-ownership was much less pronounced. Where mortgage markets were more regulated, house price increases have been less sharp and mortgage debt much shallower with significant impact in dampening female labour force participation. Catholic conformity also had an effect in some of these cases, for example, Italy and Austria, also underpinning the 'familial' regime. Married women especially were much less likely to seek to enter the labour force in these nations. The complementarity between economic restructuring, the entry of women into the labour market and the expansion of the home-owning society is key to the argument. We need to be able to see the big picture in this way to make sense of what happened. It should not go unnoticed in these final pages that the impact of the Coalition government's 'Big Society' initiative and its strategy to tackle the public-sector deficit will impact disproportionately on women. A House of Commons report showed that women's share of net personal tax increases/benefit cuts was estimated to be 72% of the total (House of Commons Library, 2010) and a Trades Union Congress study showed that public-sector spending cuts would lead to heavier job losses for women than for men (TUC, 2009), creating a dampening effect on the home-owning market.

Another key stratification effect is the clear evidence of a major intergenerational housing-generated rift in most of the home-owning nations. House price increases, the famine of mortgages arising from the credit crunch and the differential layering in of housing wealth have all impacted to create disparities and fractures in the housing landscape with major long-term impact. House price rises on the scale of the last few decades are bound to have increased wealth inequalities between tenants and owners and have caused a major intergenerational cleavage. In the UK, for example, the average age of first-time buyers *without inter-family lending* has reached 38. As referred to in Chapter Eight, a study by Steve Wilcox shows that the number of first-time buyers under 30 fell from 211,000 to only 100,900 between 2006 and 2009 and that this was entirely due to the fall in the numbers of unassisted buyers (ie those not supported by parents). Of first-time buyers in 2009, 80% relied on family money, usually in providing the mortgage deposit (Wilcox, 2010b). With increases in debt arising from student fees (likely to be £9,000 per year for a wide range of courses especially in the Russell Group and other research-based universities) and what appears to be a slow recovery after the recession of 2008/09, even the quite modest house price correction has left the cheapest flats beyond the scope of young professionals, both by income and by their inability to save up for increasingly large deposits. Instead, there is a revival of private renting, and buy-to-let landlords have again bought up a large quantity of first-time buyer properties at the bottom end of the market. Renting from private landlords has become a normal housing option for young adults and is being spoken of as a tenure of choice, although this is perhaps a rationalisation of an increasingly difficult situation. There is any amount of data on house price-to-income ratios to show what has happened here. This, too, in the big picture narrative, is a timing issue captured rather melodramatically in the title of the book by Conservative front-bench politician David Willetts (2010): *The Pinch: How the Baby Boomers Took Their Children's*

Future, and Why They Should Give it Back. As Willetts points out, the baby-boom generation, now aged 45–65, own more then half the UK's disposable wealth, valued at £3.5 trillion (£1 trillion in housing and £0.75 trillion in pension funds). The under-45s own only £0.9 trillion of assets. Although this is in part simply a factor of age, according to Willetts, the disproportionate share means that the baby boomers should be generous to their children.

Housing and the welfare state

A key theme in the book has been the synergies between the housing system, economic restructuring and the development of welfare states. The central point here is that taking a narrow view of housing and the welfare state obscures explanation of what happened and why. It is and always was wrong to think of the welfare state only as the system of state-provided services funded from central taxation. In fact, as social policy students have often pointed out, the post-war Beveridgean 'male breadwinner' model of welfare depended not only on services and income transfers, but particularly on sheltering public services in a state-managed sector and strong labour-market policies that protected and favoured *male* participation, guaranteeing work but making married women's entry into the labour market difficult (Schwartz, 2003; Hudson and Lowe, 2004). Council housing during this period played an important role in breaking poverty cycles (Feinstein et al, 2008). Stable employment and income was the bedrock of this era and was built on collective bargaining, control of markets and the bringing into national ownership of key industrial sectors such as steel and coal, which provided considerable support to the private manufacturing sector. The public utilities, road transport, the railway network and telecommunications were all significantly sheltered by the state. Of course, the formal welfare state underpinned this mixed economy. State housing, as we have seen in the earlier chapters, was part and parcel of this despite the much stronger market imperative embedded into housing from before the war. Indeed, such was the institutional momentum behind council housing that it continued to be built even when the economy was already shedding its manufacturing base. State housing was responding to demographically driven needs, and the failure to revive the private rented sector. There were specific 'housing' elements in the agenda and there was quite a long lag before the 'social housing' agenda kicked in. Difficult-to-let estates were not in the main caused by inefficient housing managers but by depopulation arising from economic restructuring and deindustrialisation.

The rise of ideas such as the competition state dovetailed with the new services-based economy and the influx of women into the labour market. As we saw in Chapter Five, privatisation of the utilities and the railways, and large swathes of state-managed activity, caused the sheltered existence of the male breadwinner model to falter and then substantially give way to a much more 'hollowed-out' state. The welfare state was reconfigured around a new economic and social paradigm. As was outlined in the earlier chapters, how we understand the role of housing in this is partly shaped by the long stories – of the early start, the rise of council housing and the coming of the home-owning society – but also connects to what happened outside the welfare state sphere of influence. The stratification effects of housing wealth are also a key outcome and seem likely to unwind in quite a complex interaction between the generations and those households who hold the most valuable housing assets.

And so, asset-based welfare

The synergies between the rise of the home-owning society, globalisation and welfare state change are significant. There is no need to rehearse the argument again. The question at this end point of 'the housing debate' is the extent to which asset-based welfare has truly played a part in reshaping 21st-century welfare institutions. Confined to the UK case, there would seem to be a growing body of evidence that home-owners do indeed 'bank' on their properties as cushions against adversity and for several decades have been unlocking their housing equity in order to service welfare needs as well as consumption, and that this applies to households of all age bands. Indeed, the most recent survey work suggests that remortgaging was particularly common among younger home-owners. This is very much in tune with recent government thinking about the nature of modern citizenship. Having a responsible attitude to saving and building up assets, principally through housing, is a major tenet of being an active citizen. The Treasury under Gordon Brown published several papers that made this connection explicit. The deserving citizen salts away savings and builds a secure future through the accumulation of assets. It is not just home-owning that matters here, but crucially the connection of these households to enormous flows of global capital through the new institutional structures of the mortgage markets that fuelled this opportunity. Also, as was outlined in Chapter Eight, this was not just a UK issue: home-ownership grew, house prices soared and mortgage debt escalated almost everywhere in the developed economies, especially the liberal-market societies with their very open mortgage markets and wide spread of home-ownership.

These developments seem likely to have had ballot-box repercussions as home-owners, cushioned by their equity, question spending on high-cost public service provision and have a strong preference for low tax and low interest rate policies. How this resonates politically depends not just on the home-owning–mortgage market nexus, but also on the wider welfare regime and its long history and degree of cultural embeddedness. In the UK case, for example, although an archetypal liberal-market nation, the legacy of the Beveridge settlement lingers, especially in widespread support for the National Health Service. As has been pointed out time and again in these pages, welfare state institutions are very resilient. Household welfare strategies in this context are built around the cushioning effect of some state services, including pensions, but clearly not council housing. This institutional stickiness suggests an enduring support for some but not other state provision. It could reasonably be argued that UK home-owners support the 'responsible citizen' approach – building up their asset base – which engenders political attitudes critical of public spending, but have *dampened* their low tax/low spend partisanship, certainly compared to the US. Britain has a much more 'mixed economy of welfare'. Note, however, that even in the UK there is a significant private health sector underpinned by health insurance schemes and almost certainly by the proceeds of remortgaging. Although in abeyance for now, the (housing) asset-based welfare state has become part of the new orthodoxy, but its articulation is nuanced by the long story and by the echo of old political paradigms. Some very deeply layered cultural echoes have lately bubbled to the surface in a new version of the Poor Law idea of 'deserving' (responsible citizen/asset-holder looking after their interests) and 'undeserving' (long-term unemployed, tenants of social housing).

The asset-based welfare state, therefore, brings new social schisms and structural cleavages to the heart of society. For all that the vast majority of home-owners have seen the price of their home increase over many decades, in real terms faster than inflation, there is a layer of low-income owners whose grip on their home is tenuous. Often dependent on two earners in the household, illness or unemployment by one of the partners can easily tip household budgets into making mortgage payments unaffordable. Although only a tiny minority of mortgagors are eventually repossessed by the lenders, it is a heartbreaking experience. As Burrows et al pointed out, because 70% of households are owner-occupiers, 'half the poor' live in the home-owning sector (Burrows et al, 2000). But this is not the whole story. The other half of the poor live in a small, 'residualised' social housing sector, and live under a number of pressures, as described earlier in the chapter. The ending of tenancies for life is a major turning point in the *longue durée* narrative of British state housing. The impact of the cap on housing benefit will unsettle millions of tenants so that the whole package of welfare reform in and around 'housing' impacts on the future in ways difficult to foresee. But there is no doubt that taken as a whole the consequences of this reform package will be very dramatic indeed. State housing, once a vision for a new social order, levels of comfort and affordability, has been reduced over three decades to a shadow of its former self, a mockery of what Addison, Unwin, Wheatley, Bevan and even enlightened Conservative politicians such as Macmillan thought was its destiny.

The division between tenants and home-owners in general has become as important as the traditional horizontally stratified social class measured and demarcated by income. Housing divides society by age, by gender, by class and wealth. Home-ownership equalised wealth inequalities very significantly over the course of the 20th century and millions of home-owners have benefited from this asset base in a way previously inconceivable. Following the globalisation of the mortgage markets, new fault lines have appeared in the distribution of assets and debts, through intergenerational inequalities, and as the home-owning society project has impacted on welfare state change, so its impact has spread across society in ways that used to be impossible. The paradigm shift from the post-war Beveridgean welfare settlement to the emergence of the post-industrial workfare state/competition state model, driven on by globalisation, marks out a major historic juncture. Part and parcel of this has been the residualisation of state housing and the emergence of the ideas around asset-based welfare. If nothing else, the lesson from these pages is that 'housing' has played a key role in the shift to the post-Beveridgean paradigm.

Of course, the unwinding of the property boom after the banking crisis leaves a huge residue of debt for home-owners and precisely at the moment when housing assets are needed to compensate for public spending cuts, prices have faltered, thousands of mortgage products have been withdrawn and *in situ* remortgaging drastically scaled back. The 'haves' will survive comfortably, as will their offspring. Parents will support their children in their housing aspirations by affording mortgage deposits (often by remortgaging their own houses) and acting as guarantors to the new array of intergenerational mortgage products. Major intergenerational fault lines have already appeared; as we have seen, the average age of first-time buyers (without family help) has risen to 38. Women will bear the brunt of the public-sector spending cuts not just in reduced benefits, but also disproportionately in losing their jobs, particularly workers in the public sector (TUC, 2010). Home-owners will most likely tend to vote for a low interest rates policy and low spending strategies when they can. Pension policy is undoubtedly significantly affected by home-owners making the 'really big trade-off' between savings and housing costs in later life.

Access to welfare dependent on accumulated assets is terribly perilous and vulnerable to boom-and-slump cycles. The power of the home-owning paradigm and the financialisation of everyday life built around it became prey to tremendously footloose global capital during the 1980s. But despite it all, what will not now change is that people continue to think of their homes not just as places to live and be themselves, but as a financial resource, a bank, that from time to time they can draw on should needs arise. There are huge, macro-level 'housing' complementarities here, particularly the connection between mortgage-backed securities and pension funds, and secure and stable welfare state regimes have been rocked and altered by this financial tsunami. New welfare state landscapes have been carved out because home-owning became connected to global capital flows in ways previously impossible. Asset-based welfare may for the time being be on the back foot, but its institutional structures have been layered into society and behaviours have been changed. What is sure is that never again will most people think of their house as only a home.

References

Atkinson, A.B., Gordon, J.P. and Harrison, A.J. (1989) 'Trends in the shares of top wealth-holders in Britain, 1923–1981, *Oxford Bulletin of Economics and Statistics*, vol 51, no 3, pp 315–32.

Bachelard, G. (1964) 'Poetics of Space' in *Rethinking Architecture*, New York: Routledge.

Baldwin, P. (1990) *The Politics of Social Solidarity: Class Bases of the European Welfare State, 1875–1975*, Cambridge: Cambridge University Press.

Bank of England (2007) 'Financial Stability Report', 15 October. Available at: www.bankofengland.co.uk/publications/fsr

Barker, K. (2004) *Review of Housing Supply: Delivering Stability – Securing Our Future Housing Needs*, London: HMSO/HM Treasury.

Belsky, E.S. (2010) 'Housing Wealth Effects and Course of the US Economy: Theory, Evidence and Policy Implications', in S.J. Smith and B.A. Searle (eds) *The Blackwell Companion to the Economics of Housing: The Housing Wealth of Nations*, Chichester: Wiley-Blackwell.

Beveridge, W. (1942) *Social Insurance and Allied Services*, London: HMSO.

Boddy, M. (1980) *The Building Societies*, Houndmills: Macmillan.

Bosanquet, N. (1980) 'Labour and Public Expenditure: an Overview', in N. Bosanquet and P. Townsend (eds) *Labour and Inequality*, London: Heinemann.

Bowley, M. (1945) *Housing and the State 1919–1944*, London: Allen and Unwin.

Bramley, G. (1998) 'Housing Surpluses and Housing Need', in S. Lowe, S. Spencer and P. Keenan (eds) *Housing Abandonment in Britain: Studies in the Causes and Effects of Low Demand Housing*, York: Centre for Housing Policy.

Bramley, G., Pawson, H. and Third, H. (2000) *Low Demand Housing and Unpopular Neighbourhoods*, London: DETR.

Bramley, G., Munro, M. and Pawson, H. (2004) *Key Issues in Housing: Policies and Markets in the 21st Century*, Basingstoke: Palgrave/Macmillan.

Burnett, J. (1986) *A Social History of Housing*, 2nd edn, London: Methuen.

Burrows, R., Ford, J. and Wilcox, S. (2000) 'Half the Poor? Policy Responses to the Growth of Low-Income Home-Ownership', in S. Wilcox (ed) *Housing Finance Review 2000/2001*, York: Joseph Rowntree Foundation.

Campbell, J. (1987) *Nye Bevan and the Mirage of British Socialism*, London: Weidenfeld and Nicolson.

Case, K.E. and Quigley, J.M. (2010) 'How Housing Busts End: Home Prices, User Cost and Rigidities During Down Cycles', in S.J. Smith and B.A. Searle (eds) *The Blackwell Companion to the Economics of Housing: The Housing Wealth of Nations*, Chichester: Wiley-Blackwell.

Castles, F.G. (1998) *Comparative Public Policy: Patterns of Post-war Transformation*, Cheltenham: Edward Elgar.

Castles, F.G. (2005) 'The Kemeny Thesis Revisited', *Housing, Theory and Society*, vol 22, no 2, pp 84–6.

Castles, F.G. and Ferrera, M. (1996) 'Home Ownership and the Welfare State: is Southern Europe Different?', *South European Society and Politics*, vol 1, pp 163–85.

Castells, M. (1996) *The Rise of the Network Society: The Information Age: Economy, Society and Culture Vol I*, Oxford: Blackwell.

Clapham, D., Kemp, P. and Smith, S.J. (1990) *Housing and Social Policy*, Basingstoke: Macmillan.

Clery, E., McKay, S., Phillips, M. and Robinson, C. (2007) *Attitudes to Pensions: The 2006 Survey*, London, DWP/HMRC.

Crouch, C. (1977) *Class Conflict and the Industrial Relations Crisis*, London: Heinemann.

Daunton, M.J. (1990) *Housing the Workers*, Leicester: Leicester University Press.

DCLG (Department for Communities and Local Government) (2010) *Review of Social Housing Regulation*, London: DCLG.

DETR (Department of the Environment, Transport and the Regions) (2000) *Quality and Choice: A Decent Home for All: The Housing Green Paper*, London: DETR.

Department of the Environment and Welsh Office (1995) *Our Future Homes: Opportunities, Choice, Responsibility*, Cm 2901, London: HMSO.

Dewilde, C. and Raeymaeckers, P. (2008) 'The Trade-Off between Home-Ownership and Pensions: Individual and Institutional Determinants of Old-Age Poverty', *Ageing and Society*, vol 28, pp 805–30.

Dickens, C. (1854) *Hard Times*, London: Bradbury and Evans.

DoE (Department of the Environment) (1977) *Housing Policy: A Consultative Document*, Cmnd 6851, London: HMSO.

Dolan, C. and Barrientos, S. (2003) 'Labour Inflexibility in African Horticulture', *Insights: Development Research*, no 47. Brighton: Institute of Development Studies, University of Sussex.

Doling, J. (2002) 'The South and East Asian Housing Policy Model', in M.R. Agus, J. Doling and D.S. Lee (eds) *Housing Policy Systems in South and East Asia*, Basingstoke: Palgrave/Macmillan.

Doling, J. (2006) 'A European Housing Policy', *European Journal of Housing Policy*, vol 6, no 3, pp 335–49.

Donnison, D. (1967) *The Government of Housing*, Harmondsworth: Penguin.

Elsinga, M. Haffner, M. and Van Der Heyden (2008) 'Threats to the Dutch Unitary Rental Market', *European Journal of Housing Policy*, vol 8, no 1, pp 21–37.

England, R. (2006) 'The Rise of Private Label', *Mortgage Banking*. Available at: www.Robertstoweengland.com/document/MBM.10-06EnglandPrivateLabel.pdf

Esping-Andersen, G. (1990) *The Three Worlds of Welfare Capitalism*, Cambridge: Polity Press.

Esping-Andersen, G. (1996) *Welfare States in Transition*, London: Sage.

Evans, M. and Cerny, P. (2003) 'Globalization and Social Policy', in N. Ellison and C. Pierson (eds) *Developments in British Social Policy 2*, Basingstoke: Palgrave.

Feiling, K. (1970) *The Life of Neville Chamberlain*, London: MacMillan.

Feinstein, L., Lupton, R., Hammond, C., Mujtaba, T., Salter, E. and Sorhaindo, A. (2008) *The Public Value of Social Housing: A Longitudinal Analysis of the Relationship between Housing and Life Chances*, London: Smith Institute.

Fitzpatrick, S. and Stephens, M. (eds) (2009) *The Future of Social Housing*, London: Shelter.

Forrest, R. and Murie, A. (1988) *Selling the Welfare State: The Privatisation of Council Housing*, London: Routledge.

Forrest, R. and Murie, A. (1990) *Moving the Market*, Aldershot: Avebury.

Forster, E. M. (1910) *Howards End*, London: Edward Arnold.

Fraser, D. (2003) *The Evolution of the British Welfare State since the Industrial Revolution*, Basingstoke: Palgrave.

Gauldie, E. (1974) *Cruel Habitations*, London: George Allen & Unwin.

Giddens, A. (1989) *Sociology*, Oxford: Polity Press.

Giddens, A. (1990) *The Consequences of Modernity*, Cambridge: Polity Press.

Giddens, A. (1999) *Runaway World: How Globalization is Reshaping Our Lives*, London: Profile Books.

Gilson, C. (2011) 'An end to "tenancy for life" in the social housing sector will not solve current acute shortages', Blog. Available at: http://blogs.lse.ac.uk/politicsandpolicy/2010/08/27.

Girouard, N. (2010) 'Housing and Mortgage Markets: an OECD Perspective', in S.J. Smith and B.A. Searle (eds) *The Blackwell Companion to the Economics of Housing: The Housing Wealth of Nations*, Chichester: Wiley-Blackwell.

Gladstone, D. (1995) *British Social Welfare: Past, Present and Future*, London: UCL Press.

Glennester, H. (1995) *British Social Policy since 1945*, Oxford: Blackwell.

Green, R.K. and Wachter, S. M. (2010) 'The Housing Finance Revolution', in S. J. Smith and B. A. Searle (eds) *The Blackwell Companion to the Economics of Housing; the Housing Wealth of Nations*, Chichester: Wiley-Blackwell.

Greenspan, A. and Kennedy, J. (2007) 'Sources and Uses of Equity Extracted from Homes', *Finance and Economics*, vol 20, Federal Reserve Board.

Greenspan, A. and Kennedy, J. (2008) 'Estimates of Home Mortgage Originations, Repayment and Debt on One-to-Four Family Residences', *Finance and Economics Discussion Series*, no 41, Washington DC: Federal Reserve Board, Division of Research & Statistics and Monetary Affairs.

Groves, R., Murie, A. and Watson, C. (2007) *Housing and the New Welfare State*, Aldershot: Ashgate.

Gurney, C. (1999a) 'Lowering the Drawbridge: a Case Study of Analogy and Metaphor in the Social Construction of Home Ownership', *Urban Studies*, vol 36, pp 1705–22.

Gurney, C. (1999b) 'Pride and Prejudice: Discourses of Normalisation in Public and Private Accounts of Home Ownership', *Housing Studies*, vol 14, pp 163–83.

Hall, P. (1993) 'Policy Paradigms, Social Learning and the State: the Case of Economic Policymaking in Britain', *Comparative Politics*, vol 25, pp 275–96.

Hall, P. A. and Soskice, D. (eds) (2001) *Varieties of Capitalism*, Oxford: Oxford University Press.

Hamnett, C. (1991) 'A Nation of Inheritors? Housing Inheritance, Wealth and Inequality in Britain', *Journal of Social Policy*, vol 20, no 4, pp 509–36.

Hamnett, C. (1999) *Winners and Losers – Home Ownership in Modern Britain*, London: UCL Press.

Hardman, I. (2011) 'Nearly Half of Councils to Reject New Tenure', *Inside Housing*, 28 April.

Harloe, M. (1985) *Private Rented Housing in the United States and Europe*, London: Croom Helm.

Harris, B. (2004) *The Origins of the British Welfare State: Social Welfare in England and Wales, 1800–1945*, Basingstoke: Palgrave/Macmillan.

Harvey, D. (1973) *Social Justice and the City*, Oxford: Blackwell.

Heffernan, R. (2002) 'The Possible as the Art of Politics: Understanding Consensus Politics', *Political Studies*, vol 50, pp 742–60.

Heidenheimer, A.J., Heclo, H. and Adams, T.C. (1990) *Comparative Public Policy, the Politics of Social Choice in America, Europe and Japan*, New York: St Martin's Press.

Held, D. and McGrew, A. (eds) (2000) *The Global Transformations Reader*, Cambridge: Polity Press.

Held, D., McGrew, A., Goldblatt, D. and Perraton, J. (1999) *Global Transformations: Politics, Economics and Culture*, Cambridge: Polity Press.

Hennigan, M. (2008) *International House Price Comparison 1970–2006*, Finfacts. Available at: www.finfacts.ie/irishfinancenews/article_1012464.shtml

Hill, M. (1993) *The Welfare State in Britain: A Political History since 1945*, Aldershot: Edward Elgar.

Hill, M. (2003) *Understanding Social Policy*, Oxford: Blackwell.

Hills, J. (2007) *Ends and Means: The Future Roles of Social Housing in England*, ESRC Research Centre for Analysis of Social Exclusion (CASE) Report 34, London: London School of Economics and Political Science.

Hirst, P. and Thompson, G. (1990) *Globalization in Question*, 2nd edn, Cambridge: Polity Press.

HM Treasury (2001a) *Savings and Assets: The Modernisation of Britain's Tax and Benefits System, Number Nine*, London: HMSO.

HM Treasury (2001b) *Delivering Savings and Assets for All: the Modernisation of Britain's Tax and Benefits System, Number Eight*, London: HMSO.

Holliday, I. and Wilding, P. (2003) 'Social Policy in the East Asian Tiger Economies: Past, Present and Future', in C. Bochel, N. Ellison and M. Powell (eds) *Social Policy Review 15*, Bristol: The Policy Press, pp 155–72.

Holmans, A.E. (1987) *Housing Policy in Britain*, London: Croom Helm.

Holmans, A.E. (2000) 'British Housing in the Twentieth Century: an End-of-Century Overview', in S. Wilcox (ed) *Housing Finance Review 1999–2000*, York: Published for the Joseph Rowntree Foundation by the Chartered Institute of Housing and the Council of Mortgage Lenders.

Holmans, A.E. and Frostzega, M. (1994) *House Property and Inheritance in the UK*, London: HMSO.

House of Commons Library (2010) 'Gender Audit of the Budget, 2010'. Available at: www.yvettecooper.com/women-bear-brunt-of-budget-cuts

Howlett, M. and Cashore, B. (2009) 'The Dependent Variable Problem in the Study of Policy Change: Understanding Policy Change as a Methodological Problem', *Journal of Comparative Policy Analysis*, vol 11, no 1, pp 33–46.

Hudson, J. and Lowe, S. (2004) *Understanding the Policy Process: Analysing Welfare Policy and Practice*, Bristol: The Policy Press.

Hudson, J. and Lowe, S. (2009) *Understanding the Policy Process: Analysing Welfare Policy and Practice*, 2nd edn, Bristol: The Policy Press.

Hughes, D. (1991) 'Tenants' Rights', in S. Lowe and D. Hughes (eds) *A New Century of Social Housing*, Leicester: Leicester University Press.

Hutton, W. and Giddens, A. (eds) (2001) *On the Edge: Living with Global Capitalism*, London: Vintage.

Immergut, E. (1992) *Health Politics: Interests and Institutions in Western Europe*, Cambridge: Cambridge University Press.

Jessop, B. (1994) 'The Transition to Post-Fordism and the Schumpeterian Welfare State', in R. Burrows and B. Loader (eds) *Towards a Post-Fordist Welfare State*, London: Routledge.

Jessop, B. (2000) 'From the KWNS to the SWPR' in G. Lewis, S. Gewirtz and J. Clarke (eds) *Rethinking Social Policy*, London: Sage Publications.

Jones, C. and Murie, A. (2006) *The Right to Buy*, Oxford: Blackwell.

Jones, K. (2000) *The Making of Social Policy in Britain: from the Poor Law to New Labour*, London: Athlone.

Jonsson, I. (1999) 'Women and Education in Europe', *International Journal of Contemporary Sociology*, vol 36, no 2, pp 145–62.

Keenan, P. (1998) 'Residential Mobility and Low Demand: a Case History from Newcastle', in S. Lowe, P. Keenan and S. Spencer (eds) *Housing Abandonment in Britain: Studies in the Causes and Effects of Low Demand Housing*, York: Centre for Housing Policy, University of York.

Kemeny, J. (1980) 'Home Ownership and Privatisation', *International Journal of Urban and Regional Research*, vol 4, no 3, pp 372–88.

Kemeny, J. (1981) *The Myth of Home Ownership: Public versus Private Choices in Housing Tenure*, London: Routledge.

Kemeny, J. (1992) *Housing and Social Theory*, London: Routledge.

Kemeny, J. (1995) *From Public Housing to the Social Market*, London: Routledge.

Kemeny, J. (2005) '"The Really Big Trade-Off" between Home Ownership and Welfare: Castles' Evaluation of the 1980 Thesis, and a Reformulation 25 Years on', *Housing, Theory and Society*, vol 22, no 2, pp 59-75.

Kemeny, J. and Lowe, S. (1998) 'Schools of Comparative Housing Research: from Convergence to Divergence', *Housing Studies*, vol 13, no 2, pp 161–76.

Kemp, P. A. (1991) 'From Solution to Problem? Council Housing and the Development of National Housing Policy', in S. Lowe and D. Hughes (eds) *A New Century of Social Housing*, Leicester: Leicester University Press.

Kemp, P. A. (2004) *Private Renting in Transition*, Coventry: Chartered Institute of Housing.

Kim, K.-H. and Renaud, B. (2009) 'The Global House Price Boom and its Unwinding: an Analysis and a Commentary', *Housing Studies*, vol 24, no 1, pp 7–24.

Kincaid, J., Samuel, R. and Slater, E. (1962) 'But Nothing Happens: the Long Pursuit: Studies in the Government's Slum Clearance Programme', *New Left Review*, nos 13–14.

Levi, M. (1997) 'A Model, a Method and a Map: Rational Choice in Comparative Historical Analysis', in M.I. Lichbach and A.S. Zuckerman (eds) *Comparative Politics: Rationality, Culture and Structure*, Cambridge: Cambridge University Press.

Linden, G., Kraemer, J. and Dedrick, J. (2007) *Who Captures Value in a Global Innovation System? The Case of Apple's iPod*, California, CA: Personal Computing Industry Center.

Lowe, S. (1988) 'New Patterns of Wealth: The Growth of Owner Occupation', in R. Walker and G. Parker (eds) *Money Matters*, London: Sage.

Lowe, S. (1990) 'Capital Accumulation in Home Ownership and Family Welfare', in N. Manning and C. Ungerson (eds) *Social Policy Review 1989–90*, Harlow: Longman.

Lowe, S. (1992a) 'Home Ownership, Wealth and Welfare: New Connections', in A. Corden, E. Robertson and K. Tolley (eds) *Meeting Needs in an Affluent Society*, Aldershot: Avebury.

Lowe, S. (1992b) 'The Social and Economic Consequences of the Growth of Home Ownership', in J. Birchall (ed) *Housing Policy in the 1990s*, London: Routledge.

Lowe, S. (2004) *Housing Policy Analysis: British Housing in Cultural and Comparative Context*, Houndmills: Palgrave/Macmillan.

Lowe, S. and Watson, S. (1989) *From First-time Buyers to Last-time Sellers: An Appraisal of the Social and Economic Consequences of Equity Withdrawal from the Housing Market 1982–1988*, York: Joseph Rowntree Memorial Trust/University of York.

Lowe, S., Keenan, P. and Spencer, S. (eds) (1998) *Housing Abandonment in Britain: Studies in the Causes and Effects of Low Demand Housing*, York: Centre for Housing Policy, University of York.

Lowe, S., Searle, B.A. and Smith, S.J. (2011 forthcoming) 'From Housing Wealth to Mortgage Debt: the Emergence of Britain's Asset-Shaped Welfare State', *Social Policy and Society*.

Lundquist, L.J., Elander, I. and Danermark, B. (1990) 'Housing Policy in Sweden – Still a Success?', *International Journal of Urban and Regional Research*, vol 14, pp 445–67.

Macpherson, C.B. (1962) *The Political Theory of Possessive Individualism: Hobbes to Locke*, Oxford: Oxford Paperbacks.

Malpass, P. (1990) *Reshaping Housing Policy: Subsidies, Rents and Residualisation*, London: Routledge.

Malpass, P. (2000) *Housing Associations and Housing Policy*, Basingstoke: Macmillan Press.

Malpass, P. (2005) *Housing and the Welfare State*, Basingstoke: Palgrave/Macmillan.

Malpass, P. and Murie, A. (1999) *Housing Policy and Practice*, 5th edn, Houndmills: Macmillan.

Malpezzi, S. and Wachter, S. (2005) 'The Role of Speculation in Real Estate Cycles', *Journal of Real Estate Literature*, vol 13, pp 143–65.

Marshall, T.H. (1950) 'Citizenship and Social Class', in T.H. Marshall (ed) *Citizenship and Social Class and Other Essays*, Cambridge: Cambridge University Press.

Merrett, S. (1979) *State Housing in Britain*, London: Routledge and Kegan Paul.

Merrett, S., with Gray, F. (1982) *Owner Occupation in Britain*, London: Routledge and Kegan Paul.

MHLG (Ministry of Housing and Local Government) (1961) *Housing in England and Wales*, Cmnd 1290, London: HMSO.

Mian, A. and Sufi, A. (2009) 'The Household Leverage-Driven Recession of 2007–2009', University of Chicago Booth School of Business and NBER. Available at: http://ssrn.com/abstract =1463596.

Miles, D. (2004) *The Miles Review of the UK Mortgage Market: Taking a Long-Term View*, Final Report, London: HMSO/HM Treasury.

Miles, D. and Pillonca, V. (2007) *Financial Innovation and European Housing and Mortgage Markets*, Morgan Stanley Research Europe, 18 July.

Ministry of Housing and Local Government (1965) *The Housing Programme 1965–70*, Cmnd 2838, London: HMSO.

Ministry of Housing and Local Government (1968) *Old Houses into New Homes*, Cmnd 3602, London: HMSO.

Mishel, L., Bernstein, J. and Boushey, H. (2003) *The State of Working America 2002/2003*, Ithaca: ILT Press.

Morgan Grenfell (1987) *Housing Inheritance and Wealth*, Morgan Grenfell Economic Review 45, London..

Mortensen, J.L. and Seabrooke, L. (2008) 'Housing as Social Right or Means to Wealth? Comparing the Politics of Property Booms in Australia and Denmark', *Comparative European Politics*, vol 6, no 3, pp 305–24.

Morton, J. (1991) 'The 1890 Act and Its Aftermath – the Era of the "New Model Dwellings"', in S. Lowe and D. Hughes (eds) *A New Century of Social Housing*, Leicester: Leicester University Press.

Muellbauer, J. (2008) 'Housing, Credit and Consumer Expenditure', CEPR Discussion Paper no 6782.

Muellbauer, J. and Murphy, A. (2008) 'Housing Markets and the Economy: the Assessment', *Oxford Review of Economic Policy*, vol 24, no 10, pp 1–33.

Murie, A. (1997) 'The social rented sector, housing and the welfare state in the UK', *Housing Studies*, vol 12, no 3, pp 457–61.

Murie, A. and Jones, C. (2006) *The Right to Buy: Analysis and Evaluation of a Housing Policy*, Oxford: Blackwell.

Myles, J. and Pierson, P. (2001) 'The Comparative Political Economy of Pension Reform', in P. Pierson (ed) *The New Politics of the Welfare State*, Oxford: Oxford University Press.

Myners, P. (2001) *Myners Review of Institutional Investment: Final Report*, London: HM Treasury.

Nadvi, K. and Thoburn, J. (2004) 'Vietnam in the Global Garment and Textile Chain: Impacts on Firms and Workers', *Journal of International Development*, vol 16, no 1, pp 111–23.

ONS (Office of National Statistics) (2009) *Wealth in Great Britain: Main Results from the Wealth and Assets Survey 2006/08*. Available at: www.statistics.gov.uk/downloads/theme_economy/wealth-assets-2006-2008/Wealth_in_GB_2006_2008.pdf

Orwell, G. (1937) *The Road to Wigan Pier*, London: Victor Gollancz.

Orwell, G. (1939) *Coming up for Air*, London: Victor Gollancz.

Pawson, H. (1998) 'The Growth of Residential Instability and Turnover', in S. Lowe, P. Keenan and S. Spencer (eds) *Housing Abandonment in Britain: Studies in the Causes and Effects of Low Demand Housing*, York: Centre for Housing Policy, University of York.

Pierson, P. (1994) *Dismantling the Welfare State? Reagan, Thatcher and the Politics of Retrenchment*, Cambridge: Cambridge University Press.

Pierson, P. (2001) *The New Politics of the Welfare State*, Oxford: Oxford University Press.

Pierson, P. (2004) *Politics in Time: History, Institutions and Social Analysis*, Princeton, NJ: Princeton University Press.

Power, A. and Mumford, K. (1999) *The Slow Death of Great Cities? Urban Abandonment or Urban Renaissance*, York: York Publishing Services/ Joseph Rowntree Foundation.

Priemus, H. (1995) 'How to Abolish Social Housing? The Dutch Case', *International Journal of Urban and Regional Research*, vol 19, no 1, pp 145–55.

Quilgars, D. and Jones, A. (2010) 'Housing Wealth: a Safety Net of Last Resort? Findings from a European Study', in S.J. Smith and B.A. Searle (eds) *The Blackwell Companion to the Economics of Housing: The Housing Wealth of Nations*, Chichester: Wiley-Blackwell.

Ravetz, A., with Turkington, R. (1995) *The Place of Home: English Domestic Environments, 1914–2000*, London: E & FN Spon.

Ravetz, A. (2001) *Council Housing and Culture: the History of a Social Experiment*, London: Routledge.

Renaud, B. and Kim, K.-H. (2007) 'The Global Housing Price Boom and its Aftermath', *Housing Finance International*, vol XXII, no 2, pp 3–15.

Rhodes, R.A.W. (1994) 'The Hollowing out of the State', *Political Quarterly*, vol 65, pp 138–51.

Royal Commission on the Housing of the Working Class (1885) *First Report (England and Wales)*, BPP (HC), 1884–5 (c 4402).

Schwartz, H.M. (2003) 'Globalisation/Welfare: What's the Preposition? And, or, versus, with?', in C. Bochel, N. Ellison and M. Powell (eds) *Social Policy Review 15*, Bristol: The Policy Press, pp 71–89.

Schwartz, H.M. (2009) *Subprime Nation: American Economic Power, Global Capital Flows and Housing*, Ithaca, NY: Cornell University Press.

Schwartz, H.M. and Seabrooke, L. (2008) 'Varieties of Residential Capitalism in the International Political Economy: Old Welfare States and the New Politics of Housing', *Comparative European Politics*, vol 6, pp 237–61.

Schwartz, H.M. and Seabrooke, L. (2010) *The Politics of Housing Booms and Busts*, Basingstoke: Palgrave/Macmillan.

Seabrooke, L. (2006) *The Social Sources of Financial Power: Domestic Legitimacy and International Financial Orders*, Ithaca, NY: Cornell University Press.

Sherraden, M. (1991) *Assets and the Poor: A New American Welfare Policy*, New York: M.E. Sharpe Inc.

Skocpol, T. (1992) *Protecting Soldiers and Mothers: The Political Origins of Social Policy in the United States*, Cambridge, MA: Harvard University Press.

Smith, S.J. and Searle, B.A. (2007) 'Banking on Housing: Spending the Home', ESRC End of Award Report, Available at www.esrc.ac.uk

Smith, S.J. and Searle, B.A. (2008) 'Dematerialising Money? Observations on the Flow of Wealth from Housing to Other Things', *Housing Studies*, vol 23, no 1, pp 21–43.

Smith, S.J. and Searle, B.A. (2010) 'Housing Wealth as Insurance: Insights from the UK', in S.J. Smith and B.A. Searle (eds) *The Blackwell Companion to the Economics of Housing: The Housing Wealth of Nations*, Chichester: Wiley-Blackwell.

Smith, S.J., Searle, B.A. and Powells, G. (2010) 'Introduction', in S.J. Smith and B.A. Searle (eds) *The Blackwell Companion to the Economics of Housing: The Housing Wealth of Nations*, Chichester: Wiley-Blackwell.

Swank, D. (2002) *Global Capital, Political Institutions and Policy Change in Developed Welfare States*, Oxford: Oxford University Press.

Szelenyi, I. (1983) *Urban Inequalities under State Socialism*, Oxford: Oxford University Press.

Thelen, K. and Steinmo, S. (1992) 'Historical Institutionalism in Comparative Politics', in S. Steinmo, K. Thelen and F. Longsteth (eds) *Structuring Politics: Historical Institutionalism in Comparative Perspective*, Cambridge: Cambridge University Press.

Torgersen, U. (1987) 'Housing: the Wobbly Pillar under the Welfare State', in B. Turner, J. Kemeny and L. Lundqvist (eds) *Between State and Market: Housing in the Post-Industrial Era*, Stockholm: Almqvist and Wicksell International.

Toussaint, J. and Elsinga, M. (2009) 'Exploring "Housing Asset-Based Welfare". Can the UK Be Held Up as an Example for Europe?', *Housing Studies*, vol 24, no 5, pp 669–92.

TUC (Trades Union Congress) (2010) *Women and the Recession – One Year On*, London: TUC.

Turok, I. and Edge, N. (1999) *The Jobs Gap in Britain's Cities: Employment Loss and Labour Market Consequences*, Bristol: The Policy Press.

UNGA (United Nations General Assembly) (1948) *Universal Declaration of Human Rights*, Lake Success, NY: UN Department of Public Information.

Watson, M. (2009) 'Planning for a Future of Asset-Based Welfare? New Labour, Financialized Economic Agency and the Housing Market', *Planning, Practice and Research*, vol 24, no 1, pp 41–56.

Webster, D. (1998) 'Employment Change, Housing Abandonment and Sustainable Development: Structural Processes and Structural Issues', in S. Lowe, P. Keenan and S. Spencer (eds) *Housing Abandonment in Britain: Studies in the Causes and Effects of Low Demand Housing*, York: Centre for Housing Policy, University of York.

Wilcox, S. (2000) *Housing Finance Review 2000/2001*, York: Joseph Rowntree Foundation.

Wilcox, S. (2010a) *Financial Barriers to Home Ownership*, York: Genworth Financial and Centre for Housing Policy, University of York.

Wilcox, S. (2010b) *Housing Finance Review 2009/2010*, York: Joseph Rowntree Foundation.

Wilensky, H.L. (1975) *The Welfare State and Equality: Structural and Ideological Roots of Public Expenditure*, Berkeley, CA: University of California Press.

Willetts, D. (2010) *The Pinch: How the Baby Boomers Took Their Children's Future, and Why They Should Give It Back*, London: Atlantic Books.

Woods, N. (2000) 'The Political Economy of Globalization', in N. Woods (ed) *The Political Economy of Globalization*, Basingstoke: Macmillan.

Zavisca, J. (2008) 'Property without Markets: Housing Policy and Politics in Post-Soviet Russia, 1992–2007', *Comparative European Politics*, vol 6, pp 365–86.

Index

The letter f indicates a figure and t a table

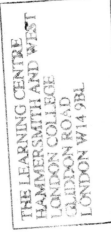